Indian Prisons

Towards Reformation, Rehabilitation and Resocialization

Indian Prisons
Towards Reformation, Rehabilitation and Resocialization

Edited by
K. Jaishankar
Tumpa Mukherjee
Priti Bharadwaj
Megha Desai Asher

ATLANTIC
PUBLISHERS & DISTRIBUTORS (P) LTD

Published by
ATLANTIC
PUBLISHERS & DISTRIBUTORS (P) LTD
7/22, Ansari Road, Darya Ganj, New Delhi-110002
Phones : +91-11-40775252, 23273880, 23275880, 23280451
Fax : +91-11-23285873
Web : www.atlanticbooks.com
E-mail : orders@atlanticbooks.com

Branch Office
5, Nallathambi Street, Wallajah Road, Chennai-600002
Phones : +91-44-64611085, 32413319
E-mail : chennai@atlanticbooks.com

ISBN 978-81-269-1950-5

Printed in India at Glorious Printers, A-13, D.S.I.D.C., Jhilmil
Industrial Area, Delhi-110095

Dedicated to

The pre-trial detainees in Indian prisons,
who continue to remain behind the bars
for years without any certainty

Foreword

As a former prison administrator, and the present criminal justice scholar, with a profound interest in prisoner rehabilitation and reintegration policies and processes from an international perspective, I am genuinely honoured to present the foreword to the first edition of this entrancing anthology aptly titled, *Indian Prisons: Towards Reformation, Rehabilitation and Resocialization*. The comprehensiveness and depth of the chapters that have been assembled in this compilation of original, quantitative and qualitative research is a true demonstration as to the dedication and commitment of the editors and the contributing authors. The contributing authors sought answers, and plausible solutions to treatment of India's prisoner population by scrutinizing and critically evaluating the current state of the Indian prison system from a theoretical and pragmatic perspective, particularly in regards to the prison system's influence on prisoner reformation, rehabilitation, and to a large extent, the success of prisoner reintegration policies and procedures.

Indian Prisons takes readers on an exploration inside the walls of India's prison system from both historical and contemporary perspectives, including a closer glimpse into Tihar Prison, one of the largest prison complexes in the world, comprised of nine central prisons and one District Prison at Rohini Prison Complex. This book is an engaging fifteen-chapter edited volume divided into four distinct, yet equally important, sections.

The first section of the book presents a critical evaluation of India's correctional system with chapters evaluating Foucault's Prison Principles and their application to colonial India's prison system. Additionally, the authors introduce readers to a critical analysis of India's current prison reformation and rehabilitation objectives.

The second section focuses heavily on existing and proposed prisoner rights within India, primarily in regards to Articles 21 and 22 within the Indian Constitution, with particular emphasis on the constitutional safeguards being applied to India's growing female offender population and equally importantly, the plight of the female offenders' children. Another significant concern pertains to the issue of the rising elderly population within Tihar's Central Prison. Simply stated, the chapters within this section examine the basic constitutional rights afforded to these protected prisoner populations, but in addition, the authors also offer sound recommendations to improve the prison conditions to ensure that the prisoners' basic legal, emotional, and physical needs are being fulfilled.

Section three addresses the all-important issues of offender rehabilitation with particular emphasis on India's community-based corrections system, specifically in regards to the rehabilitative efforts associated with existing and proposed probation and parole programs and policies within India. The chapters pertaining to criminal propensity and various criminological explanations for criminality are thoroughly explored, especially since most theories of criminal behaviour have been historically grounded in Western society and culture.

Lastly, section four presents a glimpse into current and future innovations in India. There is a specific emphasis regarding prison privatization, pharmacological correctional methods, prisoner treatment and security issues, prison management strategies, and of course, scientific and technological advancements concerning Geographic Information Systems (GIS), Global Positioning Systems (GPS), Radio Frequency Identification (RFID) and Biometrics, and their application to the management and supervision of offenders.

In closing, I am confident that the readers will find this book as interesting, instructive, and thought provoking as I have. I personally want to thank the editors and the authors who have contributed to this stimulating piece of scholarly work, which directly contributes to the advancement and betterment of the corrections field in regards to offender treatment, management, and supervision.

Michael Pittaro
Prison Expert
Owner, Crimen et Justitia Consulting
Nazareth, Pennsylvania, USA

Introduction

Prisons in India are a state subject, included in the State List (List II) of the Seventh Schedule of the Constitution. Several committees including the All India Committee on Jail Reforms, 1980-83 (commonly referred to as the Mulla Committee for its chairman, Justice A.N. Mulla) have recommended that the Constitution be amended to transfer prisons from the State to the Concurrent List. This has not found place in the Constitution yet.

A person does not become a non-person after entering the gates of a prison. The International Covenant on Civil and Political Rights (ICCPR) reiterates: "All persons deprived of their liberty shall be treated with humanity and with respect for the inherent dignity of the human person."[1] There are laws to protect the basic rights of those imprisoned. The ICCPR and the United Nations Standard Minimum Rules for the Treatment of Prisoners, 1955 are the two chief international human rights frameworks governing the administration and management of prisons universally. The UN Standard Minimum Rules for the Treatment of Prisoners set out best practices. Although these rules do not describe an extensive model system, they set out generally accepted principles on classification, accommodation, personal hygiene, clothing and bedding, food and water, medical services, discipline and punishment, contact with family and friends, grievance redressal as well as information to prisoners.

India is also obligated to follow these basic standards in its prisons. In addition, the Constitution of India, the Prisons Act of 1894, the Protection of Human Rights Act of 1993, the Supreme Court and High Court judgments, and the National Human Rights Commission guidelines oversee prisons nationwide. The state manuals based on the Prisons Act, 1894 have specific

1. Article 10(1), the International Covenant on Civil and Political Rights, 1966.

rules and regulations.[2] These regulations dictate every aspect of prison life, from admission to the release of prisoners, and from timely production of prisoners in the court, to visits by the judiciary in the prisons. It also documents the duties of prisoners and prison staff along with the basic living conditions that need to be maintained in the prison to ensure a prisoner's right to basic human dignity. None of these Acts or prison manuals[3] has a chapter or a section on the rights of prisoners. They do have an all exclusive section on discipline and punishments corresponding to every behaviour of a prisoner, and what actions should be taken for the commission or omission of such behaviour. However, there is nothing to inform the prisoners about their rights and the actions that can be taken against the custodians, if they fail or violate these rights of prisoners. These rights are found more explicitly under various Supreme Court and High Court judgments. "Unfortunately, the Central Government and the Supreme Court have left it to the states to implement their directives, and the states have proceeded slowly, if at all, in meeting their legal obligations. Frequently, individual state recommendations simply die on the vine without any attempt to implement them."[4]

Importance of Prison Reformation

Prison reformation is an attempt to improve conditions within the prisons to achieve a more effective and refined penal system. Younger criminals who have committed fewer and less severe crimes are most likely to be successfully reformed. Unfortunately, many of India's prisons date back to the era of British colonial rule, with thousands of prisoners kept in crumbling facilities largely unchanged since the beginning of the last century, which

2. Apart from these, the other Acts include Prisoners Act, 1900; The Transfer of Prisoners Act, 1950; The Prisoners (Attendance in Courts) Act, 1955; The Repatriation of Prisoners Act, 2003; and Identification of Prisoners Act, 1920.
3. Except some states that have amended their prison manuals recently.
4. Human Rights Documentation Centre (2009). "Arresting the problem: Towards prison reform in India." http://www.hrdc.net/sahrdc/hrfeatures/HRF197.htm as on 25 August 2010.

makes reformation of prisoners extremely difficult (Zora, 2005).[5] For prisoner reformation to take place, the first step required is reformation of prisons in India.

Prisoner Rehabilitation and Reformation

In Indian prisons, reformation is taking place at a slow pace due to the shortage of manpower, funds and good training skills. Most of the reformation programs are the ones that are devised by NGOs like Rotary Club, the Lions Club, the CHRI and others. *Preksha-dhyan*, *Vipasyana,* spiritual discourses, lectures and preaching on issues of healthy social life, literacy classes and de-addiction programs, adult education classes, plantation, horticulture and environment improvement with the material assistance, are some of the regular features of the prison. With good supervision and external support from social organisations, such programs help change the atmosphere within the prisons, helping prisoners change their ways for a good return into the society.

As Sri Sri Ravi Shankar states, "Expand your vision and see that inside every culprit is a victim crying for help. If you heal the victim, you will eliminate crime from the planet." Sri Sri began the Prison Program in 1990, to provide prisoners with an opportunity to integrate into the mainstream society, and heal themselves. The program features self-development workshops with an emphasis on human values, microfinance incentives and vocational training programs. The project also features programs for law enforcement officials. Recently, the Foundation also introduced the SRIJAN (Social Rehabilitation of Inmates in Jail and Aiding the Needy) initiative. SRIJAN offers inmates with a variety of opportunities such as theatre, music and dance workshops, and personality development.

However, rehabilitation is impossible if it doesn't ensure a better future for a prisoner once outside the prison. Plenty of social theorists have given enough evidence stating that the primary causes of crime are unemployment, illiteracy and poverty. Without education or skill training a prisoner is practically handicapped, once out in the real world. Hence, any rehabilitation

5. P. Zora (2005). "Fifty-four Years in Jail Without Trial: The Plight of Prison Inmates in India". World Socialist Website (ICFI).

work taking place within the walls of the prisons needs to lay emphasis on this factor.

The SRIJAN initiative also offers vocational training in commercial arts, costume jewellery, fashion technology, and weaving. Three SRIJAN workshops were recently held in New Delhi, India, where inmates were trained to produce items such as office stationery, gift boxes and lampshades. The Foundation works with local NGOs and partners to market these handicrafts in India and abroad. All proceeds go to the craftsmen, thus making them economically independent. Besides SRIJAN, there are many more ongoing projects in the prisons where the natural talent of the prisoner is tapped and used to the full potential, thereby making the prisoner realize what they are indeed capable of and how they would not have to be dependent on anyone, post acquittal.

Rehabilitation of a prisoner is a difficult task that requires a lot of patience. It is important that the prisoner is made to realize that the confinement is to ensure that they take the time out to contemplate what wrong they have done and how they can change themselves so that they won't commit the crime again. Aside from instilling skills or providing education, a must for all prisoners should be anger management therapy, wherein violent prisoners learn the art of controlling their emotions.

Today, plenty of prisons around the globe have introduced meditation in prisons. Although meditation isn't a cure-all, it can help prisoners reach a turning point by providing tools to help them take responsibility for their actions. "Many inmates carry around a lot of anger and low self-esteem. Meditation can help alleviate a lot of the anger and help people to learn self-love and compassion towards others" (Janis Masyk-Jackson, 2010). Meditation as a medium for prisoner rehabilitation may be a novel concept, one which has not been studied in depth, and reports show that, "many prisoners find it useful as a way to cope with and eliminate negative feelings like anger, while causing them to re-evaluate life, and move forward as a positive member of society" (Janis Masyk-Jackson, 2010).[6]

6. Janis Masyk-Jackson (2010). "Rehabilitation in Prison and Meditation." *Buddhist Teachings and Improving Prisoners' Mental Health*: 22 March 2010.

In India, most of these methods are already in use but a lot more needs to be done. Due to lack of manpower and the usual troubles associated with Indian prisons, prisoner reformation and rehabilitation is taking place at a very slow pace. Along with NGOs, government and private companies also need to take some responsibility towards such social movements. Many prisoners are looking for a chance to change and it is imperative that they be given a chance instead of their entire life being thrown away. The biggest problems plaguing Indian prisons are overcrowding, and corruption. It is about time that the law enforcement personnel are clearly instructed of both do's and don'ts (Mohan, 2008).[7] The instructions ought to make the police adequately humane in their attitude. The liability must be for each one of them when any breach of conduct is detected (Mohan, 2008).

Mohan (2008), clearly and very rightly states that, if immediate measures are not taken to bring the Indian prison management concurrent with times, the law and justice system will never be able to work with a positive attitude. The many subjects that require critical consideration include the infrastructure of the prisons, the state and handling of the prison inmates, training of prison personnel, upgrading of prisons, and a revamped remedy to the correctional administration. Without rectifying these, prisoner rehabilitation is almost an impossible task.

Prisons have always intrigued people. Whether it was the fear of being incarcerated, the thrill of knowing a prisoner's life within the prison, or the methods of interrogation—it all arouses curiosity. Media has always had a great impact on public, and prisons and prisoners have always had a special portrayal in media. Convicts are either shown in a bad light, where they play the role of a brute unfit to be released unconstrained into the society, or an innocent victim caught in a criminal mess by an outdated criminal justice system. Prisons have always been classically portrayed. They are unhygienic, impossible to live in, with prison guards who are sadists, and inmates who are routinely tortured for no reason. However, it has failed to show the changes that are being brought about in prisons across the country.

7. Sumitra Mohan (2008). "Reforming the Prison Administration in India." *IPCS* No. 2697: 6 October 2008.

Dynamic changes are being suggested, though implementation is taking time; it would be unfair to say that the system is not attempting to bring about a difference.

As the Prison Reform Trust (UK) rightly states, "Prisoners and their families should be treated with humanity and respect and have access to clear information and the opportunity to represent themselves and have their views taken into account. Besides, they should also provide constructive regimes in decent, safe conditions that ensure the well-being of prisoners and prepare them for resettlement in the community."

The importance of reformation in prison has now become a primary concern of NGOs and human rights activists, and is also a much debated topic. The nation should now make it a matter of primary concern. Indian criminal and penal laws and their accompanying institutions derive from archaic and punitive colonial legislation and institutional practice. It is time to think of better networking, effective prison reforms and their true application, education and overall societal contribution to the improvement of prison conditions (Sumitra Mohan, 2008). We must seek solutions both in the prisons and outside in society. Public funds now being wasted on unhealthy institutions called prisons need to be better spent on sensible pay-offs (Larrabee, 2006).[8]

Considering the various issues of prisons including the issues of reformation, rehabilitation and resocialization processes, this book emerges as a capsule which provides an overview of current prison practices, and gives an in-depth understanding of prison systems in India with solutions to problems plaguing Indian prisons.

Contents of the Book

In chapter one, Pradip Basu has made an attempt to examine the applicability of Michel Foucault's perspective on French prisons to the prisons in colonial India. Michel Foucault (1926-1984), the French philosopher of the 20th century, discussed in his book, *Discipline and Punish: The Birth of the Prison* (1975)

8. A.K. Larrabee (2006). "Punishment vs Rehabilitation in the Criminal Justice System." *Associated Content, Inc.*: 28 November 2006.

[hereinafter *DP*], a new approach to analyse the modern French prison system. Foucault contends that the modern prison system became the consistent form of punishment due to humanitarian concerns of reformists. He does so by marking out the swings in culture that lead to the prison's dominance, focusing on the body and questions of power. Prison is a form used by the *discipline*, a new technological power, which can also be found in modern schools, hospitals, psychiatric clinics, factories, workshops, military barracks, etc. It must however be noted that this chapter is only a preliminary attempt in connecting Foucault's ideas about prison with those of the prisons in colonial India, and an in-depth study is required further. This chapter gives phase to the opening of the book with a good theoretical framework.

In chapter two, Megha Desai Asher and Tumpa Mukherjee have done a critique of the Indian prisons. The authors have highlighted many issues and challenges of Indian prisons, such as lack of political will, lack of human resources, overcrowding, prison torture, deaths in custody, disproportionate undertrial to convict ratio, delay in disposal of cases for the underprivileged, criminals-jail staff nexus, and children of prisoners. This particular chapter has further given an opening to the book, apart from the Editors' Introduction. The authors have also provided some solutions to overcome the problems faced by Indian prisons.

Vijay Raghavan, in chapter three, deeply delves in the reforms that have been taking place in the prison administration in India. In this chapter, the author has given an overview of prison reforms from a historical perspective, and has provided valuable information about the legal status of prisons and prisoners. The author has analyzed various rights of the prisoners, and brought various contemporary issues that are not in tune with the reforms made in the Indian prisons. This chapter is an attempt by the author to put forth the prison reforms in a systematic manner, and that way it becomes a core chapter of the book.

Ever since the attainment of Independence, India has commenced her tryst with the much-coveted principle of democratic decentralization. The Panchayats have been envisaged as instrumentalities of both political as well as social change intended to ensure not only community participation at the grass-roots level, but also to evolve an efficient system of local justice as a bulwark against reactionary and anachronistic social practices. While the performance of the Panchayats in delivering local justice is a subject of intensive debate, one significant innovative contribution of India to the concept of democratic decentralization has been to harness the Panchayats as agents of both community participation as well as the dispensation of criminal justice inside prisons. This requires a progressive democratization of the prison administration. A positive step in this direction was taken by Dr. Kiran Bedi in Tihar Jail after assuming charge as Inspector General of Prisons in May 1993. The novelty of her mission lay in her resolve to demonstrate that a system of Panchayats could be set in operation even inside the four walls of the prison for the purpose of delivery of justice to the prisoners. The fourth chapter by Sumit Mukherjee seeks to examine the extent to which this proved successful as a mechanism of local justice.

Prison as a penal institution, and a formal agency of control, has a significant role to play in the criminal justice administration. Chapter five by Jeevan Ballav Panda explores those aspects of criminal law in India which relate to the deplorable condition of prisoners, and the legislative and judicial reforms, which have been taken with suitable suggestions for improving their status in this era of human rights. The chapter also aims at identifying challenges posed by the criminal justice system and to find out ways and means for addressing these challenges through suitable mechanism. Furthermore, it concentrates on the recent developments which have taken place through judicial approach by making a transition from an obsolete retributive or deterrent approach towards punishment to a modern reformative or rehabilitative approach. In the absence of a specific legislation emphasizing the rights of a prisoner and very few outdated legislations addressing the issue indirectly, the primary focus of the chapter is to create awareness among the readers by emphasizing the existence of prisoners' rights and their importance through various judicial pronouncements. This chapter suggests that the present (emerging) system of criminal justice does not adequately address such concerns. Accordingly, it considers and analyses the adequacy of the criminal justice system, and the need for a transformation in our approach in order to address the entire range of concerns. The chapter concludes by raising some fundamental questions about the need for change of the course to a new direction with appropriate recommendations and suggestions about prisoners' rights, and the need for a humane approach.

Articles 21 and 22 of the Constitution of India protect and safeguard the rights of convicts, undertrials and offenders. Chapter six, by Debarati Halder tries to find out different types of safeguards guaranteed to women prisoners. The core of the analysis orbits around the concept of right to life; the author has attempted to bring out the various facets of right to life in the arena of rights guaranteed to women prisoners. This chapter is a doctrinal research analysis of case laws, and tries to look at the concept of right to life under the Indian Constitution from the perspective of women prisoners' rights.

Chapter seven, by T. Lakshmi Narayana, tries to explore the plight of children of women prisoners. It also examines the condition of the children of prisoners in the light of previous studies conducted. A critical analysis of the law and practice by the various states, and the need for prison reforms is also attempted by the author. Finally, it lays down the rationale for the extension of a range of child development schemes sponsored by the Central Government to the children of prisoners.

Elderly prisoners now constitute only a small proportion of those incarcerated at any one time in the prison system. The need to recognize them as a special group within the prison population is gaining importance but at slower pace. The elderly have the basic needs that are substantially different from those of an average offender. As the people in society grow older, the number of adult prisoners in prisons is also bound to grow, even if the current patterns in crime and sentencing remain unchanged. Chapter eight, by Megha Shree and Honey Aggarwal, provides a comprehensive profile of elderly prisoners in Tihar Prison. The study attempts to explore whether the basic rights of elderly prisoners are being carried out or not. It is hoped that the outcome of this study will help focus attention on this "forgotten group which always remains under the shade", and cause some debate on their situation among the policymakers.

As far as India is concerned, the alternatives available to imprisonment are fine, probation, and community service order. Of these, probation is most widely used in almost all states in India. S. Ramdoss, in chapter nine, gives an overview of probation in India, and examines it as an alternative to punishment. The author feels that probation brings out positive results in terms of the rehabilitation and correction of the offenders. Probation is also cost-effective (only about 1/50th of the expenditure for the probationer compared to that of the prisoner). The author further feels that probation prevents the offender from becoming a recidivist, and it plays a vital role in crime prevention. In this chapter, probation is referred to as community-based correction and vice versa.

Chapter ten, by Amit Chaturvedi, is an effort to analyze the impact of parole on the psychology and the social adjustability of an inmate. "Criminal Propensity" and "Psychological Well-Being" were the two parameters studied on a sample of one hundred prisoners (fifty that had been at least once granted parole, and fifty others who never had this opportunity). The samples were randomly drawn from District Jail Rohini, New Delhi, that consisted of inmates sentenced for periods of seven years or more. The results showed that parole has a definite positive effect on the psychological well-being of the inmate, although, it does not affect his 'criminal propensity'.

The reasons why people commit crime willfully has been a matter of great concern. However, most theories of criminal behaviour are grounded in Western society and culture. Attempts to explore the causes of crime in the Indian context and situation have been sporadic and generally non-empirical in nature. Arvind Verma and Manish Kumar explore the causes for criminal motivations in India in chapter eleven. This chapter describes and analyzes the major reasons of criminality amongst convicted offenders. The results provided in this chapter suggest that growing urbanization, breakdown of extended family system, lure of consumerism, and influence of criminal associates are some of the main reasons for these people to fall into a life of criminality.

Open prisons and open colonies for prisoners, in the recent past, have emerged as effective institutional reformatory and correctional measures. These institutions, which ostensibly eliminate the 'tensions' and 'barriers' created by the restrictions and physical restraints placed on inmates of a 'closed' jail—a prison with walls—and provide them better opportunity for re-interaction and re-assimilation with 'free community' and 'family', and strive to bridge the gulf between the traditional 'closed prison' and 'free community'. They in fact furnish a 'half-way-home' to their inmates for their smooth and effective socio-psychological rehabilitation and re-integration into the social mainstream. By providing maximum opportunity to their inmates to re-mould their 'attitudes' and to bring about positive changes in their 'behavioural patterns', these institutions, it is believed, make prisoners 'fit' to lead a law-abiding and self-supporting life after their release. Tumpa Mukherjee and Periakaruppan, in chapter twelve, give an overview of open prisons in India, and give an example of a successful experiment, i.e. Lalgola Open Prison in West Bengal.

Managing crime is everyone's business, more so, the correctional wing of the criminal justice system. As a developing society, bulk of our resources is spent on the most expensive response: incarceration. While it may be difficult to predict the future rate of prison population growth, it is comparatively easy to ideate the contribution of 'a la mode' developments in science, technology and management, to the correctional planners and the correctional regimen of the future. Chapter thirteen, by P. Madhava Soma Sundaram, mainly pivots on a whole gamut of issues related to the future of corrections like privatization of prisons, pharmacological correctional methods, contemporary in-community correctional methods, prisoner treatment and security issues, prison management issues and the like. Suggestions are advanced for addressing and implementing these methods in India.

The prison systems of the developed and less developed countries are turning towards information technology (IT). In the new millennium it can be seen as a paradigm shift from the conventional prison systems. Technologies ranging from basic Microsoft application such as MS Word to advanced technologies like Geographic Information Systems (GIS), Global Positioning Systems (GPS), RFID and Biometrics have now become part and parcel of the prison managements all over the world. IT applications have taken firm roots in both institutional as well as community corrections. Chapter fourteen by K. Jaishankar gives an overview of advanced information technologies and computation developments in prisons across the world, and its effects in the management of offenders from an international perspective.

The final chapter of the book (chapter fifteen), by Priti Bharadwaj, serves as the conclusion chapter of the book. Priti identifies some specific problems of the Indian prisons, and provides various strategies to revamp Indian prisons. The chapter focuses on some contemporary solutions to the problems of Indian prisons, and that way it stands apart.

K. Jaishankar, Tumpa Mukherjee,
Priti Bharadwaj and Megha Desai Asher

Contents

Foreword vii

Introduction xi

Section One: Indian Corrections: Critical Appraisals

1. Foucault's Prison Principles and the Colonial Indian Prison System.. 3
Pradip Basu

2. Indian Prisons: A Critique 21
Megha Desai Asher and *Tumpa Mukherjee*

3. Prison Reforms: Historical and Contemporary Perspectives.. 38
Vijay Raghavan

4. *Panchayats* and Decentralization of Prisons: Role of Kiran Bedi in Transforming Tihar Jail 64
Sumit Mukherjee

Section Two: Rights of the Prisoners

5. Rights of the Prisoners.. 79
Jeevan Ballav Panda

6. Women Prisoners and their Rights.................................. 98
Debarati Halder

7. Rights of Children of Prisoners.................................. 122
T. Lakshmi Narayana

8. Rights of Elderly Prisoners: A Study in Tihar Central Prison 142
Megha Shree and *Honey Aggarwal*

Section Three: Issues of Offender Rehabilitation

9. Probation: An Appraisal of Community-based Corrections 167
S. Ramdoss

10. Is Parole Rehabilitating Offenders? An Analysis of Criminal Propensity and Psychological Well-being of Convicts 187
Amit Chaturvedi

11. Criminality Among Convicted Offenders 201
Arvind Verma and *Manish Kumar*

Section Four: Innovations in Corrections

12. Open Prisons in India 233
Tumpa Mukherjee and *P. Periakaruppan*

13. Towards Techno-Corrections: A Frontline View of Hot New Practices and Technologies 246
P. Madhava Soma Sundaram

14. Info-Tech Prisons in the New Millennium: International Perspectives 258
K. Jaishankar

15. Strategies for Revamping the Indian Prison System... 282
Priti Bharadwaj

Contributors 293

SECTION ONE

INDIAN CORRECTIONS: CRITICAL APPRAISALS

1

Foucault's Prison Principles and the Colonial Indian Prison System

Pradip Basu

Introduction

Michel Foucault (1926-1984), the French philosopher (Armstrong, 1992; Gane & Johnson, 1993; Rabinow, 1984; Simons, 1995) of the 20th century, discussed in his book, *Discipline and Punish: The Birth of the Prison* (1975) (Sheridan, 1987) [hereinafter *DP*], a new approach to analyze the modern French prison system. In 1972, he also joined the GIP (Group for Prison Information) to support prisoners' rights. His book is an examination of the social and theoretical mechanisms behind the substantial changes that came about in western penal systems during the modern age. It focuses on historical documents from France, but the anxieties it conveys are relevant to many modern western societies (For general discussions on poststructuralism and postmodernism, see Bertens, 1995; Sarup, 1988; White, 1991).

Foucault contends the widely accepted notion that the modern prison system became the consistent form of punishment due to humanitarian[1] concerns of reformists. He does so by marking out the swings in culture that leads to the prison's dominance, focusing on the body and questions of power. The main ideas of *DP* can be summarized into five parts: torture, punishment, discipline, panopticism and prison (Foucault, 1975; Sheridan, 1987). The present chapter seeks to examine to what extent

1. Humanism based on the so-called universal principles of Enlightenment claimed to have been emancipatory, progressivist and rationalist. Foucault and many other postmodern thinkers have made critique of humanism and its emancipatory project.

this analysis undertaken by Foucault is applicable in context to colonial India. It must however be noted that this is only a preliminary attempt which needs further study.

Foucault begins the book by contrasting two forms of penalty: (a) the violent and chaotic public torture (Foucault, 1975) and execution of Damiens who was convicted of regicide in 1757, and (b) the highly regimented daily schedule for inmates from an early 19th century prison. Foucault lists the daily activities in the House of Young Prisoners in Paris. This routine was written 80 years from the time of Damiens' execution. Foucault's point is to show how drastically the penal system changed in those 80 years. He argues that the public spectacle of torture was a theatrical forum which served several purposes for society. It sought to reflect the violence of the original crime onto the convict's body for all to see. The law was considered an extension of the sovereign's body, and so the revenge must take the form of harming the convict's body. Crimes committed during this time were not crimes against the public good, but a personal injury to the King himself. The public visuals of torture and execution were public assertion of the King's authority to rule and to punish. But at the same time, it made available a forum for the convict's body to turn into a locus of compassion and appreciation. Public executions often led to riots in support of the prisoner. He argues that public execution and torture were ultimately non-economical. It was applied non-uniformly and haphazardly. Hence, its political cost was too high.

Punishment

Foucault then showed in *DP* how in the French society toward the end of the 18th century protests against public execution and torture sustained (Foucault, 1975; Sheridan, 1987). The public cried out for punishment without torture, which ultimately led to the invention of the modern prison. Deprivation of liberty became the main form of punishment. Fines upset the poor more than the rich, but depriving one of freedom caused the same level of distress to all. Reformists were unhappy with the unpredictable, unevenly distributed nature of violence which the sovereign would focus on the body of the convict. Reformists felt that the power to punish and judge should become more evenly distributed; the state's power must be a form of public power. This, according to Foucault, was of more concern to reformists than humanitarian arguments. Prisoners would have been compelled to do work which reflected their crime, thus repaying society for their violations. This would have allowed the public to observe the convicts' bodies enacting their punishment, and thus to reflect on the crime. Foucault argues that this theory of 'gentle' punishment signified the first step away from the terrific force of the sovereign, and towards more generalized and controlled means of punishment. But, he proposes that the shift towards prison which followed was the outcome of a new 'technology' and ontology for the body being developed in the 18th century, the 'technology'.of discipline, and the ontology of 'man as machine'.

Foucault's analysis has induced countless scholars to look for its relevance in many other modern western societies (Bertens, 1995; Sarup, 1988; White, 1991). Some have, however, raised the question as to how far it is helpful in understanding the situations of the colonial times and for that matter postcolonial modernity? For instance, in contrast to the French conditions, in India under British rule, torture continued to be practised as the dominant mode. Certainly it was non-economic in any long-term consideration. But for short-term interest, it was the easiest resort to crush infringement of law. This means in India torture could be afforded. If we look specifically at the Indian situation, we find that although western colonial power tried to introduce the modern disciplinary regime in India, it was still constrained by the compulsions of the situation of colonial modernity (Chakrabarty, 2001; Chatterjee, 1994, 1996; Choudhury, Das, & Chakrabarty, 2000).

According to Chatterjee (1996):

> We must remind ourselves; however, that though the fully developed colonial regime of the Victorian period was precisely the agency that supervised the introduction of most of the institutions characteristics of modern disciplinary power in India, the project of modernity was insurmountably limited by the nature

> of colonial rule itself. Hence, while the superior reach and effectiveness of modern power would justify the introduction into colonial governance of appropriate disciplinary institutions and practices, they would at the same time be compromised, and even subverted, by the need to maintain a specifically colonial form of power. Indeed, since it could continue to exist only by reproducing the difference between the colonizer and the colonized, the colonial state was necessarily incapable of fulfilling the criterion of representativeness of the fundamental conditions that makes modern power a matter of interiorized self-discipline, rather than external coercion (p. 8).

No wonder Indian prisons remained more an organ of torture than an instrument of disciplinary regime.

Discipline

The advent of modern prison as a form of punishment for every crime grew out of the development of discipline in the 18th and 19th centuries, according to Foucault (Foucault, 1975; Sheridan, 1987). Highly sophisticated forms of discipline grew up concerned with the smallest and most precise aspects of a person's body. Discipline developed a new economy and politics for bodies. Modern institutions required that bodies must be individuated according to their tasks, as well as for training, observation, and control. Discipline created a whole new form of individuality for bodies, which enabled them to perform their duty within the new forms of economic, political, and military organizations emerging in the modern age. 'Discipline' according to Foucault may be identified neither with an institution nor with an apparatus; it is a type of power, a modality for its exercise, comprising a whole set of instruments, techniques, procedures, levels of application, and targets; it is a 'physics' or an 'anatomy' of power, a technology (Foucault, 1975; Sheridan, 1987). It assures an infinitesimal distribution of the power relations. Modern society is one not of spectacle, but of surveillance; under the surface of images, one invests bodies in depth. It is not that the totality of the individual is amputated; it is rather that the individual is carefully fabricated in it.

Foucault (1975) argues:

> Historically, the process by which the bourgeoisie in the course of the 18th century became the politically dominant class was masked by the establishment of an explicit, coded and formally egalitarian juridical framework, made possible by the organization of a parliamentary, representative regime. But the development and generalization of disciplinary mechanisms constituted the other dark side of these processes. The general juridical form that guaranteed a system of rights that were egalitarian in principle was supported by these tiny, everyday, physical mechanisms, by all those systems of micro-power that are essentially non-egalitarian and asymmetrical that we call the disciplines (p. 222).

It is true that in India too the colonial machinery served the imperialist English bourgeoisie. The political domination of the imperialist bourgeoisie was shrouded by the establishment of an overt, coded and formal juridical structure, made possible by the organization of a few legal reforms. But these were extremely limited in scope though they formally assumed the parliamentary, representative gesture. Here also the development and generalization of disciplinary mechanisms constituted the other, gloomy side of these processes, but these were marked by their very narrow fields of application (Foucault, 1975; Sheridan, 1987).

It is true there were a series of attempts for prison reforms (Ahuja, 2002) in India in various forms. The Indian Jails Committee (1836) gave its Report in 1838. On the recommendations of the 1864 Committee, Jail Manual was framed in 1870 and the segregation system was introduced. On the recommendations of the 1889 Committee, the under trials were segregated. The 1892 Committee recommended 9 hours work in jail. The 1919 Jails Committee recommendations overhauled the prison system: segregating offenders, classification system for residence, training inmates, educating offenders, recreation measures, maintaining social contacts, moral and religious lectures, remission system, etc. There were provincial prison reform committees as well, e.g.

Punjab (1925), U.P. (1946). The first open prison was started in 1905 in Bombay Presidency but was closed in 1910. Statutes like the Prisons Act (1894), Prisoners Act (1900) confer some rights on prisoners. In fact, the colonial rulers proclaimed with great enthusiasm that the European juridical form supposedly guaranteed a system of rights that pretended to be egalitarian in principle. But unlike in England, these were not supported by these minuscule, everyday, physical mechanisms, by disciplines, and by systems of micro-power that are in essence non-egalitarian and asymmetrical. On the contrary, juridical form and the system of rights themselves were extremely constrained. The newly introduced disciplinary mechanisms were incomplete, partial and restricted in their span of functioning. Even in their truncated extent, these were supported by the naked violence of the colonial machinery.

The formation of the disciplinary society is connected with a number of broad historical processes—economic, juridico-political and, lastly, scientific—of which it forms part. If the economic take-off of the West began with the techniques that made possible the accumulation of capital (Poster, 1985), it might perhaps be said that the methods for administering the accumulation of men made possible a political take-off in relation to the traditional, habitual, costly, violent forms of power, which soon fell into disuse and were superseded by a subtle, calculated technology of subjection. In fact, the two processes —the accumulation of men and the accumulation of capital—cannot be separated; discipline is the unitary technique by which the body is reduced as a 'political' force at the least cost and maximized as a useful force. The growth of a capitalist economy gave rise to the specific modality of disciplinary power whose general formulas, techniques of submitting forces and bodies, in short, 'political anatomy', could be operated in the most diverse political regimes, apparatuses or institutions.

Foucault said constant supervision and forced discipline broke the will of the criminal and made him into a 'docile body'. The 'docile body' was easy to control. Discipline creates 'docile bodies', ideal for the new economics, politics and warfare of the modern industrial age—bodies which function in factories, military regiments, and school classrooms. But, to construct this individuality the disciplinary institutions must be able to (a) constantly observe and record the bodies they control, and (b) ensure the internalization of the disciplinary individuality within the bodies being controlled. That is, discipline must come about without excessive force, but rather through careful observation, and moulding of the bodies into the correct form through this observation. Discipline requires a particular form of institution, which Foucault argues, was exemplified by Bentham's new prison model: *Panopticon*.

Panopticism

The Panopticon was, according to Foucault, the ultimate realization of a modern disciplinary institution in Europe. It allowed for constant observation and was designed so that the prisoner could never be sure whether he was being observed or not. Through this, it caused the internalization of disciplinary individuality, and the docile body required of its inmates. Thus, prison and the model of the Panopticon, provide the ideal form of modern punishment. It was the ideal modernization of punishment, so its eventual dominance was natural. Hence was the emergence of the prison as the dominant form of punishment. Behind these disciplinary mechanisms the haunting memory of 'contagions', of the plague, of rebellions, crimes, vagabondage, desertions, people who appear and disappear, live and die in disorder can be read. It individualizes the excluded, operated regularly by disciplinary power from the beginning of the 19th century in the psychiatric asylum, the penitentiary, the reformatory, the approved school and the hospital. The authorities function according to a double mode; that of binary division and branding (mad/sane; dangerous/harmless; normal/abnormal); and that of coercive assignment of differential distribution (who he is; where he must be; how he is to be characterized; how he is to be recognized; how a constant surveillance is to be exercised over him in an individual way, etc.) (Foucault, 1975; Sheridan, 1987).

Bentham's *Panopticon* is an architectural figure: at the periphery, is an annular building, at the centre, is a tower, this tower has windows that open onto the inner side of the ring, the peripheral building is divided into cells that they have two windows, one on the inside, corresponding to the windows of the tower and the other on the outside which allows the light into the cell. Place a supervisor in a central tower and shut up in each cell a madman, a patient, a condemned man, a worker or a schoolboy. Lighting and the eye of a supervisor capture better than darkness in old dungeons and as Foucault maintains, "Visibility is a trap." Each is seen by the supervisor; but the side walls prevent him from coming into contact with his companions. He is seen, but he does not see; he is the object of information, never a subject in communication. The arrangement imposes on him an axial visibility but a lateral invisibility. And this invisibility is a guarantee of order. If the inmates are convicts, there is no hazard of a plot; if they are patients, there is no danger of contagion; if they are madmen there is no risk of their committing violence; if they are schoolchildren, there is no copying, no noise; if they are workers, there are no disorders, no slowing down the rate of work. A compact mass, through individualities merging together, is replaced by a collection of separated individualities.

Foucault (1975) observes:

> Hence the major effect of the Panopticon is to induce in the inmate a state of conscious and permanent visibility that assures the automatic functioning of power. So to ensure that the surveillance is permanent in its effects, even if it is discontinuous in its action; that renders its actual exercise unnecessary; this is a machine for creating and sustaining a power relation independent of the person who exercises it; in short, that the inmates should be caught up in a power situation of which they themselves are the bearers (p. 201).

Bentham's principles are: power should be visible and unverifiable. In case of visible, the inmate will constantly have before his eyes the central tower from which he is spied upon and in unverifiable, the inmate must never know whether he is being looked at by any one at any given time. It is an important mechanism, for it automatizes and de-individualizes power. It does not matter what motive animates the supervisor. The Panopticon produces homogeneous effects of power. A real subjection is born mechanically from a fictitious relation. So it is not necessary to use force to constrain the convict to good behaviour, the madman to calm, the worker to work, the schoolboy to application, and the patient to the observation of the regulations. Bentham was surprised that panoptic institutions could be so light: there were no more bars, chains, or heavy locks; one finds in the program of the Panopticon a concern which individualizes observation, with characterization and classification, with the analytical arrangement of space. The Panopticon makes it possible to draw up differences, among patients, to observe the symptoms of each individual, without the proximity of beds, among schoolchildren, it makes it possible to observe performances, to draw up rigorous classifications and among workers, it makes it possible to compare the time each takes to perform a task, and to calculate their wages.

The Panopticon was, said Foucault, also a laboratory; it could be used as a machine to carry out experiments, to alter behaviour, to train or correct individuals, to experiment with medicines and monitor their effects, to try out different punishments on prisoners, and to seek the most effective ones and to teach different techniques simultaneously to the workers, to decide which is the best. To try out pedagogical experiments: one could bring up different children according to different systems of thought. The Panopticon must be understood as a generalizable model of functioning; a way of defining power relations in terms of the everyday life. No doubt Bentham presents it as a particular institution. As opposed to the ruined prisons of torture, the Panopticon presents a cruel, ingenious cage.

Foucault further observes:

> It is polyvalent in its applications as it serves to reform prisoners, to treat patients, to instruct schoolchildren, to confine the insane, to supervise workers, and to put beggars and idlers to work. It is a type of location of bodies in space, of distribution of individuals, of hierarchical organization, of disposition of centres and channels of power, of definition of the instruments and modes of intervention of power, which can be implemented in hospitals, workshops, schools, and prisons (p. 205).

It arranges things so that power is not exercised from the outside, like a rigid, heavy constraint, but is so subtly present so as to increase their efficiency. Its enclosed nature does not preclude a permanent presence from the outside: anyone may come and exercise in the tower surveillance. Even if it is rigorously closed, it may be subjected to irregular and constant inspections not only by the inspectors, but also by the public and society. There is no risk that the increase of power may degenerate into tyranny; the disciplinary mechanism will be democratically controlled. The seeing machine is now transparent.

The panoptic schema was, Foucault further states, destined to spread throughout the social body. Although, it is to make power more economical and more effective, its aim is to strengthen the social forces, to increase production, to develop the economy, spread education, and raise the level of public morality. Power is strengthened in such a way that, far from impeding progress, it actually facilitates such progress. It can be exercised continuously in the very foundations of society, in the subtlest possible way. On the other hand, it functions outside the sudden, violent, discontinuous forms associated with the exercise of sovereignty. The sovereignty of the king is at the opposite extreme of this new physics of power. Its domain is that the whole lower region of irregular bodies, with their details, their multiple movements, their heterogeneous forces, their spatial relations, all of which have its maximum intensity not in the person of the king, but in the bodies that can be individualized by these relations. Panopticism is the general principle of a new 'political anatomy' whose object and end are not the relations of sovereignty but the relations of discipline. Bentham also set out to show how one may get the disciplines to function in a diffused, multiple, polyvalent way throughout the whole social body. Bentham dreamt of transforming these disciplines into a network of mechanisms that would be everywhere and always be alert, running through society without interruption in space or in time. In Foucault's words,

> There are two images, then, of discipline. At one extreme, the discipline-blockade, the enclosed institution, established on the edges of society, turned inwards

> towards negative functions: arresting evil, breaking communications, suspending time and at the other extreme, panopticism, a functional mechanism that must improve the exercise of power by making it lighter, more rapid, more effective, a design of subtle coercion for a society to come. The movement from...exceptional discipline to one of a generalized surveillance rests on a historical transformation, i.e. the gradual extension of the mechanisms of discipline throughout the seventeenth and eighteenth centuries, their spread throughout the whole social body, the formation of what might be called in general the disciplinary society (p. 209).

According to Foucault, the panoptic modality of power—at the elementary, technical, merely physical level at which it is situated is not under the immediate dependence or a direct extension of the great juridico-political structures of a society; it is nonetheless not absolutely independent. Although, in a formal way, the representative regime makes it possible, directly or indirectly, for the will of all to form the fundamental authority of sovereignty, the disciplines provide, at the base, a guarantee of the submission of forces and bodies. The real, corporal disciplines constituted the foundation of the formal, juridical liberties. The constant pressure acts even before the offences are committed. Its strength is that it never intervenes, it is exercised spontaneously, without any physical instrument other than architecture and geometry, it acts directly on individuals; it gives 'power of mind over mind'. It assures its economy (in material, in personnel, in time) and it assures its efficacy by its preventative character, its continuous functioning and its automatic mechanisms.

In the political sphere, it can constitute a mixed mechanism in which relations of power (and of knowledge) may be precisely adjusted, in the smallest detail, to the processes that are to be supervised. It can establish a direct proportion between 'surplus power' and 'surplus production'. Thanks to its mechanisms of observation, it gains in efficiency and in the ability to penetrate into men's behaviour; knowledge follows the advances of power, discovering new objects of knowledge over all the surfaces on which power is exercised. The 'Enlightenment', which discovered the liberties, also invented the disciplines. The sciences of man, psychology, psychiatry, pedagogy, criminology, etc., which have so delighted our 'humanity' for over a century, have their technical matrix in the petty, malicious details of their investigations. Its appearance in the form of tests, interviews, interrogations and consultations is apparently in order to rectify the mechanisms of discipline. But these techniques merely refer individuals from one disciplinary authority to another, and they reproduce, in a concentrated or formalized form, the schema of power-knowledge (Gordon, 1980) proper to each discipline.

Prison

No doubt in modernizing India too, colonial modernity brought with it western institutions such as modern schools, new prisons, contemporary psychiatric asylums, latest hospitals, most recent workshops, currently fashioned military, etc. To a remarkable extent these institutions are implicated with the kind of disciplinary power described by Foucault which is, on the one hand, the tactics of individualizing disciplines are imposed on the excluded; and, on the other hand, the universality of disciplinary controls makes it possible to brand the person and to bring into play against him the dualistic mechanisms of exclusion. The existence of a whole set of techniques and institutions for measuring, supervising and correcting the abnormal brings into play the disciplinary mechanisms. But at the same time it must be remembered that colonial modernity was itself restricted in its reach by the compulsions of its own unique situation. In every detail of the functioning of this modernity it was bearing the signs of colonialism, which left indelible marks on the modernist or humanitarian reforms brought about by the British in Indian penal system.

In spite of the obvious differences between the modern French society and colonial India with respect to the extent of a full-fledged disciplinary regime, there is remarkable similarity between the objectives and functioning of the prisons in both. For instance, Foucault explores that prisons became more than just places where liberty was deprived; they were places where discipline could be instilled. Discipline was a drive to inculcate useful, social qualities into the convicts. It was an attempt to reform the criminal. One will be rewarded for achievement, while punished for non-conformity. Forcing the prisoners to live and work under strict guidelines implanted discipline. The prisoners were forced to 'constructively' use every minute. This was social training to prepare criminals for a life of productivity when released. No doubt in colonial India too, as Foucault described in the European context, prison's much professed goal was to reduce crime by punishing the criminal. Prisons should also deter others from committing crimes. But, according to Foucault, prisons did not meet their objective; in fact they made criminals worse (Foucault, 1975; Sheridan, 1987).

Any expert on the colonial Indian penal system would note the remarkable accuracy, appropriateness and relevance in the observations made by Foucault (1975) on French prisons:

> Prisons do not diminish the crime rate: they can be extended, multiplied or transformed, the quantity of crime and criminals remains stable or, worse, increases.... Detention causes recidivism; those leaving prison have more chance than before of going back to it; convicts are, in a very high proportion, former inmates.... The prison cannot fail to produce delinquents. It does so by the very type of exercise that it imposes on its inmates: whether they are isolated in cells or whether they are given useless work, for which they will find no employment, it is, in any case, not 'to think of man in society; it is to create an unnatural, useless and dangerous existence'.... The prison also produces delinquents by imposing violent constraints on its inmates; it is supposed to apply law, and to teach respect for it; but all its functioning operates in the form of an abuse of power.... The prison makes possible, even encourages, the organization of a milieu of delinquents, loyal to one another, hierarchized, ready to aid and abet any future criminal act.... The conditions to which the free inmates are subjected necessarily condemn them to recidivism: they are under the surveillance of the police; they are assigned to a particular residence, or forbidden others.... Lastly, the prison indirectly

> produces delinquents by throwing the inmate's family into destitution... (pp. 265-68).

One would find it relevant in colonial India also, the comments Foucault makes to indicate that there must be a reason why prisons are still around today, even if they are unsuccessful at preventing crime:

> But perhaps one should reverse the problem and ask oneself what is served by the failure of the prison; what is the use of these different phenomena that are continually being criticized; the maintenance of delinquency, the encouragement of recidivism, the transformation of the occasional offender into a habitual delinquent, and the organization of a closed milieu of delinquency. Perhaps one should look for what is hidden beneath the apparent cynicism of the penal institution which after purging the convicts by means of their sentence, continue to follow them by a whole series of 'brandings'...and which thus pursues as a 'delinquent' someone who has acquitted himself of his punishment as an offender? Can we not see here a consequence rather than a contradiction? If so, one would be forced to suppose that the prison, and no doubt punishment in general, is not intended to eliminate offences, but rather to distinguish them, to distribute them, to use them; that is not so much that they render docile those that are likely to transgress the law, but that they tend to assimilate the transgression of the laws in a general tactics of subjection (Foucault, 1975, p. 272).

Foucault hypothesized that the prison system has lasted so long as it benefits the ruling class. The ruling class makes use of criminality as a way of averting confrontation that could lead to revolution. The dynamic groups of the lower social class commit crime by which they were calling for a change and rebelling against the powerful elite. The ruling class utilizes the law as a means to lessen the power of these rebellions. The legal systems segregated the most dynamic of the lowest class from the rest of society, posed them as a separate group from the 'normal' lower class, and forced them together as a group of outcasts, thus rendering them politically harmless. This group, branded as criminals, is easier to supervise and keep disorganized by letting the members in and out of the prison system.

> ...It would be hypocritical or naive to believe that the law was made for all in the name of all; that it would be more prudent to recognize that it was made for the few and that it was brought to bear upon others; that in principle it applies to all citizens, but that it is addressed principally to the most numerous and least enlightened classes.... For the observation that prison fails to eliminate crime, one should perhaps substitute the hypothesis that prison has succeeded extremely well in producing delinquency, a specific type, a politically or economically less dangerous—and on occasion, usable—form of illegality; in producing delinquents, in an apparently marginal, but in fact centrally supervised milieu; in producing the delinquent as a pathologized subject (Foucault, 1975, pp. 276-77).

He further said:

> To this was added a patient attempt to impose a highly specific grid on the common perception of delinquents: to present them as close by, everywhere and everywhere to be feared (Foucault, 1975, p. 286).

Foucault explained how the penal system with its outreaching arms affects society as a whole. He believed other governmental programmes, such as welfare and new educational techniques, expanded from the penal system. He called this expansion of disciplinary control the carceral archipelago. It created a whole society of docile bodies submitting to the will of the state. "We have seen that, in penal justice, the prison transformed the punitive procedure into a penitentiary technique; the carceral archipelago transported this technique from penal institutions to the entire social body" (Foucault, 1975, p. 298). But in this regard we must point out that the Indian colonial situation was different; different in the sense that the British Indian penal system as a part of a greater disciplinary regime did not affect 'the entire social body' in India. Unlike that in France, therefore, the discipline of the colonial Indian prison system had not spilled out into rest of society. Other governmental programs, welfare measures and educational institutions, had not expanded from this penal system. Further, the Indian prisons were more characterized by naked force, vulgar coercion and brutal torture and less by the subtle mechanisms of disciplinary regime. Foucault's assessment of the prison as part of a larger 'carceral system' which has supposedly become an all-encompassing institution in modern society is not so much appropriate in the specific context of British India. No doubt prison was here too part of a modern power network, including schools, psychiatric clinics, military institutions, hospitals, and factories, a system which operated under the scientific authority of medicine, psychology, and criminology. But its extension and efficacy were only partial. It failed to build up a panoptic society for all its members all over India.

Conclusion

My contention is: first, in the colonizing set up of France, it was far more possible to meet up the economic demands of the people by the ruling class, since, a certain degree of economic well-being could be afforded through the all-pervasive economic exploitation of the colonies. In colonial India, on the contrary, economic plunder was boundless and the colonized people were subjected to abject poverty and utter distress. Disciplinary regime could be established in its full-fledged shape in France within the framework of a developed imperialist economy. However, in India, the starving population had to desperately take resort to violent forms of resistance too often in order to compel the colonial rulers to yield to even some bare minimum of their needs. The colonial economic plunder was so profitable, even, while based on violence on the colonized, that, the rulers did not have to be concerned about a more economic penal system. More often than not these movements for bare existence and survival were suppressed by the colonial monster with brute force denying all legal-civil and political rights and norms whatsoever.

Secondly, the British rulers were so blinded by white racism that they were not bothered by any sort of pressure of public opinion against torture of the 'niggars' or non-white and 'inferior' 'subhuman' natives. Curiously enough, such a voice of public opinion either in India or in England was amazingly feeble and pitiably weak too. Likewise, the enlightened citizen's criticisms, the autonomy of the civil society, the call for democratic rights, the claim for Rule of Law, freedom of expression and opinion, individual liberty, all were theoretically, or for that matter even epistemologically, restricted to the domain of the white Europeans. The innumerable colonized Indians and their low quality of life, the colour of their skin, their supposedly inferior culture, the presumed absence of knowledge practices in their lives, the dominance of superstitions and lack of rational faculty, and the lack of secular approach provided both epistemologically and morally justifiable grounds for their being easy victims to the unbridled greed of the power-crazy colonizer. Because of this racist cultural and ideological foundation of the colonial rule the whole terms of rule had to be raw, vulgar, brutal and crude. Disciplinary regime could only work as an exception, within a limited compass.

References

Ahuja, R. (2002). *Criminology*. Jaipur: Rawat Publications, pp. 303-34.

Armstrong, T.J. (tr.) (1992). *Michel Foucault: Philosopher*. New York: Harvester Wheatsheaf.

Bertens, H. (1995). *The Idea of the Postmodern*. London: Routledge.

Chakrabarty, D. (2001). *Provincializing Europe*. Delhi: Oxford University Press.

Chatterjee, P. (1994). *The Nation and its Fragments: Colonial and Postcolonial Histories*. Delhi: Oxford University Press.

Chatterjee, P. (Ed.) (1996). *Texts of Power*. Calcutta: Samya.

Choudhury, A., Das, D. and Chakrabarty, A. (2000). *Margin of Margin*. Calcutta: Anustup.

Foucault, M. (1975). *Discipline and Punish: The Birth of the Prison*. New York: Random House. (Originally published in 1975 in French under the title *Surveiller et punir: Naissance de la prison*, it was translated into English in 1977).

Gane, M. and Johnson, T. (Ed.) (1985). *Foucault's New Domains*. London: Routledge.

Gordon, C. (Ed.) (1980). *Michel Foucault, Power/Knowledge*. New York: Pantheon Books.

Poster, M. (1985). *Foucault, Marxism and History*. Cambridge: Polity Press.

Rabinow, P. (Ed.) (1984). *The Foucault Reader*. New York: Pantheon Books.

Sarup, M. (1988). *An Introductory Guide to Post-structuralism and Post-modernism*. New York: Harvester Wheat Sheaf.

Sheridan, A. (tr.) (1987). *Discipline and Punish: The Birth of the Prison*. London: Penguin Books. (Originally published in 1975 in French under the title *Surveiller et punir: Naissance de la prison*, by Foucault and was translated into English in 1977).

Simons, J. (1995). *Foucault and the Political*. London: Routledge.

White, S.K. (1991). *Political Theory and Post-Modernism*. Cambridge: Cambridge University Press.

2

Indian Prisons: A Critique

Megha Desai Asher and Tumpa Mukherjee

Introduction

In India the institution of prisons was a mechanism of social control meant for punishing offenders. It is a legacy of the British rule. The first Committee on Prison Administration known as the Prison Discipline Committee was set up in January 1836 and its report was received in 1838 (Bali-Mahabal, n.d). It drew attention to the existing horrible condition and corruption prevalent in the lower staff, but it did not give any suggestions for the improvement of conditions (Ahuja, 2000). It rejected education, moral lectures, and rewards to inmates and laid stress on hard and monotonous life in jail, i.e., on retributive punishment (Ahuja, 2000).

A Commission of Enquiry into Jail Management and Discipline was next set up in 1864 (Bali-Mahabal, n.d). But the reports pointed out that the colonial rulers were interested in prison only from the point of view of administration and discipline. On the recommendations of the 1864 Committee, two significant changes were made: 1. Jail Manual was framed in 1870 and 2. Segregation System was introduced in prisons, segregating males from females, adults from children and 'civil offenders' from 'criminal offenders' (Bali-Mahabal, n.d). A conference of experts held in 1877 resulted in a draft bill being prepared governing the principles and practices of prison management (Bali-Mahabal, n.d). In 1888, the Fourth Jail Commission was appointed and the Prison Act of 1894 is the result of Fourth Jail Commission, intended to standardize the rules governing the lives of the prisoners.

Modern prison reform in the country can be said to have originated from the Report of the Indian Jail Committee of 1919-20. This report was a landmark in the history of prison administration in India, as it threw new light and adopted a humanistic approach for the prisoners. The report identified reformation and rehabilitation as the true objective of prison administration.

In post-independent India, the first systematic study on the conditions of the prisoners and the prison system was undertaken by a United Nations sponsored team in 1952 with Dr. W.C. Reckless as the Head. He pointed out the need for career oriented training for jail administrators rather than being picked up from other services and inducted in jails to look after prisoners. His recommendations resulted in the revival of the conference of the Inspector Generals of Prison after a lapse of seventeen years. However, the Indian Constitution, followed the colonial model, kept the prison administration in the state list, under the jurisdiction of the state administration and all the state laws could be traced to the two main laws that governed the administration of prisons in colonial India—the Prisons Act of 1894 and Prisoners Act of 1900.

In the year 1957-59 the All India Jail Manual Committee was set up. It submitted its report in 1960. This resulted in the setting up of the Central Bureau of Correctional Services, which was later renamed as National Institute of Social Defense. A Working Group in 1973 suggested that the government should make effective use of alternatives to imprisonment as a policy measure and also highlighted the desirability of proper training of prison personnel and improvements in their service conditions. Further it made important recommendations with regard to the classification and treatment of offenders and laid down the principle of follow-ups and after care procedures. It pointed out that the development of prisons and correctional administration should no longer be divorced from the national development process and prison administration should be treated as an integral part of the social defense component of national planning (Bali-Mahabal, n.d).

Alarmed by the rise in criticism regarding the issue of prison malfunctioning in India the Government of India appointed the All India Committee on Jail Reforms in 1980, under the Chairmanship of Justice A.N. Mulla in 1980, popularly known as the Mulla Committee. The Mulla Committee examined all aspects of prison administration and made wide ranging recommendations which if implemented would go a long way to make prison administration efficient, humane and professional. The recommendations of Mulla Committee touched upon legislative, operational, security aspects, besides matters like classification of prisoners, living condition in prisons, medical and psychiatric services, treatment programs, vocational training for prison inmate, problems related to under trials, and other non-convicted prisoners, problems of women prisoners, etc. The report laid emphasis on the management of prisons to be entrusted to a cadre of professionals (Bali-Mahabal, n.d). The modalities suggesting for priority action entail a thorough restructuring of laws and procedures based on criminological and penological thinking (Shankardass, 2000).

Deplorably, India's prison system continues to be plagued by age old myriad problems, in spite of all reforms made by the Central and State Governments. Overcrowded prisons, disproportionately high undertrial population, lack of sufficient resources, frustrated and overburdened prison staff, lack of escorts to produce prisoners in court, unnecessary detention of undertrials for undue period are among some of the major concerns weighing down the Indian prisons. This chapter critically analyses the existing issues and challenges of Indian prisons and provide suitable solutions.

Issues and Challenges of Indian Prisons

1. Lack of Political Will

Having curtailed their liberty, prisoners do not enjoy voting rights. Even though they can contest elections being in the prison, they cannot vote. This lack of power in deciding the next ruling party has made them forgotten souls behind bars. The 3,76,396 (Government of India, 2007) votes do not count and hence the politicians disregard spending any time or money to curb the challenges faced by both the prisoners and the prison administration. Even the society does not have a sympathetic attitude towards those imprisoned. A person in the prison, irrespective of the fact that s/he has not been proven guilty, is already considered a criminal in the eyes of the community. Hence, reforming prisons has never been a priority on the agenda of a political party. In 1996, the National Human Rights Commission (NHRC) suggested a prison reform bill, which has been conveniently ignored by all the governments, as prisons is not their priority (Zora, 2005). The importance of political will in reforming prisons cannot be undermined. The United Nations report emphasizes "encouraging national ownership, generating political will, and civil society involvement in the prison system are complex and difficult processes, yet are key to success of program support" (United Nations, 2005, p. 6).

2. Lack of Human Resources

Jail staff constitutes the dynamic security of the jail. According to the Mulla Committees' recommendations, one warder should be entrusted with keeping watch over 25 prisoners. But in most of the prisons the available warder prisoner ratio does not follow the Mulla Committee's recommendations. In Jharkhand, even if all the warders are available round the clock, the warder inmate ratio is 1 : 27. There exists an acute shortage of staff, taking into account the shifts or when the warders go on leave or are entrusted with other work. Only one-fifth of the number is available which means that one warder has to manage 145 prisoners (Bali—Mahabal, n.d). According to an official of the Ranchi circle of jails, which has three divisional jails under its jurisdiction, central jails warders were last recruited in 1985. Against the 362 sanctioned posts, the circle has 192 vacancies. While in the jails under the Hazaribagh Circle, 138 posts of the 513 sanctioned posts remain vacant (*The Statesman*, 2004, March 10).

3. Overcrowding

On 19 June, 2000, at about 6.30 p.m., two of the inmates in an overcrowded cell apparently started fighting. A senior prison official, the Circle Officer, and other prison officers, reportedly attacked the prisoners in the cell indiscriminately with razors and wooden poles (lathis). There were 180 inmates in the cell, designed to hold 50. Some 40 inmates were injured, three reportedly suffering broken bones. Four have filed complaints in the Sessions Court [Amnesty International (2000), India: Fear of Torture—Detainees in Arthur Road Jail, Mumbai].

The above example is just one of the many news reports on the condition of inmates in Indian Prisons. Overcrowding, torture, inhuman conditions, etc. are all the primary ongoing activities within the walls of Indian Prisons. It is a shame that in this day and age our Criminal Justice Systems has still not been able to bring about the drastic reformations required in prisons. The Comptroller and Auditor General of India (CAG) in its report for the financial year ending March 31, 2008, observed that the average rate of occupancy in prisons was as high as 147 per cent, as per the records during the period of 2003-07 (*The Indian News*, 12th June, 2009). Currently too, in a special report by the Commonwealth Human Rights Initiative Indian Prisons are overcrowded by over 135%, and the Union State Minister for Home Affairs Ajay Maken told Lok Sabha, "The overcrowding in Indian prisons exists to the extent of 135.7 per cent."

The CAG report also stated that, "Overcrowding in prisons resulted in denial of the required ground, air and lateral ventilation spaces to the prisoners, which could affect their physical and mental health. It also put pressure on utilities such as water supply and sewerage systems. The workload of security staff also increased, hampering their ability to control crime and violence in the prisons" (*The Indian News*, 12th June, 2009). Delays in investigations, rising number of undertrial prisoners, and difficulties in granting bail have all resulted in overcrowding in prisons. Indian prisons in most instances do not match up to international standards. They lack the very basic amenities, such as sufficient food, clean drinking water, good hygienic spaces and health care.

"The occupancy rate of more than 100 per cent results in overcrowding in the jail" (Government of India, 2007, Glossary). One of the striking features of Indian prisons is the 141.4 per cent overcrowding across the 35 states and union territories. India was accommodating 3,76,396 prisoners in 2007 in its 1276 prisons having a capacity of 2,77,304 prisoners. 141.4 per cent is the overall average, with some states exceeding way beyond (Government of India, 2007). Uttar Pradesh reported the highest overcrowding of prisons (201.3%) followed by Chhattisgarh (193.3%) and Delhi (185.7%). Seventy-four per cent of the states struggle with overcrowded prisons. Only Jammu and Kashmir, Manipur, Mizoram, Nagaland, Rajasthan, West Bengal, Chandigarh, Dadar & Nagar Haveli, and Daman & Diu, have their prison population within the prison capacity.

Overcrowded prisons is one of the root causes that has branched out into several problems such as inadequate resources for every prisoner; increased burden on the limited prison staff, disgruntled and frustrated staff, lack of sufficient escort for the production of prisoners in court; delay in delivery of justice; deteriorating hygiene and sanitation conditions; and inadequate health care facilities, etc. It also causes surveillance and security issues which ordinarily is one of the key concerns of prison officers. This has been identified by the Apex Court on several occasions including in *Ramamurthy* v. *State of Karnataka,*[1] when a prisoner from Bangalore Central Jail complained about the general living conditions in a letter to the Chief Justice of India. The letter was treated as a writ petition and an inquiry was carried out by a District Judge who submitted a comprehensive report on the same. The Supreme Court observed the various problems that cropped as a result of the overcrowded prison.

Overcrowding has innumerable negative effects. The outbreak of diseases like malaria, diarrhea and cholera is quite frequent. The practice of homosexuality (though not officially acknowledged) may enhance the risk of prisoners becoming AIDS victim. The presence of a large number of under trial prisoners has also exaggerated the problem of overcrowding. According to the National Human Rights Commission's report the under-trial comprises of 70-75 per cent of all jail inmates (*The Statesman*, 2004, July 4). The National Crime Records Bureau had put their

1. AIR 1997 SC 1739.

number at 2,17,659 towards the end of 2003. Inordinate delay in disposal of their cases often keeps them behind the bars (*The Statesman*, 2004, July 4). According to the National Crime Record Bureau (NCRB) study, Crime in India, 2002, nearly 220,000 cases took more than 3 years to reach court and about 25,600 exhausted 10 years before they were completed (Zora, 2005).

For the delays in trial, the entire criminal justice system comprising of police, judiciary and legal profession are to be blamed. In many cases, charge sheets are filed by the police very late leading to a long chain reaction (Bali-Mahabal, n.d). The maximum delay takes place in examining witnesses and recording evidence. There are also lapses in producing undertrial in courts on the date of hearing as a result hearing get adjourned causing unnecessary delay (Bali-Mahabal, n.d). Due to the resource crunch, it has become difficult to either augment the police escort in each district or add to the number of jail vans. As the number of jail vans is not enough, often prisoners are brought in the court in less secure police vehicles, requiring deployment of more policemen in the escort party (Bali-Mahabal, n.d). However many undertrial prisoners are in jails simply because they are so poor and the provision of bails are beyond their reach. They belong to the underprivileged section of our society (lowest strata in terms of caste, economy), belonging to rural areas with an agricultural background and are involved in some minor violation of the law. Most of the persons who land up on Indian prisons are those who come in conflict with the law under various kind of situational compulsion or victimizing circumstances. When such persons are made to stay with juveniles, hardened criminals, or even first time offenders, minor criminals can be turned into hardened one's in a short time.

The National Human Rights Commission (NHRC) in a letter to the state governments has asked to prepare a list of convicts serving life sentence who are 'eligible for premature release'. The commission has kept certain kinds of crime out of this privilege. For instance, convicts sentenced to life for terrorism, those convicted of organized crime, professional murderers, murders during cross border smuggling and those convicted for murdering on duty public servant should not be considered at all. In setting the guidelines for the possibility of an early release, NHRC has updated the provisions listed under Criminal Procedure Code, 1973, Section 433-A, Constitution of India, Article 161. Early provisions were favourable for those convicted who had a good record under captivity or were overaged and has lost the potential to be involved in new crime. The act of release was contingent upon the fact that the released convict would not be in a position to group with other criminals or that the original offense had been an individual act of crime and did not affect the society in a big way. Most importantly, the witnesses who had deposed at the trial were not apprehensive of retaliation in the event of premature release. According to NHRC, all male lifers who have served a 14-year imprisonment could be eligible for pre-mature release. For females it could be considered after the completion of a ten-year jail term. Aged life convicts those who have crossed 65 years and have already spent seven years behind bars including remission can be considered. NHRC has also been very elaborate on 'terminally-ill' life convicts. Those suffering from diseases like cancer, tuberculosis, AIDs, irreversible kidney failure, cardiorespiratory failure, leprosy or any other infectious disease and have spent five to seven years behind bars are also eligible for premature release (*Times of India*, 2004, August 17). Yet in India, a large section of aged prisoners are languishing in jails. Though the all India figure of such aged population was not available, a considerable section of this aged class should have been free (thereby reducing overcrowding considerably) had the respective state governments heeded the directives of the NHRC to release elderly prisoners.

4. Torture

Torture is an integral part of the Indian prison system; sexual harassment, rape, violent methods of interrogation, are all a part and parcel of our justice system. Custodial violence against women very often includes rape and other forms of sexual violence such as threats of rape, touching, "virginity testing", being stripped naked, invasive body searches, insults and humiliations of a sexual nature, etc. (Asian Center for Human Rights, 2008). Torture of women in custody including rape is reported regularly in

India. Custodial rape remains one of the worst forms of torture perpetrated on women by law enforcement personnel including prison officials.

5. Deaths in Custody

Custodial deaths in India are a reality which is hard to deny. Instances of inhuman, degrading treatment, concealed physical and mental torture like exposure to sun for long hours during summer, delay or refusal to provide medical care, prolonged physical work even during ill health, are manifestations of the various forms of torture inflicted upon prison inmates. According to the Indian Home Ministry records, deaths while in remand or custody increased from 1340 in 2002 to 1462 by the end of 2003. According to the National Human Rights Commission report, a large proportion of the deaths in custody were from natural and easily curable causes aggravated by poor prison conditions. Tuberculosis caused many deaths, and HIV/AIDS remained a serious health threat among prison inmates (Zora, 2005). According to the Crime in India, eighty-six custodial deaths were reported in the country in the year 2004 (Government of India, 2004). Non-Government Organizations (NGO) that deal with prison abuses alleges that death in police custody, which occurred within hours or days of initial detention often, implied violent abuse and torture. The rape of persons in custody is also a part of the broader pattern of custodial abuse.

In West Bengal, high rates of undertrial deaths have blotted the State's record. In early 2002, an enquiry was launched into the death of the under trialprisoner Samir Kunthia, and the post mortem revealed no less than 30 injuries on his body (*Times of India*, 2004, November 13).

In July 2004, the National Human Rights Commission requested a report from the Inspector General of Prisons, Punjab, after a man incarcerated in Amritsar's Central Jail claimed that the Deputy Superintendent and other prison officials branded him on his back when he demanded water and better treatment. Doctors found fresh scars on his back that proved had been inflicted with hot iron rods. By the end of the year no action had been taken (Zora, 2005).

According to the United Nations Principles on the Effective Prevention and Investigation of Extra-Legal, Arbitrary and Summary Executions provide that there shall be:

> There shall be a thorough, prompt and impartial investigation of all suspected cases of unlawful killing, including where complaints by relatives suggest unnatural death. The principles state that if the body has been buried and it later appears that an investigation is required, the body shall be promptly and competently exhumed for an autopsy [which] shall be available to those conducting the autopsy for a sufficient amount of time to enable a thorough investigation to be carried out.... In order to ensure objective results, those conducting the autopsy must be able to function impartially and independently of any potentially implicated persons or organizations or entities.

The principles also state that families of the deceased and their legal representatives shall have access to all information relevant to the investigation, and have the right to insist that a medical representative be present at the autopsy.

On 19th August, 2009, *The New Indian Express* (South Indian Edition), printed an article by R. Guhambika, titled, "Around 40 custodial deaths in 3 years" in the state of Tamil Nadu. While, the figures are hard to believe in comparison to other states, as the number is considerably low, the state is known to have one of the best justice systems in the country. However, the interrogation methods used by the police are '*crude and obsolete*'. While some of the prisoners are capable of handling the pain, many of them are scarred for life. "Custodial death victims usually hail from backward sections of society—many of them are Dalits—with little or no means to seek legal help", according to rights activists.

It's important to understand the problems prisoners undergo in prisons, as there are many who want to bring about a change in their lifestyle but are unable to because of the torture they have been put through. Many prisoners who have chosen to live a reformed life after their release from prison have found it frustratingly impossible to do so, because every time a crime is committed in their neighbourhood the police approach them, or they are directly taken to the police station where they are abused endlessly. Eventually out of mere frustration, many choose to end their lives. Torture in prisons continues to be a growing problem and a solution is the need of the hour.

6. Disproportionate Undertrial to Convict Ratio

Indian prisons have a strikingly high undertrial population. Undertrials are persons kept in prison (judicial custody) while the charges against them are being tried (Government of India, 2007). Undertrials are prisoners who are innocent in the eyes of the law. Yet, Indian prisons house prisoners of which 66.6 per cent are undertrials (Government of India, 2007, p. i). Only 31.9 per cent of Indian prison population are convicted. The highest number of undertrials at the end of 2007 were reported from Uttar Pradesh (53,992), followed by Bihar (33,316) and Madhya Pradesh (16,537), (Government of India, 2007, p. 29).

A lot of these prisoners continue to remain in prisons, despite being charged of bailable offences. In bailable offences, it is the right of the accused to be out on bail. However, since the bail system is biased and favours those that are economically well-off, it cannot be called impartial or fair. It is a challenge for the indigent to produce such huge monetary amounts for their release and so they continue to stay in prisons.

> Democracy's very life depends upon making the machinery of justice so effective that every citizen shall believe in and benefit by its impartiality and fairness [*M.H. Hoskot* v. *State of Maharashtra*, (1978) 3 SSC 544].
>
> With imprisonment, a radical transformation comes over a prisoner, which can be described as prisonisation. He loses his identity. He is known by a number. He loses personal possessions. He has no personal relationships. Psychological problems result from loss of freedom, status, possessions, dignity and autonomy of personal life (*A Convict Prisoner in the Central Prison* vs. *State of Kerala*, 1993 Cri LJ 3242).

Just like Machang Lalung (Zora, 2005) and Syed Maqbool Shah (Rafiq, 2010) who had completely forgotten how life would be outside the four walls on their release after fifty-four and fourteen years respectively. While Machang, had he been convicted would have been given a maximum punishment of ten years imprisonment, was released after paying a token bond amount of one rupee, Syed was acquitted after serving fourteen years in prison. There are several Syed's and Machang's who continue to stay in prison without being given an opportunity to prove their innocence. The legislators identified this and in 2005 amended the Cr.P.C. to set a maximum period that an under-trial prisoner can be kept in prison. The 2005 amendment of the Cr.P.C. has brought some respite to a small section of undertrial prisoners.

7. Delay in Disposal of Cases for the Underprivileged

Most prisoners are poor and belong to the underprivileged sections of society. The state that deprives them of liberty is duty bound to provide them the basic necessities. The Supreme Court in *Hussainara Khatoon and Others (II)* v. *Home Secretary, State of Bihar* case found that "though speedy trial is not specifically enumerated as a fundamental right, it is implicit in the broad sweep and content of Article 21".[2] One of the critical problems plaguing Indian criminal justice system is the colossal delay in disposal of cases. This delay in disposal of cases may be attributed to three primary causes namely: large number of vacancies for the position of judicial officers; inability/failure of the police to complete investigation on a timely basis; and lack of police escort to produce the accused in court (Bharadwaj, 2009).

8. Criminals-Jail Staff Nexus

In recent times innumerable incidents have taken place which for the umpteenth time proves that vices like criminals-jail staff nexus exists within the institution of prison.

The five undertrials who escaped from Dum Dum Central Correctional Home did so with the connivance of the jail staff who helped them break open the cells at the prodding of

2. AIR 1979 SC 1369.

Chaitanya Pal, the undertrial prisoner who was released on bail (*The Telegraph*, 2003, September 23).

A jail warder supplied the mobile phone and cash to Aftab Ansari (who allegedly masterminded the American Center Attack, Kolkata in January 2002). This was revealed in an inquiry report which stated that the warder Ruplal Majumdar supplied the mobile phone and two ₹ 500 notes in connivance with outsiders (*The Statesman*, 2003, March 2).

Jail Officials found nearly ₹ 2000 inside notorious criminal Gudda's cell in the Presidency Correctional Home, Kolkata, during a surprise raid. Noted criminals like Sheikh Vinod have been running an extortion racket from behind the jail walls by issuing instructions over the cell phone. Officers of Alipore Central Correctional Home went on a search and dug out a set from the courtyard facing his cell. Wrapped in polythene the cell phone was hidden in the mud (*The Statesman*, 2004, November 13).

9. Children of Prisoners

One of the most important areas of concern is the treatment of children of women prisoners. A survey on the children of women prisoners conducted by the National Institute of Criminology and Forensic Science between 1997-2000 reveals that they are forced to grow up in conditions of deprivation and criminality, along with lack of proper nutrition, inadequate medical care and little opportunity for education (*The Statesman*, 2003, March 2). Most prisons didn't have crèches, medical care or recreational and educational opportunities. Some did not even have segregated barracks for women and children and were found to live in the male section.

The Supreme Court of India has issued a directive to the Central government and the states to ensure basic minimum rights to children of women prisoners. A three-judge bench, headed by Chief Justice Y.K. Sabharwal said that jails should ensure that children accompanying their mothers to jail are not treated as prisoners but as free individuals. Moreover, the court has ordered that the jail administration should ensure that pregnant undertrials or convicted women be provided with alternatives to giving birth inside the jail. The Supreme Court's directive has sought an amendment of jail manuals to provide women with extra facilities, which includes them being shifted to hospitals with proper facilities. The directive also states that birth certificates of children born to incarcerated mothers must not mention jail as their place of birth (*The Telegraph*, 2006, May 3).

Yet hundreds of innocent children live in jails across India only because their mothers have been imprisoned. Some may be stigmatized or physically or emotionally harassed by other children and at times even by jail staff. Jails in Mumbai have unmistakable signs of destroyed childhood: dusty teddy bears with gouged out eyes, broken red toys and decapitated dolls, no cribs, baby food or warm milk. Officials admit in private that the children are viewed as a liability and a drain on their already meager jail budget (Asia Child Rights, 2004).

Conclusion

All the above-mentioned challenges can be resolved, however due to a lack of political will and desire among the key players, nothing has been done to remedy the situation. Judges can be appointed, a dedicated branch of police can be appointed to look into investigations; and similarly with less overcrowded prisons, proper coordination between police and prisons appropriate number of escorts can be managed. However, if there is no will among the police officers to complete investigation on a timely basis, and if there is no desire among the judicial officers to complete a case without prolonging it to more dates and letting the prisoners languish in prison, nothing can be done to better the situation.

Certain steps may be taken to ensure effective functioning of prisons in India. These include:

- The photograph and fingerprints of the convict may be kept.
- New technology in locking system as well as biometric system such as fingerprint or retinal eye identification may be used.
- The ion spectrometry drug detection machines may be installed inside the prison. Such machines help to detect tiny levels of drug on people's hand and clothing.

- The effective use of this machine may ensure that drugs don't reach inside the prisons.
- Latest technological devices may be used for the management of prison.
- Manual counting may be replaced by Technological System International Prison Security Management devices. These latest technological devices can perform a perfect inmate 'headcount' every two seconds, thereby helping to trace out any prison escape immediately.
- It is necessary to convert some of the cells where high profile, hardened prisoners are present into the 'Supermax' prisons of the West.
- Perimeter fencing should be provided outside the jails. Constant mobile patrolling is necessary in and around the jail premises. The case histories of inmates in all the prisons in India have not yet been fully computerized and must be computerized. Methods of preservation of historical records/data should be given due attention.
- It is necessary to speed up the judicial process so that some innocent undertrials don't have to languish in jails for long time. It is an unnecessary financial burden on the state.
- Video-conferencing trial system may be implemented for undertrial. Alternatives to prisons may be created. Non-custodial punishments can serve as a viable alternative to prisons.
- Those accused for drug related problems may be sent to drug rehabilitation centers.
- Restorative justice in form of victim-offender interaction may be used.
- For the first time offenders community service scheme may be implemented. Under this scheme an offender is required to perform certain hours of community service at a particular institution (like old age home, clinics, hospitals). The bottom line is that some convicts are not really serious offenders/habitual criminals and that

with some help they can become ordinary law abiding members of the country.

- It is necessary to recruit sociologists, psychologists and professional counsellors in the jail department.
- It is necessary to create an All India Cadre of officers to manage the prisons.

Furthermore, a National Assessment and Accreditation Council for accessing Correctional Homes in India may be set up with the help of human rights activists, judges, lawyers and eminent sociologists, and criminologists. Prisons throughout the country may be evaluated by setting parameters like presence of humanitarian reforming conditions, jail management, and convict-correctional staff interactions. Such a move may facilitate healthy competition among the jails in India to improve their infrastructure (both material and non-material resources).

The National Human Rights Commission has been advocating the replacement of the archaic Indian Prison Act of 1894 by a Model Prison Bill which would be uniformly applicable throughout the country. In the year 1996, the Commission had prepared and circulated an outline of a Model Prison Bill and urged all the states to have appropriate resolutions passed in their respective legislatures so that a new Act could be adopted by the Parliament under Article 252 of the Constitution of India. While this process was underway, the Ministry of the Home Affairs entrusted a related task to the Bureau of Police Research and Development. On 27th December 2002, the Commission thus received for its comments, from the Union Home Secretary, a Draft Model Prison Manual prepared by a Committee headed by the Director General, Bureau of Police and Research Development. After the Draft Prison Manual was examined by the Custodial Justice Cell, the Commission considered the matter and forwarded its comments to the Ministry of Home Affairs on 11th February 2003 (NHRC, 2003). It is necessary that the Central Government should create a standard jail manual applicable throughout the country with the help of human rights activists, judges, lawyers, sociologists, criminologists and professionals dealing with issues related to prison. Community participation should be encouraged.

It is to be remembered that cosmetic reform or aping western model of correctional administration and management will not solve the problems of jail administration in India, unless discipline be blended with humanitarian jail administration.

References

Ahuja, R. (2000). *Criminology.* Jaipur & New Delhi: Rawat Publications.

Asia Child Rights (2004). "India: Children Stay in Indian Prison with their Mothers". *ACR Weekly Newsletter, 3*(15), 14 April 2004.

Bali-Mahabal, K. (n.d.). Prison Conditions in India. Human Rights behind the Prison wall. *Human Rights Law Network.*

Bharadwaj, P. (2009). *Liberty at the Cost of Innocence—A Report on Jail Adalats in India.* Commonwealth Human Rights Initiative. New Delhi.

Government of India. (2007). *Prison Statistics India.* National Crime Records Bureau, Ministry of Home Affairs, Government of India.

——. (2004). *Crime in India.* National Crime Records Bureau, Ministry of Home Affairs, Government of India.

National Human Rights Commission (NHRC) (2003). *Annual Report* (2002-03).

Rafiq, Z. (2010). After 14 years, free 'strange' to acquitted man. Retrieved on 15th July 2011 from http://www.indianexpress.com/news/after-14-years-freedom-strange-to-acquitted-man/610236/0

The Statesman. (2004, March 10). Where jail is no bar to freedom.

——. (2005, July 4). Prison Evils. Need for Urgent Reforms.

——. (2003, March 2). Warder supplied cash, mobile phone to Ansari.

The Telegraph. (2003, September 23). It can happen only in India. Missiles find Home in Delhi house, Prisoners find ladder in jail.

——. (2006, May 3). Free in prison.

The Times of India. (2004, November 13). State prison hotbed of crime.

——. (2004, August 17). NHRC set new rules for early release of lifers.

United Nations. (2005). *Supporting National Prison Systems: Lessons Learned and Best Practices for Peacekeeping Operations.*

Zora, P. (2005). Fifty-four Years in Jail without Trial: The Plight of Prison Inmates in India. Retrieved on 15th July 2011 from http://www.countercurrents.org/hr-zora260805.htm

3

Prison Reforms: Historical and Contemporary Perspectives

Vijay Raghavan

Introduction

Prison populations have remained at the margins of welfare and development, and have seldom been viewed as in need of deserving social services. With the development of criminology as a subject of enquiry, a gradual shift has taken place, whereby the individual alone is no more held responsible for his/her norm or law breaking behaviour. This shift in perspective has led to the development of an understanding of crime causation that includes psychological, social, economic and political factors as being responsible for deviant behaviour in human beings. The shift has included a gradual policy shift away from capital punishment, torture and debilitating forms of punishment, imprisonment as and not for punishment, more humane custodial conditions, protection of legal and human rights, and finally a focus on retraining, rehabilitation and social inclusion.

The history of the correctional movement could be traced to developments which first took place in the U.K. in the early twentieth century. The turning point, in the humane treatment of custodial populations came with the Universal Declaration of Human Rights. These standards were further strengthened by the U.N. Standard Minimum Rules for Treatment of Prisoners, 1955. In the Indian scenario, the Indian Constitution, the Prisons Act, 1894, the rulings of the Supreme Court and the various High Courts in the country and the reports of various prison reform committees set up by the government from time to time have adequately highlighted the problems and concerns with regard to the situation of prisoners and the suggested roadmap to address these concerns. In contrast, the situation at the ground level continues to a cause for concern. It warrants urgent steps to be taken with regard to deinstitutionalization of prison populations, improving custodial conditions and taking steps to create human resource and infrastructure to fulfil the correctional and rehabilitation objectives of Indian criminal justice system. In this chapter, an attempt is made to provide an overview of the past and current prison reforms in India and some suggestions for the improvement of prison conditions in India.

A Situational Analysis of Prisons in India

The system of prison welfare in the country was set in the context of reformation and rehabilitation of the convicted prisoner. Prisons were originally meant to house those who had been convicted by the law for the offences they were charged with. A minor focus of prisons was the housing of untried or undertrial prisoners, i.e. those awaiting trial and kept in judicial custody, till the completion of their cases in courts. They were in prison either because they were unable to produce suitable sureties or because they had been denied bail due to the nature of the offence they were charged with. The basic duty of the prison and judicial authorities towards this population was to ensure their physical and mental health and safety and access to their legal rights. The question of any correctional or treatment programs for this group did not arise, as they had not yet been found 'guilty' of the offence they had been charged with.

However, one fact that the authorities and civil society did not take note of was the rising numbers of undertrials in prisons. Owing to the rising crime rate, it is observed that the number of prisoners has expanded since the last century. However, the number of prisons has not increased post-independence, thus resulting in overcrowding and non-classification of prisoners according to correctional principles. According to the National Crime Records Bureau (2006), there are a total of 1336 prisons in the country, housing a total population of 373,271 prisoners as against a stipulated capacity of 263,911 prisoners. Out of this number, as of 2006, 31.3 per cent were convicts, 65.7 per cent were undertrials and the balance 3 per cent being detainees and others. As far as the male-female ratio is concerned, 96.1 per cent were males and 3.9 per cent were females.

The average occupancy of prisons in the country was 144.1 per cent for males and 97.5 per cent for females. This implies an overcrowding of 44.1 per cent for males against the stipulated/authorized capacity, while for female wards/prison are underpopulated to the tune of 2.5 per cent. The worst scenario in terms of overcrowding of male prisoners was found in Sikkim and Delhi (222 per cent and 221.1 per cent, i.e. overcrowding of 122 per cent and 121.1 per cent respectively). Among the smaller states, the most manageable situation was found to be in Nagaland (57.2 per cent, i.e. underpopulated by 42.8 per cent) and among the larger states, it was Rajasthan and West Bengal (81.8 per cent and 92.9 per cent).

The delays in trials in courts have also taken menacing dimensions, leading to the overcrowding of prisons. The Law Commission in its 120th Report recommended that the strength of judges per million population may be increased from 10.5 to 50 judges. The present judge strength in India is 14 per million population (Twocircles.net, 2009). India has one of the poorest judge-population ratios when compared to countries such as Australia (47 per million), UK (50 per million), Canada (75 per million) and USA (107 per million) (Hansaria, 2005). This is despite the fact that the pendency of cases in the country is about 26.3 million in the subordinate courts and over 3 million in the High Courts in India (*Hindustan Times*, 2007).

By the early eighties, the situation had become alarming, the array of public interest litigations that have clogged the courts since then, is an indicator of the seriousness of the problem at hand. A system that was designed to handle a specific target group, i.e. convicts had now been taken over by another, for which the system was poorly prepared, i.e. undertrials. Investments in the welfare sector by the government reduced considerably in terms of institutional set up, manpower, training, and service delivery. There was a gradual neglect of the criminal justice system, and custodial institutions in particular.

As urbanization increased, it has led to 'atomization' of individuals coupled with dilution of traditional mechanisms of social control. This in turn has led to increased crime rates, particularly in the urban centres. As more people migrated to cities and towns in search of livelihoods, a plethora of archaic laws, designed by the British primarily to maintain law and order, were used by the police to take charge of persons who were seen as 'disturbing law and order', resulting in the criminalization of persons primarily migrants in search of employment and coming from poverty groups. The prison system came to be crushed under the weight of petty offenders, ticketless travellers, those arrested for 'loitering' in suspicious circumstances, drunken behaviour, hawkers, those arrested under the forest act, theft of railway property, and a host of other property crimes which could be linked to the overall lack of employment options and social security benefits that any 'caring' State should have. These cases in turn clogged the courts of the country, crippling the criminal justice system in the process.

As per the Prison Statistics India 2006 (Government of India, 2006), out of a total of 245,244 undertrial prisoners in the country, the pendency of cases in the courts is as follows:

- Pending for 6 months 156,937 cases (63.9%)
- Pending for 6 months to 1 year 42,671 cases (17.3%)
- Pending for 1 to 2 years 26,982 cases (11.0%)
- Pending for 2 to 3 years 11,343 cases (4.62%)
- Pending for 3 to 5 years 5,742 cases (2.34%)
- Pending above 5 years 1,569 cases (0.63%)

The situation of interminable delays in the justice delivery system in turn, has led to a very poor conviction rate. Collection of evidence, summoning of witnesses, ensuring they do not turn hostile at the trial stage and retaining the interest of the complainant in convicting the offender became a huge task for the prosecuting agencies. Most persons arrested finally get either acquitted or discharged in their cases. The police machinery routinely arrests people rather than use their discretion of arrest.[1] The courts then remand them to judicial custody after police investigation is over, thus increasing the load on the prisons. The prisons in turn have no choice but to keep them as undertrials till they go out on bail or their cases in court end up in a discharge, acquittal, release on probation or a sentence of imprisonment. Correctional and vocational training facilities are provided only to the last mentioned category, as in classical understanding, these are the only persons who constitute the client population of the prison systems.

As far as the higher judiciary and enlightened forces within the system is concerned, the system should be accessible to the marginalized, but in practice, the rights and facilities offered by the system somehow eludes those who are most in need. The major reason is that the structures and investments required in implementing the court judgments and reform committee reports simply do not exist. In consonance with the changing realities there have been little or no investments made to increase trained manpower, ensure legal rights, create rehabilitation structures and reduce overload on the system.

According to the Prison Statistics India, 2006 (Government of India, 2006), the total number of prisoners provided with:

- Educational facilities was 100,959 (around 27 per cent of total prison population),
- Vocational training was 40,338 (around 11 per cent),
- Financial assistance was an insignificant 1709 prisoners, and
- Rehabilitated convicts was 1632.

Shockingly, as many as 18 states have reported that the number of cases officially given financial assistance as zero and 19 states have reported that the number of cases rehabilitated during the same period as zero.

1. The power of arrest is a discretionary power given to the police by the law, to be selectively used by them only in cases where they apprehend the accused may abscond or tamper with evidence. The Criminal Procedure Code Amendment 2008 has further clarified this position under section 41 of the Code.

Prison Reforms: Historical Perspective

The history of the correctional movement could be traced to developments which first took place in the U.K. in the early twentieth century. The Gladstone Committee Report (1894) was one of the first such attempts to bring reforms in the British prison system. The Report highlighted the overemphasis on the deterrent aim of imprisonment and under emphasis on reformation of the prisoner. It reiterated that the prisoner should not be merely taken as condemned but the system should be designed so as to be able to 'individualise' him/her. It condemned hard labour, hard fare and hard bed as outdated concepts.

The report laid down the basic principles of the existing prison system in England:

1. Imprisonment should lead to constructive training—moral, mental and vocational.
2. Such training should be lawfully carried out in homogenous establishments specifically created for the purpose.
3. Special training prisons need not provide security of normal prison buildings.
4. Services of the community outside prisons should be enlisted to help in training of the prisoners.
5. Continuing responsibility of society should be maintained for discharged prisoners towards their social rehabilitation (cited in Government of India, 1987, Vol. II).

In India under the British rule, it was Lord Macaulay, who drew attention to the terrible prison conditions prevailing in the country. A Committee was set up in 1836 to examine the issue and make recommendations. However, the Committee did not give any reform oriented recommendations on the pretext of laxity of discipline (cited in Government of India, 1987, Vol. II).

The defining moment in the humane treatment of custodial populations came with the Universal Declaration of Human Rights (United Nations, 1948). It resolved that member nations shall ensure that citizens are given equal treatment, and have the right to life and liberty. It further resolved that the State shall ensure security of persons, freedom from torture, cruel, inhuman and degrading treatment, right to recognition as persons before the law, no arbitrary arrests, detention or exile, equality before law, fair, public, independent and impartial trial with necessary guarantees for defense.

These standards were further strengthened by the U.N. Standard Minimum Rules for Treatment of Prisoners, 1955 (United Nations, 1955). The Standard Minimum Rules was approved by the Economic and Social Council of the United Nations in 1957, of which India is a signatory. These rules mandate that 'the prisoner should be encouraged and assisted in cultivating relations with persons or extra-institutional agencies conducive to his rehabilitation and best interest after release'. It stipulates that 'representatives of such agencies shall have access to prisoners during their term of incarceration and be taken into consultation for the future of each prisoner from the beginning of his sentence'. Some of its specific recommendations relating to treatment of prisoners are:

(i) *General rules*: There shall be no discrimination on the basis of race, sex, colour, religion, political, or other opinion, national or social origin, property, birth, or other status. The States shall respect the religious beliefs and moral precepts of the community to which a prisoner belongs [rule 6(1) and (2)].

(ii) *Rules regarding separation of prisoners*: There shall be rules for separation of prisoners on the basis of sex, age, criminal record and other circumstances (rule 8). Woman prisoners shall be kept separately from male prisoners. Untried prisoners shall be kept separately from the convicted prisoners; civil prisoner from criminal prisoner and young prisoner from the adult prisoner [rule 8(a), (b), (c) and (d)].

(iii) *Rules for providing minimum facilities*: There shall be separate accommodation for different types of prisoners, separate bedding and clothing giving due consideration to hygiene, food of nutritional value, adequate health facilities, qualified medical staff, and facilities of T.V., radio, newspapers, magazines and books shall be provided. Communication with family and friends at regular intervals shall be allowed [rules 8(d), 15, 16, 19, 20(1), 22(1), 23(1), 37, 38 and 39].

(iv) *Rules for undertrials:* There shall be separation of under trials on age basis (young and adults should be kept in separate premises), allowing home food, and wearing their own clothing.

(v) *Social relations and aftercare*: The purpose of punishment should be to reform and not torture. Necessary steps shall be taken before completion of sentence, to ensure that the prisoner is able to return to normal life, through pre-release programs, and release on trial under supervision (not by the police) combined with provision of social aid.

The Fourth United Nations Congress on Prevention of Crime and Treatment of Offenders, held in Japan, 1970, devoted a full session to the theme of public participation of prevention and control of crime and juvenile delinquency.

The U.N. Declaration on Protection from Torture, 1975 (United Nations, 1975) laid down guidelines for member nations to ensure protection from torture:

- Article 2: Any act of torture or other cruel inhuman or degrading treatment or punishment is an offence to human dignity shall be condemned as a denial of the purposes of the Charter of the UN and as violation of human rights and fundamental freedoms proclaimed in the Universal declaration of Human Rights.
- Article 3: No State may permit or tolerate torture or other cruel, inhuman, degrading treatment or punishment.

Legal Status of Prisoners

A. Constitutional Provisions

While the UN resolutions are not legally binding on member States, the Indian Constitution (Government of India, 2007) contains comprehensive provisions to ensure that citizens are treated in consonance with the above-mentioned resolutions.

- Article 14 states that the State shall not deny any person, equality before the law or equal protection of the laws within the territory of India.
- Article 19 guarantees six freedoms to citizens of India. Freedoms like the freedom of movement, freedom to reside and to settle. However, freedom of profession, occupation, trade, or business cannot be enjoyed by the prisoners because of the very nature of these freedoms and due to the conditions of imprisonment. But other freedoms like freedom of speech and expression, or freedom to become member of an association, can be enjoyed by prisoners, within the limitations of prisons.
- Article 20(1) protects persons from ex-post-facto laws, i.e. no person shall be convicted for any offence except for violation of a law in force at the time of commission of the act charged as an offence.
- Article 20(2) protects persons from being prosecuted and punished more than once for the same offence, i.e. the principle of double jeopardy.
- Article 20(3) safeguards the undertrial or a detenue from being compelled by the prison or police authorities to give testimony which is likely to expose them for criminal consequences.
- Article 21 states that no person shall be deprived of his life or personal liberty except according to the procedure established by law.
- Article 22(1) provides the right of a person accused of an offence to be defended by an advocate of his choice. The right makes it mandatory on the part of the State to provide for free and competent legal representation to the accused in his case in the court of law, from the time of arrest through the entire trial.
- Article 39-A provides for free legal aid services to be established by the State.
- Article 22(4) to (7) provides for special safeguards to detenues detained under preventive laws.

B. Prisons Act, 1894

The Prisons Act of 1894 (Government of India, 1957) lays down the minimum conditions for upkeep and treatment of prisoners and imposes limitations on custodial authorities to the type of treatment that can be given to those in penal custody.

- Section 4 provides for proper accommodation for prisoners.
- Section 7 casts an obligation on the State Government to provide for temporary accommodation in case of overcrowding and outbreak of epidemic.
- Section 13 makes the Medical Officer (M.O.) responsible for sanitary conditions in prisons.
- Section 14 provides that the M.O. is required to submit a report regarding the mental condition of a prisoner whenever it appears that he is not fit.

The Act also provides for separation of male from female prisoners, undertrial from convicted prisoners and male prisoners under the age of 21 years from those above 21 years. The various provisions of the Act are the guiding force behind the Prison Manuals formulated by each State. The Model Prison Manual (1970) drafted by the All India Jail Manual Committee, has also laid down the guiding principles based on which many States have drafted or upgraded their respective State Prison Manuals. Some of the common features of these Manuals are:

- ➢ Undertrial prisoners are permitted to wear their own clothing, eat home-cooked food and bring books inside and subscribe to newspapers/magazines, etc. from their own sources.
- ➢ Convicted prisoners, who have been sentenced to rigorous imprisonment, are not allowed to work for more than nine hours a day. The type of work to be assigned to a prisoner is to be decided by the M.O. based on the physical examination of the prisoner every fifteen days.
- ➢ Punishments in prison are for offences like wilful disobedience, use of force, foul language, etc. The punishments include hard labour, separate confinement,

reduction of diet, etc., but no two punishments can be combined, which may have adverse effect on the health of the prisoner.

- Meetings (*mulakat*) with family members is allowed in a regulated manner at specified intervals, both for convicts as well as undertrials, as per the Prison Manuals of different States, ranging from twice a week to once a month, depending on the State Manual and the category of the prisoner (undertrial or convict).
- Rules on release on parole and furlough (short leave) are also specified in the various Prison Manuals for prisoners as a means of maintaining contact with the family and society, which would be helpful in rehabilitation. Rules existing in the Prisons Act state that prisoners should be temporarily released subject to certain conditions for a period not exceeding ten days, excluding time required for journey.
- Prisoners enjoy all political rights as ordinary citizens, such as right to vote or right to fight elections. These rights are subject to certain disqualifications, as per the Representation of Peoples' Act, i.e. those who have been sentenced for offences involving moral turpitude.

C. Supreme Court and High Court Rulings

The Supreme Court and various High Court rulings on prisoners' rights also need mention, as these rulings have interpreted the laws of the land based on writ petitions and Public Interest Litigations (PILs) filed from time to time on the issue.

(1) Protection of the Fundamental Rights of Prisoners

In the case of Patnaik (AIR 1974 SC 2092), Justice Chandrachud held that "Convicts are not, be mere reason of the conviction, denuded of all the fundamental rights which they otherwise possess. A compulsion under the authority of law, following upon a conviction, to live in a prison-house entails by its own force the deprivation of fundamental freedoms like the right to move freely throughout the territory of India or the right to practice a profession.... But the Constitution guarantees other freedoms like the right to acquire, hold and dispose off property for the exercise of which incarceration can be no impediment."

In Writ Petition No. 1822 of 1985 of the A.P. High Court, while considering the question of wages for work done by prisoners, said that "In the general realm of reason too, one can find no support for the view that the State can deny payment to the prisoner's work or that the State is under no obligation to provide any work to the prisoner. Idleness, particularly forced idleness, is sure to destroy a man's life and personal liberty."

In Hussainara Khatoon (1979 Cr.L.J. 1045) and earlier in Hoskot (AIR 1978 SC 1548), the Supreme Court declared that "the right to free legal services is an essential ingredient of reasonable, fair and just procedure implicit in the right to personal liberty under Article 21".

In the Francis Coralie case (AIR 1981 SC 746), it was observed that the right to life for prisoners includes the right to live with human dignity and includes adequate nutrition, clothing, shelter, facilities for reading, writing and expressing oneself in diverse forms, freely moving about and mixing with fellow human beings.

(2) Right to Fair Procedure

(i) Right to bail: In Babu Singh's case [(1978) 2 SCR 777], the Supreme Court laid down that the rejection of bail without any reason, amounts to unreasonable deprivation of an individual's liberty.

(ii) Right to be represented in court: In the Hoskot case (AIR 1978 SC 1548), the Supreme Court laid down two ingredients of fair procedure:

(a) A convict should be provided with a copy of the judgment within a reasonable period so that he may exercise his right to appeal, and

(a) Free legal aid should be provided to the person if he is not able to arrange the same owing to disability or poverty.

(iii) Right to speedy trial: Fair procedure includes a reasonable speedy trial. In the Hussainara Khatoon case (AIR 1979 SC 1360), the Court stated that a speedy trial is implicit in the broad sweep and content of Article 21, as interpreted in the Maneka Gandhi case (AIR 1978 SC 597).

(3) Political Rights

(i) Freedom of expression: Freedom of thought and expression includes the right to express one's views—including in writing or by publishing one's writings. This right is available to prisoners within reasonable restrictions (as laid down in the censorship rules of Prison Manuals). The Supreme Court in the Pandurang Sanzgiri case (AIR 1966 SC 424) observed that any procedure which permits the impairment of the individual's rights without giving him a reasonable opportunity of being heard should be condemned as unfair and unreasonable.

(ii) Press interviews: In the Prabha Dutt case, the Supreme Court (AIR 1982 SC 6), ruled that a prisoner is entitled to give a press interview, if the press is willing to take his interview. A death sentence prisoner, who is willing to write something which is of great scientific, historical or educational value may be given enough opportunity and time to complete his work by suspending execution of death penalty for a reasonable period of time.

(iii) Freedom of association: Prisoners can become a member of any organization, social, cultural or political, as per Article 19(1)(c) of the Constitution.

(4) Some Specific Rulings Regarding the Role of Social Workers in Prison

In the landmark judgment of Sunil Batra (AIR 1980 SC 1579), the Supreme Court laid stress on the U.N. Declaration:

> The treatment of prisoners should emphasise not their exclusion from the community but their continuing part in it. Community agencies should therefore, be enlisted wherever possible to assist the staff of the institution in the task of the social rehabilitation of the prisoners. There should be, in connection with every institution, social workers, charged with the duty of maintaining and improving the desirable relations of a prisoner with his family and with valuable social agencies. Steps

should be taken to safeguard to the maximum extent compatible with law and the sentence, the rights relating civil interests, social security and physical security of prisoners.

In Kishor Singh's case (AIR 1981 SC 625), the Supreme Court has observed that solitary confinement violates the spirit of the Constitution, if applied without any judicial control, on flimsy grounds, without giving the prisoner a reasonable opportunity of being heard and cannot be regarded as 'fair, just and reasonable' within the sense of Article 21 of the Indian Constitution (Government of India, 1987).

Recommendations of Reform Committees

The first initiative towards reforming the prison system in the country was made with the setting up of the Indian Jails Committee in 1919, which made some far-reaching recommendations on the issue. After independence, the All India Jail Manual Committee was set up in 1957 as an effort by the Government of India, to standardize the practices and facilities offered to prisoners in the various States in the country. An expert from the United Nations, Professor Walter C. Reckless was invited to help formulate the correctional policy of the nation and he played an instrumental role in the setting up of this Committee. Based on the recommendations of this Committee, the Model Prison Manual was published by the Central Government in 1970. This Manual was to serve as a standard for the States and Union Territories to upgrade their manuals. A Working Group on Prisons was set up in 1972 which gave its report a year later, reiterating some of the recommendations of earlier committees and reports and adding some new ones.

The findings of the National Police Commission (Government of India, 1977) shook the conscience of the nation, when one of its members and a distinguished police officer, K.F. Rustomji, made public the pitiable condition of undertrial prisoners in the country. These findings became the substance for a slew of public interest litigations on the issue and paved the way for the landmark judgment of Justice Bhagwati in the Supreme Court in which he deemed that even a postcard written by an aggrieved person or a citizen can be converted into a writ petition in 'public interest'.

Following these developments, the Government of India constituted the now much discussed Mulla Committee (Government of India, 1983) to enquire into prison conditions and make recommendations to improve the situation of prisoners. The report is still an oft-quoted one by experts and officials as a standard document which needs implementation. Some of the recommendations of the Report are as follows:

- Creation of separate institutions for women offenders [Vol. I, Para (ii) of Annexure V-A, p. 68].
- Classification of prisons and prisons/annexes for women offenders [Vol. I, Annexure IV-A, Chapter III, p. 45].
- Appointment of a full-time lady medical officer for prisons/annexes where there are a sufficient number of women prisoners. At other places, appointment of part-time and/or visiting lady medical officers (from the nearest hospital) [Chapter VII, Para 13.5, p. 85].
- Special consideration is to be given to women prisoners towards their segregation, protection, care, treatment, training and rehabilitation. It further recommends that police should treat women with due courtesy and dignity during investigations, in the presence of a lawyer or a relative and a female staff, and she should not be called to the police station for investigation. Women should be kept in separate lock-ups and should be escorted by female escorts. It also states that bail should be liberally granted to women undertrial prisoners and the Probation of Offenders Act should be extensively used to keep them away from prisons [Vol. I, Chapter XIII, Para 13.11, p. 187].
- Special emphasis is to be given on the involvement of community participation and NGOs in corrections. It recommends a two pronged approach to tackle the problem of crime and treatment and rehabilitation of offenders—to counter socio-economic conditions which contribute to crime and extend all possible help

to released prisoners to re-settle in society. It spells out creation of community based treatment programs and the involvement of the community with institutional, aftercare and rehabilitation of offenders. It calls for involvement of the services of experts from the field of education, medicine, psychiatry, law, social work and journalism in framing and running the correctional policy at functional and advisory levels [Vol. I, Chapter XXI].

- Involvement of the voluntary sector in adult education, legal aid, health, recreation, cultural activities, victim support, family support, counselling and guidance and rehabilitation. It also lays down the need for the creation of a Committee at the State level for this purpose and giving financial and non-financial support to NGOs interested to work in this field.

Another landmark report in this connection is the report of the National Expert Committee on Women Prisoners headed by Justice Krishna Iyer (Government of India, 1987). This Committee was set up by the Department of Women and Child Development, Government of India to make recommendations to ameliorate the conditions of women in custody. Some of the recommendations of this Committee are supportive of reformative, correctional and rehabilitative aspects. These are:

- *National Prison Service*: Setting up of a National Prison Service to professionalise prison staff (Vol. I, Para 359, p. 242). This has been also dealt with in Chapter XXIV of the Report of the All India Committee on Jail Reforms, 1983.
- *Gender Sensitization of Prison Staff*: The Committee has given a strong recommendation to orient custodial officers to adopt a progressive approach to correctional work, especially as it affects women inmates (Vol. I, Para 361, p. 243).
- *Role of Social Workers*: The Committee has recommended an active reaching out to the prisoner to effectively deal with the anxieties of inmates, particularly undertrials, with respect to their families and children. To assist the

prisoners more usefully, and especially to serve as a liaison between the prisoner and her family, it is necessary to have trained social workers whose specific duties would not be custody and security, but to work towards the social integration of the prisoners. Such social workers could also arrange activities for undertrial inmates to help them to spend their time meaningfully, without compulsion. Such social workers would be useful as a tool to prison management to understand social and group dynamics and to use it to the advantage of the prisoner as well as the custodial staff. The social worker's counselling input should encompass the custodial staff as well as the inmates (Vol. I, Paras 363 and 364, pp. 243-44).

- *Separate Volume on Women Prisoners in Prison Manuals*: In order to address the special needs of women prisoners and to increase the visibility of such a document, the Committee has recommended developing a separate volume in the prison manuals for the custody and treatment of women prisoners (Vol. I, Para 378, p. 250). A draft separate volume has been prepared by the Committee (Vol. I, Part II, pp. 332-50).
- *Association of Para-legal and Social Workers*: To increase legal literacy and assist in social and emotional mainstreaming of women prisoners, the Committee has recommended the induction of para-legal and social workers to help solve personal, family and legal problems of prisoners. It has also recommended activating the system of prison visitors, setting up socio-legal counselling services, organizing legal camps and offering functional and legal literacy to prisoners (Vol. I, Paras 380 and 381, p. 251).
- *Non-official Visitors*: The Committee has recommended the appointment of women social workers in the districts as non-official visitors. The panel's terms of reference should include monitoring of prison conditions, implementation of prison reforms, legal, mental and

rehabilitative assistance, prisoners' grievances and staff problems (Vol. I, Para 383, p. 252).

- *Socio-legal Counselling Cell*: For improved legal and social preparedness of the prisoner, and aid to the overall adjustment process in prison as well as release from custody, the Committee has recommended setting up of socio-legal counselling cells in prisons, consisting of social workers and lawyers, law students or para-legal workers (Vol. I, Para 384, p. 253).
- *Aftercare Services*: As per the Committee recommendations aftercare and aid to prisoners after release, should be viewed as an extension of probation and of prisoner well-being programs in prison. These activities should be seen as a continuum of care extended to the offender, whether before, during or after custody. It has endorsed the recommendation of the All India Committee on Jail Reforms, 1983, that probation and aftercare should be merged with the prison department and operate as one. The Committee has suggested:
  - Setting up of at least one aftercare hostel per district with temporary or long-term accommodation.
  - Employment placement program.
  - Quota for recruitment in government jobs.
  - Bank loans and subsidies for self-employment.
  - Follow-up of cases.
  - Dissemination of information through media.
- *Nodal Point for Aftercare*: The Committee has recommended the setting up of a nodal point, embracing probation, socio-legal counselling cells and aftercare services, designated as Centre for Relief to the Discharged Prisoner. This will serve as an accredited forum where social welfare, legal, social work and economic assistance can get together to offer total care under a single umbrella. It may operate under the overall supervision of the prison department and managed by voluntary agencies (Vol. I, Paras 417 to 422, pp. 264-67).

- *Parole and Premature Release*: The Committee has recommended the inclusion of prison welfare officers, district social welfare officers, district probation officers and voluntary agencies working for the welfare of prisoners in the Review or Advisory Boards set up in the States for grant of parole or premature release of convicted prisoners (Vol. I, Para 424, p. 267).

A recent initiative in the series of such exercises is the Model Prison Manual (Government of India, 2003). The report has separate chapters related to education, vocational training and work programs, welfare, aftercare and rehabilitation of prisoners. Some of the recommendations from the Model Prison Manual are:

- *Education*: The report states that the policy should aim at making every illiterate prisoner literate and developing educational qualifications of prisoners. It should consist of physical and health, academic, social, vocational, moral and spiritual and cultural education. Specialised personnel should be appointed and trained with the above objectives in mind and NGOs should be extensively involved in these programs. Teachers from the Adult Education Department could be deputed for this purpose. Open school/university and distance learning systems and the use of audio-visual aids should be extensively used to achieve the objectives. Libraries should be set up and manned by trained staff to promote the habit of reading and for upgrading their skills of neo and semi literates, as well as for fulfilment of intellectual and knowledge needs of prisoners.
- *Vocational Training and Work Programs*: This chapter lays down detailed guidelines relating to aims, methods, types, safeguards and facilities, wages, personnel required to conduct such programs. The chapter also recommends the creation of a policy on creation of employment opportunities in the sector, cooperative and agro-based industries promoted by the State, for released prisoners based on the training received inside prison.

- *Welfare of Prisoners*: This chapter makes specific provisions for counselling, psychotherapy and guidance of prisoners. It makes recommendations for appointment of welfare officers, psychiatrists and involvement of NGOs for this purpose.
- *Aftercare and Rehabilitation*: This chapter divides the aftercare needs and rehabilitation work into intervention required while the individual is under institutional care, immediately on release from prison and post-release period. It again reiterates the role of the welfare officer and NGOs for this purpose. The scope of such work is laid down from emergency assistance on release, to temporary accommodation, assistance in securing housing, employment, family support, counselling and guidance, legal aid and protection from police harassment.

The latest draft on National Policy on Prison Reforms and Correctional Administration (Government of India, 2007) has further improved on these recommendations in at least some of the areas of suggested reforms. The 2007 Draft Policy includes some welcome suggestions as far as amendments to the Prisons Act of 1894 are concerned, such as the introduction of a provision to provide for aftercare and rehabilitation services and the appointment of officers to provide legal aid for prisoners, the establishment of a Research and Development wing, financial assistance to non-governmental organizations working for the rehabilitation of prisoners and community-based alternatives to imprisonment for offenders convicted for relatively minor offences.

However, there are some rather disconcerting suggestions in the policy. These include:

1. Prisoners sentenced to simple imprisonment should be compulsorily made to work. This suggestion *de facto* eliminates the difference between simple and rigorous imprisonment, and goes against the principle of deterrence, one of the foundations of modern criminal jurisprudence. The prison administration should instead

create educational and vocational training avenues for undertrial prisoners and prisoners sentenced to simple imprisonment.

2. Amending Section 305-B of the Code of Criminal Procedure, making it mandatory for the trial judge to award the maximum sentence in cases where the accused contests the charge levelled against him or her.
3. Awarding compensation to victims of crimes from the wages earned by prisoners serving rigorous imprisonment. Deductions from the wages of a prisoner after he or she has been sentenced to imprisonment (as punishment) amounts to punishing the person twice over—a case of double jeopardy. In countries across the world where a system of victim compensation exists, it is awarded out of state funds (as in Australia), and not by pinching the pocket of the prisoner, who in any case gets a pittance as wages in prison.
4. The inclusion of senior police officers in prison administration to elicit the cooperation of the police is a worrying suggestion. This is in keeping with the recent trend of deputing Indian Police Service officers in prison departments, instead of the earlier practice of prison cadre officers leading their departments. Ensuring the cooperation of the police cannot be a ground for the inclusion of police officers in prison administration. As with the police or the judiciary, correctional services form a specialized area that requires training and qualification. Each cannot be replaced by the other: they have very specific roles and functions based on the principle of separation of powers, a foundation of any functioning democracy.

Conclusion

It is clear from the above discussion that there is no dearth of policy recommendations as far as the issue of prison reforms is concerned. The situation at the ground level however, presents a rather disturbing picture (as highlighted in the earlier section on Situational Analysis). As far as undertrial prisoners are concerned, persons charged under relatively minor offences and in bailable sections are in a majority, mainly owing to the system of cash and surety bail applied by the judiciary in our country, rather than using provision of Personal Recognizance Bond (PR Bond), a practice that is heavily loaded against the poor and the dispossessed.

Another factor leading to overcrowding of our prisons is the principle of using imprisonment as the primary penal policy. The under-use of the Probation of Offenders (P.O.) Act, 1958 and non-introduction of community-based correctional policies such as community service, bail hostels, weekend imprisonment, etc. is putting tremendous pressure on existing institutions. In order to implement the P.O. Act and introduce non-institutional penal measures, one has to strengthen the human resource and rehabilitation infrastructure by way of appointing correctional personnel such as probation officers, welfare officers, parole and aftercare officers and creation of structures such as counselling and guidance/rehabilitation centres, aftercare and homes, and a comprehensive rehabilitation scheme for released prisoners.

With regard to custodial management and vocational training, the existing situation in prisons requires much to be desired. Most prisons go very little beyond providing basic diet, amenities and medical care, not to speak of complaints about the quality of the same from prisoners which come to light through the media and petitions filed in the courts of law. There is little by the way of a proactive policy to facilitate family visits and arranging legal aid and guidance for prisoners and their families. A simple innovation such as installing a public telephone system whereby prisoners can speak to their *bonafide* family members is being resisted by prison authorities in most states. Such a system has been tried out and is being implemented in some of the prisons in Karnataka to good effect and without any threat to security concerns. Such a practice has considerably reduced the load on the prison administration as far as personal visits by family members (*mulakats*) are concerned.

Similarly, there is poor coordination between the legal service authorities and prison administration towards providing free legal aid and guidance to needy prisoners, at the bail, trial and appeal stages. For this purpose, the suggestion of the reform committees to appoint para-legal workers and law officers in prisons has largely been neglected. Secondly, the very poor honorarium being paid to lawyers on the legal aid panels is a major contributory factor in the poor quality of services being provided by them. The poor allocation of financial resources to the legal services authorities by the State indicates the lack of political will to make this Constitutional right a reality. Suggestions have been made to the Bar Council of India to make it mandatory for law graduates to act as *pro bono* lawyers for a year before they get their *sanads* (license) to practice law, but to no effect so far.

The situation of children of prisoners both inside (below the age of six years, accompanying their incarcerated mothers) and left outside is another cause for concern. The Supreme Court judgment in 2006 in the *R.D. Upadhyay* v. *State of Andhra Pradesh and Others*[2] has alleviated the situation of children living with their mothers in prisons to some extent. The situation of children left outside, either living under the care of a relative or guardian or by themselves, or living in childcare institutions still needs corrective steps to be taken as brought out through the Prayas study (2002).

The issue of education and vocational training facilities for prisoners perhaps presents a more varied picture across prisons in the country. Most such facilities are primarily being provided to convicts and not to undertrial prisoners, though the latter constitute nearly 70 per cent of the prison population. The reason for this is prisons were originally designed to cater to the rehabilitation needs of convicted prisoners, since the question of their rehabilitation theoretically arises only after they have been proved to be guilty, and therefore in need of correction and rehabilitation. However, the reality of our country's prisons is that undertrials spend considerable periods of time in prisons (from a few months to a few years) and the social stigma of imprisonment invariably sticks whether they are convicted in the offence or not. The time spent by an undertrial inside prison

2. 2006 AIR 1946, 2006(3) SCR 1132, 2006(4) SCALE336, 2006(5) JT18.

usually goes waste and he/she loses touch with the work world, making it more difficult to get back to the mainstream after release. This time could be well spent by involving the prisoner in educational and vocational activities.

The standard vocational training activities in most prisons include carpentry, tailoring, weaving, carpet making, welding, doll making, candle making, chalk making, phenyl making, etc. These trades do not necessarily lead to creation of livelihoods after release. Of late, wiring, motor winding, electrical repairs, air conditioning repairs, computer hardware and software and mobile repairing courses have been started in some of the prisons, but largely with the help of NGOs and civil society organizations (Bharadwaj, 2008). Such trainings suffer from shortage of trained teachers and financial resources. They usually do not lead to any government recognized certificate being awarded to the trainee, thus making the entire exercise of questionable import. The number of prisoners being given such trainings is also very small.

As far as educational programs are concerned, the situation presents a worse picture. Minimal efforts are being made in this direction. Skeletal staff is involved in providing literacy classes. Some prisons have tied up with the open schooling and university system to impart distance education programs. NGOs have also been involved in imparting educational programs, mostly non-formal in nature. But such efforts are few and far between. The same can be said about library facilities in prisons today.

Prison welfare officers are hardly appointed in most prisons and where they exist, their work is mostly limited to writing petitions to courts or letters to their families, on the request of the prisoners. Provision of professional counselling services and mental health programs, is essential as a component in prisoners' rehabilitation, but it is almost non-existent. In fact, the welfare component in prisons is more like an after thought, and personnel involved in the delivery of such services come very low in the prison hierarchy and they suffer from low morale and self-esteem in the prison system.

Since prison management and custodial care are seen as a part of maintenance of law and order, it is therefore a State subject whereby the role of the Union Government is recommendatory and persuasive in nature. In this context, there is a need to create a national debate on the issue to create pressure on the state governments to move in the direction of bringing far-reaching reforms in this sector. In sum, in seeking to improve prison conditions, one has to address a range of issues such as the low personnel-population ratio compared to countries that have more effective justice delivery systems, creating a specialised cadre of correctional staff at both junior and senior levels, strengthening the legal aid system towards access to justice for marginalized sections, restructuring of the educational, library facilities and vocational programs in prisons, providing financial and infrastructure support to voluntary organizations working on the rights, welfare and rehabilitation of custodialised populations, and creating accountability systems in both government and civil society actors working in this sector.

References

Bharadwaj, P. (Ed.), (2008). *Community Participation in Prisons: A Civil Society Perspective.* New Delhi: Commonwealth Human Rights Initiative. Retrieved on June 12, 2009 from http://www.humanrightsinitiative.org/publications/prisons/community_participation_in_prisons.pdf

Government of India (1957). *The Prisons Act, 1894* (Act IX of 1894) (As modified upto the 1st January, 1957). Retrieved on July 23, 2009 from http://www.mha.nic.in/pdfs/Prisons_act1894.pdf

Government of India (1977). The National Police Commission (NPC). Retrieved on July 22, 2009 from http://www.humanrightsinitiative.org/publications/police/npc_recommendations.pdf

Government of India (1983). *Report of the all India Committee on Jail Reforms 1980-83.* Delhi: Ministry of Home Affairs, Government of India.

Government of India (1987). *National Expert Committee on Women Prisoners, 1986-87.* Delhi: Ministry of Women and Child Development, Government of India.

Government of India (2003). *Model Prison Manual for the Superintendence and Management of Prisons in India.* New Delhi: Bureau of Police Research and Development, Ministry of Home Affairs, Government of India. Retrieved on June 12, 2009 from http://bprd.nic.in/index3.asp?sslid=438&subsublinkid=153&lang=1

Government of India (2006). *Prison Statistics, India 2006*. New Delhi: National Crime Records Bureau, Ministry of Home Affairs, Government of India. Retrieved on June 12, 2009 from http://ncrb.nic.in/PSI2006/prison2006.htm

Government of India (2007). *Draft National Policy on Prison Reforms and Correctional Administration*. Delhi: Ministry of Home Affairs, Government of India.

Government of India (2007). *The Constitution of India*. (As modified up to the 1st December, 2007). Retrieved on July 23, 2009 from http://lawmin.nic.in/coi/coiason29july08.pdf

Hansaria, V. (2005). Welcome Address on Law Day. Retrieved on July 22, 2009 from http://www.ebc-india.com/lawyer/articles/2005_2_19.htm

Hindustan Times (May 23, 2007). Nearly 30 million cases pending in courts. Retrieved on July 22, 2009 from http://www.hindustantimes.com/News-Feed/india/Nearly-30-million-cases-pending-in-courts/Article1-224578.aspx

Prayas (2002). *Forced Separation: Children of Imprisoned Mothers*. Mumbai: Prayas, Social Work in Criminal Justice (TISS).

Twocircles.net (2009). Judiciary. Retrieved on June 12, 2009 from http://twocircles.net/book/export/html/70143

United Nations (1948). *The Universal Declaration of Human Rights*. Retrieved on July 23, 2009 from http://www.un.org/en/documents/udhr/index.shtml

United Nations (1975). Declaration on the Protection of All Persons from Being Subjected to Torture and Other Cruel, Inhuman or Degrading Treatment or Punishment. Retrieved on July 23, 2009 from http://www.cirp.org/library/ethics/UN-torture/

United Nations (30 August 1955). Standard Minimum Rules for the Treatment of Prisoners. Retrieved on July 22, 2009 from http://www.unhcr.org/refworld/docid/3ae6b36e8.html

4

Panchayats and Decentralization of Prisons: Role of Kiran Bedi in Transforming Tihar Jail

Sumit Mukherjee

Introduction

Ever since the attainment of independence, India has commenced her tryst with the much-coveted principle of democratic decentralization. The *Panchayats* have been envisaged as instruments of both political as well as social change intended to ensure not only community participation at the grass-root level but also to evolve an efficient system of local justice as a bulwark against reactionary and anachronistic social practices. While the performance of the *Panchayats* in delivering local justice is a subject of intensive debate, one significant innovative contribution of India to the concept of democratic decentralization has been to harness the *Panchayats* as agents of both community participation as well as the dispensation of criminal justice inside prisons. As the movement for Human Rights has gained momentum both in India and the world at large, India has embarked on a concerted drive to transform prisons into reformatories. The central idea behind this is the reformation of criminals and their rehabilitation in the mainstream of social life as social assets rather than a social menace.

For this purpose the radical transformation of the jail environment is necessary because these dehumanizing conditions render access to justice impossible. Consequently many of the inmates who are not born criminals become hardened criminals under the impact of the insalubrious, suffocating and repressive prison system. The concept of reformatory is however based on an implicit assumption of the perfectibility of human nature and the right of every prisoner to the basic norms of justice. This requires a progressive democratization of the prison administration. A positive step in this direction was taken by Dr. Kiran Bedi[1] in Tihar Jail after assuming charge as Inspector General Prisons in May 1993. The novelty of her mission lay in her resolve to demonstrate that a system of *Panchayats* could be set in operation even inside the four walls of the prison for the purpose of delivery of justice to the prisoners. The present chapter seeks to examine the extent to which this proved successful as a mechanism of local justice.

The Idea of Decentralization in Prison

While the reforms introduced by Dr. Kiran Bedi at Tihar Jail signified the translation of the idea of application of the *Panchayat* system to prison management into a reality the process was initiated in India much earlier. In the Model Prison Lucknow, an Inmate *Panchayat* or the Assembly of Inmates was set in operation in 1970. It was 'the visible expression of the prisoner's determination and cooperation in all matters concerned with life in the institution' (Bhushan, 1970, p. 81). In most of the jails in Uttar Pradesh (UP) the *Panchayat* system in prison acquired a reputation for being quite advanced particularly in Lucknow where it consisted of four *Panchas* each headed by one *Sarpanch* totalling five. They were not elected but nominated by the Jail Superintendent. There was no fixed time schedule or date for the nomination of the *Panchas* and was made whenever any *Panchayat* Office bearer was charged with misconduct or was released from the institution (Trivedi, 1987). Currently the *Panchayat* system is operative in all the Central Correctional Homes of West Bengal where a missionary drive has been launched

1. Dr. Kiran Bedi has been India's first woman officer who joined the Indian Police Service in 1972. Her expertise includes more than 35 years of creative and reformative policing and prison management. She is a recipient of the prestigious Ramon Magsaysay Award (also called the Asian Nobel Prize), and several other national and international decorations. For more information on her please visit her website www.kiranbedi.org or www.kiranbedi.com

to transform jails into reformatories. At present the Central Jail of Patiala and the Open Air Jail of Nabha have *Panchayats* elected by the prisoners. In the bigger jails a committee of prisoners is selected for each year by prisoners themselves and the Jailor and Superintendent consult the Jail Panchayat Committee in matters of disciple and genuine welfare of prisoners. Thus, the idea of ensuring justice through *Panchayats* in prison originated long before the reforms introduced by Dr. Kiran Bedi in Tihar Jail. However, the expanse and extent of the reforms was wider and more comprehensive than its counterparts anywhere else in India.

Democratic Decentralization at Tihar Jail: Origin and Genesis

Immediately after assuming charge of Tihar Jail, Dr. Kiran Bedi discovered that the mindset of the prison staff needed to be radically changed. The prison officials were utterly impervious to the welfare of the prisoners and the question of prisoner's justice was wilfully consigned to oblivion. The officials inherited the colonial mindset and the idea of democratization of the prison management was foreign to their imagination. There was rampant corruption, dishonesty and dereliction of duty on the part of the prison doctors. To quote Bedi's own testimony, "their only real interest was to find out about the family backgrounds of the patients (prisoners) in order to ascertain their paying capacity" (2002, p. 35). Various other interesting details regarding the inhuman conditions prevailing in the Tihar Jail may be found in Kiran Bedi's own account of the subject. She diagnosed the malaise of prison administration as complete lack of motivation among the prison staff for any reformatory action intended to benefit the prisoners and ensure justice to them. In her steadfast exploration of an effective remedy Kiran Bedi was convinced about the need to introduce a system of *Panchayat* within the prison with the purpose of dispensation of justice (The Panchayat system is also a provision in the jail manual can be referred to back up the argument). Prior to this she devised an ingenious system of ascertaining the feed back of the prisoners through the prisoners' petition box along with daily on-the-round observations. The original practice of suggestion boxes proved ineffective because of certain inherent flaws in the system. The erstwhile jail staff would destroy any complaints made against them, as the key of the suggestion box would be in their custody. Under the new system the petition box was made mobile and a constable appointed by the jail would carry this box on his bicycle around the jail during the prisoner's free time. A gazetted officer of the Head Quarters who would sort out the petitions kept the keys of the box. This was followed by expeditious enquiries and appropriate action information about which was communicated to the prisoners at the earliest (Dangwal, 2001). This was supplemented by a daily feedback system through staff and prison councils called *Panchayat*. The model which evolved was called the Prisoners *Panchayat* (Cooperative) System which was put into practice on June 26, 1993 after a brainstorming session on June 16. According to the testimony of Dr. Kiran Bedi the decision was taken during a lunch meeting to introduce the *Panchayat* system in all the wards. Head Warder. The *Panchayat* would regulate discipline and also organize educational, sports and cultural activities.

The Ward *Lambardar* and *Munshi* would be members of the *Panchayat*. It was decided further that a Superintendent or a Deputy Superintendent would be appointed to ensure that *Panchayat* were formed in each ward. An orientation program conducted by jail officials who would explain to the inmates the objectives and benefits of the new system thereby instilling in the latter, the ability to develop self-management skills would precede this (Bedi, 2002, pp. 218-19). The response from the prisoners was by and large positive. The ward inmates began to evolve into self-organized groups and the individual Warder of each ward was deputed to be the head of each group and was called *Sarpanch* or headman. The necessary spadework was done for the *Panchayat* to blossom in full-fledged form.

From Injustice and Mis-government (rephrase) to Justice and Self-governance

The inauguration of the *Panchayat* system at Tihar Jail was a landmark event in the history of jail reforms in India. While the idea itself was not new the mode of its operationalization undoubtedly bore marks of ingenuity and creativity. Once the individual ward *Panchayats* was formed, the Superintendents summoned a *Maha-panchayat* a collective assembly of all *Panchayats*. Its main functions included the coordination of relevant activities, streamlining of the reform process, evolving a workable consensus on the acceptable methods of functioning, identification of existing problems with suggestions for solution, recommendations for further reformative activities, etc. One instant beneficial effect was the elimination of the prisoner's feeling of isolation and inferiority complex. The opportunity they now had to participate in their own correctional activities instilled in them a new conviction of a certain meaning and value of their existence. Moreover the relations between the staff and the inmates as well as between the inmates themselves were upgraded qualitatively. According to Dr. Bedi the *Panchayats* were summoned for explanation with regard to those problems whose solution lay within their ambit of operation and this helped to foster accountability in community management (Bedi, 2002, p. 20).

A number of specific *Panchayats* were formed which included the Teacher's *Panchayat* aimed at the eradication of illiteracy and the teachers were chosen from the literate sections of the prisoners. The response was so spontaneous that an Assistant Superintendent was exclusively placed as head of the Teacher's *Panchayat*. This was followed by the formation of the Medical *Panchayat*. The members of this *Panchayat* were collectively responsible for identifying those inmates who needed medical attention. This was supposed to act as an effective antidote to medical negligence, which was a regular and universal feature of prison life earlier on.

On September 25, 1993 a Maha-panchayat was summoned consisting of members from all the Ward Panchayats. This according to Dr. Kiran Bedi was a 'turning point in the internal administration of Tihar Jail' (Bedi, 2002, p. 221). The response was enthusiastic and it signalled the advent of the 3C system (Collective-Corrective-Community). This was a milestone on the path of self-governance of prisoners.

Kiran Bedi observes that the most significant *Panchayat* set up at Tihar was the Legal Panchayat. It went on to create legal history (Bedi, 2002, p. 224). Its largest single achievement was to make the inmates aware of their legal rights and enable them to exercise the same. This effected a change in the mindset of the inmates who 'perceived it as a legal maze from which all escape routes were blocked' (Bedi, 2002, p. 225). As this misplaced apprehension was overcome, participation of the inmates in the Legal *Panchayats* increased and practical solutions to complex legal problems were worked out. The core of the Legal *Panchayats* was formed by those inmates who had a legal background and who could draft petitions and type out affidavits. They were provided with typewriters and stationery. In order to supplement the Legal *Panchayat* with a foolproof data bank, Superintendent K.R. Kishore and his colleagues procured five complete sets of new books and other related literature. The costs of photocopying and the paper required were procured from the Prisoner's Welfare Fund. Each Superintendent earmarked a room for the prisoner's legal experts, which the fellow residents could also use for consultation purposes. This legal assistance was provided free of charge and the entire approach was positive and constructive. The Legal *Panchayat* deputed a team of 'inside lawyers' to solve the problem associated with the inordinate delay of trials which has led to the coining of the aphorism 'justice delayed is justice denied'. Mufti Mirazuddin Farooqi, a former senior law officer from Jammu and Kashmir led this team. It was he who devised an effective Court Diary for undertrial prisoners, using which they could keep a methodical record of the trial. It could always be placed in court in case of delay. The format was distributed free of cost among poor inmates and those who could afford to pay were charged a nominal amount. The *Panchayat* was thus motivated not only by considerations of legality but also cost effectiveness, which testified its pragmatic spirit.

A most appreciative account of the performance of the Legal *Panchayat* at Tihar Jail appeared in the noted daily *The Asian Age*.

> Over 7,000 undertrials in Tihar Jail are taking the law into their own hands. Fed up with the endless rounds of court that can stretch their cases to 10 years and beyond,

> the undertrials have decided to keep a written record of what happens in the interminable rounds they make to a court for a hearing. The Legal *Panchayats* that have been set up among the prisoners in the last two months have hit upon a way to prod awake the judicial system, reported to be among the tardiest in the world. According to one judge who spoke at a seminar on criminal justice over 20 million cases were pending in the lower courts and 2.2 million cases were pending in the 18 High Courts in the country. The judges say this is because of an explosion of litigation in the country in recent years with the passing of new legislation and population growth. But in Tihar Jail, the largest in the Asia Pacific region, prisoners are not as despairing as they used to be a year or so ago of getting a speedy trial. In the women's jail a Lok Adalat is in session (*Asian Age*, 1994).

This is a clear indication that the system of criminal justice delivery in Tihar Jail provided one of the few silver linings on the cloud.

The workload the Legal *Panchayats* were required to shoulder was enormous. To streamline its activities it was necessary to form ward-wise sub-Panchayats to create a wider base for the former. The members of the Legal *Panchayat* made indefatigable efforts to alleviate the sufferings of the inmates. They petitioned the Supreme Court, the High Courts and also the District Courts. Mufti Mirazuddin Farooqi was personally instrumental in securing bail orders for a number of prisoners. In one case, he was also able to secure commutation of a death penalty to life imprisonment. On the Performance Declaration Day in 1994 the Legal *Panchayat* submitted the following information: Out of 192 petitions for bail in High Court: 60 were relieved; 177 petitions were filed; 69 persons were released in Sessions Court; 272 appeals were made of which 225 appellants were benefited (Bedi, 2002, pp. 227-28). The Legal *Panchayat* was patronized by the Delhi Legal Aid Bureau, which energetically disseminated legal education among the inmates. Leading legal journals and bulletins published news about the Legal Aid Panchayat at Tihar. It also had a futuristic vision and chalked out the priorities for the years ahead. It sought to devise a system for monitoring the progress of appeal in various courts, make provisions for a panel of advocates to represent the prisoners and draw up a program for the rehabilitation of convicts so that they can be socially integrated after their release. An inmate of Tihar named Satendra Kumar wrote in the monthly magazine *Nav Chetana* published by Central Jail No. 4:

> A large number of prisoners have been benefited by the Legal Aid Cell which is provided by the Delhi Legal Aid and Advice Board. Many prisoners have been granted bail by the petitions filed by this cell. The Legal Aid Cell Advocate used to visit this jail three times a week earlier. But now the visiting days have increased for educating the prisoners about legal matters connected with their cases (Dangwal, 2001, pp. 254-55).

As a sequel to the Legal Aid *Panchayat* the *Insaaf* (Justice) *Panchayat* consisting of elderly persons was formed to resolve disputes among barrack mates. A Patrolling *Panchayat* was set up to ensure that any inmate did not misuse justice. The PWD *Panchayat* also did immense work in utilizing the expertise possessed by some inmates in mechanics and engineering for the sake of repair purposes and minor construction works. It was largely due to the Herculean efforts of this *Panchayat* that a full-fledged bazaar began to flourish within the jail premises and it was run by the canteen *Panchayat* members. It also did phenomenal work in garbage clearance. Several other *Panchayats* were also formed though detailed discussion of all of them does not come within the purview of the present chapter.

Transformation of Tihar Jail: Success and Critique

Mrs. Kiran Bedi is avowedly an adherent of the Gandhian philosophy of dignity of labour and this is what she has tried to uphold through the *Panchayats* in Tihar prison. Gandhi was an ardent advocate of prison reforms and as early as 1922, he provided a blueprint for prison reforms in India. He was also an eloquent votary of the system of *Panchayat*, which was the linchpin of his conception of village self-governance. Whether he visualized any such system in prison is not known, but the idea existed in India much before Kiran Bedi's reforms in Tihar as noted before. Yet the way in which the *Panchayat* system flourished in Tihar was an innovative contribution to Gandhism. Kiran Bedi writes in an unmistakably Gandhian vein:

> We decided on the Gandhian concept of *Shram Daan* (voluntary labour or service). We allotted Wednesday afternoons for *Shram Daan* following the morning literacy classes. During this course all inmates would dust and clean their own barracks/cells and also tidy their personal belongings. They would also brighten up the areas within the ward compound (Bedi, 2002, p. 222).

Superintendent of Jail 3, D.P. Diwedi requested the inmates to donate their labour under a *Shram Daan* scheme and in a week's time the complete prison bore a new look with the entire premises cleaned up and the buildings whitewashed (Dangwal, 2001, p. 255). This was in the truest sense a befitting tribute to the Father of the Nation. The women inmates were also provided with Charkhas or spinning wheels, which were symbols of Mahatma Gandhi's historic movement for *Atmashakti* or self-reliance. Though the situational context was different but the motive force was the same.

It would be worthwhile to ponder whether the drive to transform prisons into reformatories is a pious dream or a reality. Bimalendu Mukherjee, Jailor of the Correctional Home, Cooch-behar, testified that the *Panchayat* system was operative amongst the inmates (Mukherjee, September 28, 2007, by personal communication). Soumit Sarkar, Jailor of Alipore Central Jail Kolkata, also said that the *Panchayat* consisted of elected members who were entrusted with the task of catering to the welfare of the prisoners. He was however very pessimistic and negative in his perception of the very idea of prison reform and was of the decided view that unless the society was reformed sufficiently so as to ensure that it accepted the reformed prisoners when they aspired to return to the mainstream of social life after their release from prison, the latter were sure to return to the world of crime once again. Mr. Sarkar was also not particularly appreciative of the reforms at Tihar Jail though one of his officers who worked in Tihar Jail testified in his presence that the *Panchayat* system was introduced in Tihar Jail only after the arrival of Kiran Bedi (Sarkar, October 15, 2007, by personal communication). Sarkar's main point was that reforms have very little meaning for lifers who have no prospect in life. Taking an objective view of the matter it may be stated that without exaggerating the achievements of Tihar Jail under Kiran Bedi, it would be improper to ignore its incremental advantage. Kiran Bedi had a valid point when she said that during her visits to foreign prisons she found that the concept of Prison Councils, the counterpart of the system of Prison *Panchayats* in India was most casual. The interaction system was formal and lacked the element of personal human touch.

> The Panchayat system too has invaded Tihar. A system of Panchayats is functional within each barrack, which is responsible for looking after the needs of its inmates. At the same time, it facilitates greater scrutiny and accountability as functions pertaining to discipline are being undertaken by fellow inmates who are much tougher of one another (*Hindustan Times*, 1993).

The Superintendent of Jail 2, Tarsem Kumar elaborated on the *Panchayat* system in prison as a stepping stone to participatory management:

> We have worked out a system of Panchayats to aid us in our effort towards improving the quality of time the prisoners spend here. We have a cultural Panchayat; a mess Panchayat, an education Panchayat and the prisoners do not find it at all uncomfortable to follow, as this system is very indigenous to our country. A large portion of the problems, which are mostly minor administrative problems, are resolved and sorted out at these Panchayats by the prisoners themselves. This has taken a big load off us (Dangwal, 2001, p. 253).

At the same time it must be noted that there was a rapid deterioration of the prison conditions in Tihar after Bedi's departure and there were allegations of return from *Ram Raj* to *Ravana Raj* (Dangwal, 2001), seminal problem is how to ensure that the society welcomes the prisoners at the end of their captivity. In Tihar Jail special care was taken to initiate the participation of the outside community in prison to see for themselves how the inmates had been reformed. This would be the surest guarantee against social ostracisation of the prisoners after their release. At the same time one cannot suppress a feeling that for those who are lifers' reformatory measures can be at best a temporary palliative and no more. They may be gainfully employed in *Panchayat* activities but the very fact that the remainder of their life would be spent within the four walls of the prison leads one to the conclusion that the idea of reform and life sentence cannot go together. The movement for reform of inmates must however go on because it is the aspiration for a greater goal, which keeps one up, and going. But the approach must be balanced and realistic, as one must resist the temptation to envisage grandiose schemes incapable of fulfilment. The targets should be kept within reasonable limits so that non-achievement does not create a crisis of credibility.

Conclusion

The *Panchayat* system introduced in Tihar Jail demonstrated that even within a limited canvas decentralized democracy could become a reality if the people concerned had the requisite will and determination to practice it in observance and not in breach. It also proved that the concept of local government through the *Panchayats* was not merely a political concept but had a higher dimension signifying self-governance central to which was the spiritual uplift of the inmates. The prisoners for the first time inhaled the air of freedom in captivity. They were lifted from the morass of despondency, fear and humiliation and life for the first time had a meaning and purpose for them. The *Panchayat* system has been able to create not only a sense of self-esteem among the inmates but has also inculcated in them enhanced capacity for problem-solving skills.

The need of the hour is to create a congenial social atmosphere for the rehabilitation of the prisoners after their emancipation. The *Panchayat* system can serve as the means to an end but not an end in itself. It can help to infuse a new hope and spirit in the shattered mind of the prisoners and to inspire them in the words of poet Shelly to 'hope till hope creates from its very wreck the thing it contemplates'. The primary responsibility however rests with the society, which must take a wider and more liberal view of the matter and abet in its own way the transition from the idea of retributive to reconstructive justice and proclaim in the words of Tagore 'Grant me, Oh Lord! A new life from the realm of fear to fearlessness'.

References

Bedi, K. (2002). *It is Always Possible*. New Delhi: Sterling Paperbacks.

Bhushan, V. (1970). *Prison Administration in India*. New Delhi: S. Chand Group.

Dangwal, P. (2001). *I Dare!: Kiran Bedi: A Biography*. New Delhi: UBS Publishers Distributors Ltd.

Hindustan Times, December 17, 1993.

The Asian Age, May 10, 1994.

Trivedi, B.V. (1987). *Prison Administration in India—Model Prison Programmes in U.P.* New Delhi: Uppal Publishing House.

SECTION TWO

RIGHTS OF THE PRISONERS

5

Rights of the Prisoners*

Jeevan Ballav Panda

Introduction

Right from the inception of the society, criminal law occupies a predominant place among the agencies of social control and is regarded as a formidable weapon that society has forged to protect itself against anti-social behaviour. Whatever views one holds about the penal law, no one will question its importance to society. This is the law on which men place their ultimate reliance for protection against all the deepest injuries that human conduct can inflict on individuals and institutions. By the same token, penal law governs the strongest force that we permit official agencies to bring to bear on individuals. Its promise as an instrument of safety is matched only by its power to destroy. Nowhere in the entire legal field, is more at stake for the community or for the individual (Government of India, 2003).

The oldest penal institution is actually the 'Jail' which is also commonly called a 'Prison' in many countries (Chakraborti, 1997). Prisons, as a formal agency of control, have a unique role especially in a democratic society. As a vital agency of criminal justice administration they perform the twin role of incarcerating

---

* This chapter was originally published as: Panda, J.B. (2009). "Prisoner's Rights in India: Time for a Humane Approach?" In K. Jaishankar (Ed.), *International Perspectives on Crime and Justice* (pp. 326-42). Newcastle upon Tyne, UK: Cambridge Scholars publishing. The author sincerely thanks the Editor of International Perspectives on Crime and Justice for providing permission to reprint this chapter.

the convicts as well as providing custodial care for the undertrials and detained. Thus, contrary to the common belief, prisons come into picture not only after trial and conviction but also right from the stage of investigation and the commitment of the accused to judicial remand or in the course of preventive detention. Such an overbearing role of prisons become almost a routine in cases of poor, ignorant and helpless accused who are not in a position to secure release on bail. They remain undertrials for long periods and are subjected to varied forms of discriminations within prisons (Vibhute, 2004).

Imprisonment as a mode of punishment started in the 16th century, but spread widely as the main punishment for crime only in the 19th century. Before then the few prisons that existed were used mainly to hold those destined for some other punishment such as execution or to contain people unable to pay their debts (Vibhute, 2004). From 19th century onwards and following in to the 20th century, certain individualized measures of offenders were introduced into prison sentences. Thus began the concept of institutional correction (Chakraborti, 1997). By the end of the 20th century imprisonment was part of the penal code of every country and those countries too small to maintain a prison system sent their prisoners to neighbouring States for incarceration (Stern, 1998). The process of replacing physical punishments with imprisonment continues even today as more countries remove the death penalty from their statute books and substitute life imprisonment as the punishment for the most serious crimes (Amnesty International, 2002).

Indian Prison System: A Critical Appraisal

The Indian prison system, just like the other agencies of the criminal justice administration can be described to exist perpetually in a state of crisis. The reasons for such deplorable state of affairs are: *First*, antiquated and over-worked nature of prison institution. *Secondly*, lack of proper training, skills and motivation of the prison staff. *Thirdly*, policy-level ideological conflicts brought about by the modern ideas of prisoners rights and egalitarianism and *fourthly*, internationalization of the prison system.

The aforesaid reasons manifest in several specific problems that may assume different forms in the vast network of prisons. However, some of the notable problems that afflict and substantially determine the very character of the system itself that needs immediate attention can be described as follows:

1. Overcrowding.
2. Inadequate provision for basic needs.
3. Torture, ill-treatment and repressive control.
4. Unequal treatment and privileges.

Overcrowding

Imprisonment as a mode of punishment has increased surprisingly when its drawbacks in social policy and human rights terms are considered. Overcrowding has almost become a hallmark of most of the prisons and its intensity can be estimated from Tihar prison itself, which started with an average prison population of 900 inmates in 1958 and has reached 9000 by 1996 (almost ten times in four decades). During this period the Tihar complex from one Prison in 1958, opened in 1996 the 5th Jail to house mainly adolescent category prisoners (16-21 age group) (Ministry of Home Affairs, 1977).

In some countries overcrowding reaches levels where it can be described as 'cruel, inhuman, degrading treatment or punishment'. For example, the Special Rapporteur on Prisons and Conditions of Detention in Africa found on a visit to Mozambique in 1997 that the overcrowding was so acute that the inmates did not have sufficient space even to sit down comfortably although 96 of them had been transferred the previous day (African Commission on Human & Peoples Rights, 1999). In Brazil, prisoners tied themselves to the window bars so as to be able to sleep standing up (Human Rights Watch, 2006); prisoners taking it in turns to use the beds or bunks and suffocating from shortage of air (Radio Free Europe, 1996).

The main reason for prison overcrowding is that over seventy-six per cent inmates are undertrials, which are a composite outcome of powers of arrest and remand under the Indian law, delay in investigation, and trial and unequal administration of right to bail. Subsequently, it may be a cause for many other prison problems such as greater risk of disease, higher noise levels, denial of conservancy facilities, difficulties in surveillance, consequent danger levels, etc. This issue was recently raised before the Supreme Court by public interest litigation in *Rama Murthy* v. *State of Karnataka,*[1] seeking wide ranging reforms in prison conditions. The Supreme Court did not consider overcrowding *per se* as unconstitutional, but held that:

> [T]here is no doubt that the same does affect the health of prisoners.... The same also adversely affects hygienic conditions....[2] There is yet another baneful effect of overcrowding. The same is that it does not permit segregation among convicts. Those punished for serious offences and for minor. The result may be that hardened criminals spread their influence over others. Then juvenile offenders kept in jails (because of inadequacy of alternative places where they are required to be confined) get mixed up with others and they are likely to get spoiled further.... So, the problem of overcrowding is required to be tackled in right earnest for a better future.[3]

The Seventy-Eighth Report of the Law Commission of India on 'Congestion of Undertrial Prisoners in Jails' under Chapter 9, made some recommendations acceptance of which would relieve congestion in jails. These suggestions include liberalization of conditions of release on bail or by taking recourse to alternatives to incarceration (Ministry of Home Affairs, 1983). These being:

- Fine;
- Civil commitment; and
- Probation

As to release on *probation*, it may be stated that it really results in suspension of required to execute bond under the provisions of the Probation of Offenders Act, 1958, requiring maintenance of good conduct during the probationary period, the failure to do which finds the concerned persons in prison again.

1. (1997) 2 SCC 642.
2. *Ibid.* at 654.
3. *Ibid.* at 655.

That Act has provision of varying conditions of probation and has also set down the procedure to be followed in case of the offenders failing to observe conditions. Overcrowding is reduced by releases on *parole* as well, which is a conditional release of an individual from prison after serving the imposed sentence he has served part of the sentence imposed upon him. Chapter 20 of the Report of All India Committee on Jail Reforms, 1980-83 makes recommendations to streamline the system of remission, leave and premature release. As to premature release, which is the effect of parole, the Committee has stated that this is an accepted mode of incentive to a prisoner, as it saves the prisoner from the extra period of incarceration; it also helps in reformation and rehabilitation (Ministry of Home Affairs, 1983). Building more prisons is one obvious solution to overcrowding and indeed the number of prison places available in the world has increased over the past decade.

The recent amendment to the Criminal Procedure Code, 1973 (Cr.P.C.) is indeed commendable. Section 436-A of the Criminal Procedure Code is good news for undertrials languishing in prisons. The law states that if a person has been detained in prison for a specified period and if that period extends the period for which he can be sentenced then he cannot be imprisoned any longer. However, this amendment shall not be fruitful for those accused of an offence, which carries death penalty. This amendment also states that even if the accused does not have sufficient money to pay off the bail bond then also he can be released on the furnishing of a personal bond. This amendment is indeed a boon for several undertrials languishing in prisons since for a long period of time.

Inadequate Provision for Basic Needs

There is not much to doubt that though the Jail Manuals do provide rules and standards for food, clothing and other basic needs to be given to prisoners, they are rarely complied with.[4] This puts the prison inmate in a specially disadvantaged position, because his incarceration places limitations on his ability to organize any kind of basic needs on his own, while the prison

4. *Rama Murthy* v. *State of Karnataka*, (1997) 2 SCC 642.

system ties him up with substandard need satisfaction. The All India Committee on Jail Reforms, 1980-83, has observed:

> The Committee recognized that the Central Jail, Tihar had been widely criticized on account of maltreatment of, and indiscipline amongst prisoners on the one hand and improper attitudes, incompetence, corruption and abuse of power by the staff on the other. (Ministry of Home Affairs, 1983)

Furthermore, prisons being places with concentrations of poor people, overcrowding and poor food, it is not therefore surprising to find neglect of health and hygiene leading to infections and diseases. The society has an obligation towards prisoners' health for two reasons. First, the prisoners do not enjoy the access to medical expertise that free citizens have. Their incarceration places limitations on such access; no physician of choice, no second opinions, and few if any specialists. Secondly, because of the conditions of their incarceration, inmates are exposed to more health hazards than free citizens. Prisoners therefore, suffer from a double handicap.

Torture, Ill-Treatment and Repressive Control

As a custodial institution prisons have a basic responsibility for protecting the inmates from being subjected to any harm or suffering. But in actual practice the absolute dependence and powerlessness of the inmate makes an accused or undertrial an ideal target for torture, ill-treatment and repression. Prison torture and repression emanates from three distinct sources, namely (a) Prison officials who recognize torture and repression as the best means of control, if not the most satisfying form of sadism, (b) 'Convict officers' who are pressed into prison services mostly on account of their past repressive experience,[5] and (c) 'Prison mafia' which is making its presence felt in most of the prisons as an extra-legal source of control.

Unequal Treatment and Privileges

Prison society is inherently unequal. There exist within the prison several hierarchies, most of which have no formal or legal

5. *Watchdogs International* v. *Union of India*, (1998) 7 SCC 338.

recognition. The vast bulk of resource less, lower-class, inmates invariably occupy the lowest position in the hierarchy. They are not only subject to the lawful and legitimate commands of prison officials but are also treated as subjects by the influential 'convict officers' and the mafia undertrials. The issue of perpetuating the outside class and status hierarchies within the prison was examined by the Jail Manual Committee and the All-India Committee on Jail Reforms which recommended for doing away with the issue of classification based on social status, education and mode of living. In 1997, the issue of classification of prisoners into B and C classes on the basis of social status, education and mode of living under Rule 34(1)(b) and Rule 38 of the Delhi Prison (Admission, Classification, Separation, Remission, Reward and Release of Prisoners) Rules, 1988 was examined by the Justice Duggal Committee in terms of the equality guarantee under the Constitution of India. The Committee recommended the striking down on constitutional grounds the classification into 'B' and 'C' class prisoners in vogue in Delhi prisons.

The prison system both at the Central as well as the State levels has been trying to resolve these basic problems through short-term and long-term measures. The State has only partially succeeded in resolving some of the problems, but like any other human rights institution the resolution of one sets off the generation of new sorts of problems.

Prisoners' Rights: A Global Perspective

The mood and temper of the public in regard to the treatment of crime and criminals is one of the most unfailing tests of the civilization of any country (Carney, 1979). A prisoner, be he a convict or undertrial or a detainee, does not cease to be a human being, and hence continues to enjoy all his basic human rights. On being convicted of crime and deprived of their liberty in accordance with the procedure established by law, prisoners shall retain the residue of the human rights. The Universal Declaration of Human Rights, 1948 under Article 5 stipulates that "No one shall be subjected to torture or to cruel, inhuman or degrading treatment or punishment". Thus, a prison atmosphere can be accepted as civilized only if it recognizes the basic human rights of the prisoners and makes efforts for the effective and meaningful enjoyment of the same by means of prison reforms.

These abuses and injustices continue in spite of an international and regional framework of human rights conventions, treaties and instruments. The United Nation's conventions and standards on the treatment of all detained persons constitute the reference point for all States that have signed up to the International Covenant on Civil and Political Rights (ICCPR). Article 10 of the Covenant requires that people in any form of detention should be treated 'with humanity and with respect for the inherent dignity of the human person'. Similar expressions of this message can be found in the European Charter on Human Rights (Article 3), African Charter on Human and People's Right (Article 5) and the American Convention on Human Rights (Article 5).

However, the first document exclusively dealing with prisoners was the United Nations Standard Minimum Rules for the Treatment of Prisoners. This document is concerned not only with the rights of prisoners, but with the proper management of a penal institution, with a view to avoiding indiscipline, disease, and the induction of inmates into lives of crime; these objectives can be derived from the nature of the recommendations, particularly under Rules 57 and 58. These include the separation of different classes of prisoners, individual sleeping accommodation (except where the system deliberately embraces dormitories), decent sanitation, food, clothing and exercise, medical services, fair and not excessive punishment regime for disciplinary offences, complaint procedures, contact with family and 'reputable friends', access to general news, to reading materials, to respect and facilities for religious observance, respect for property, protection from unnecessary exposure to public insult and curiosity, general respect for dignity, freedom from discrimination, and a regime designed to reintegrate the prisoner into the society, with appropriate education and rehabilitative measures.

But these rules are not law, and the only treaty obligations which touch on the rights of prisoners are the ICCPR and the Declaration against Torture and other Cruel, Inhuman or Degrading Treatment or Punishment (1975) and the Convention against Torture and other Cruel, Inhuman or Degrading Treatment or Punishment (1985). These instruments clarify that torture and ill-treatment of prisoners is outlawed (Article 10, ICCPR). Clearly, some rights are lost when a person is incarcerated, but basic human rights remain. The rights accorded to all human beings, the right to life (Article 6, ICCPR), to justice and redress in all proceedings (Article 9, ICCPR) and to family life (Article 23, ICCPR), remain.

Prison should be places where justice reigns. The noted jurist, Lord Woolf, now Chief Justice of England, said that 'the system of justice which has put a person in prison cannot end at the prison doors. It must accompany the prisoner into the prison...' (Home Office Prison Disturbances, 1990). When considered on the whole, the international instruments about the treatment of detained people do put certain obligations on all prison administrations. First, it is clear that the purpose of prison is, as the American Convention on Human Rights says, the 'reform and social re-adaptation' of the prisoners. When prisoners are accused of offences against prison rules they should be dealt with according to the principles of natural justice. They should be able to appeal against decisions made against them (Article 2, ICCPR). Pre-trial prisoners are accorded special protection and must be presumed innocent until found guilty [Article 14(2), ICCPR]. Their access to their legal advisers must be assured and they should be held separately from convicted prisoners [Article 10(2a), ICCPR].

In UK, the House of Lords has said, 'a convicted prisoner, in spite of his imprisonment, retains all civil rights which are not taken away expressly or by necessary implication.'[6] Similarly, US Courts have established that prisoners do not lose all their rights: 'there is no iron curtain drawn between the Constitution and the prisons of this country'.[7] The same view has been reiterated and reaffirmed by the Constitutional Court of South Africa.[8] Furthermore, as Penal Reform International says, the human

6. *Raymond* v. *Honey*, (1983) AC 1 (10) quoted from *Secretary of State for the Home Department, ex parte Simms ex parte O' Brien, R.*, (1999) UKHL 33: (2000) 2 AC 115.
7. *Wolff* v. *McDonell*, 418 US 539 (555-56) (1974).
8. *August* v. *Electoral Commission*, CCT 8/99 Judgment April 1, 1999, para 18.

rights of prisoners with which it is concerned are derived from 'universal general human rights' and are applicable to every individual (Penal Reform International, 2001). One might argue that it would be enough to do as the recently adopted Constitution of East Timor does and provide that prisoners remain entitled to the fundamental rights except to the extent that these are inherently incompatible with the situation of being a prisoner (Article 32, Constitution of East Timor). However, prisoners are not adequately protected by the inclusion in national Constitutions of human rights provisions such as are found in the ICCPR and the International Covenant on Economic, Social and Cultural Rights (ICESCR).

Prison Reforms in India: A Legislative and Judicial Appraisal

One of the significant post-independence developments in the field of prisons has been the emergence of the prisoners' right touchstone, which has been responsible both for the demystification of prisons, as well as the movement towards standardization. Though the rights discourse has its roots in the United Nations initiatives concerning civil and political rights at the international level, and the enactment of the Universal Fundamental Rights by the Constitution of India at the national level, the real impetus came from the activist appellate court rulings, particularly in the post-emergency era.

Legislative enactments regarding prisoners are obsolete and are not comprehensive, to address the issue of protection of prisoners' rights. The first legislation regarding prisons regulation in India was The Prisons Act of 1894, which was largely based on deterrent principles reflected mainly from the British policies on the subject. The legislators took little pains to look into the other side of the problem. They were concerned more with the prison working than with treatment of the prisoners. This Prison Act has remained unchanged for the last one hundred years except for some very minor changes (Mohanty, 1997). The Prisoners Act, 1900 referred to appropriate places for confinement of prisoners and also included reformatory schools within the meaning of confinement and detention.[9] The Transfer of Prisoners

9. *Communist Party of India, Nagpur* v. *State of Maharashtra*, AIR 1989 Bom. 29.

Act, 1950 was enacted to provide for removal of prisoners from one state to another. The Prisoners (Attendance in Courts) Act, 1955 contains provisions authorizing the removal of prisoners to a civil or criminal court for giving evidence or for answering to the charge of an offence.

The Indian Constitution is also silent on the issue of prisoners' rights and there are no specific provisions as such, yet certain rights, particularly under Part III of our Constitution have been interpreted and extended through some landmark judicial pronouncements. Article 14 of the Constitution of India contemplated that like should be treated alike, and also provided the concept of reasonable classification. This Article is an essential guide and basis for the prison authorities to determine various categories of prisoners and their classifications with the object of reformation. Moreover, Article 19 of the Indian Constitution guarantees six freedoms to all the citizens of India. Amongst those freedoms there are certain freedoms which the prisoners cannot enjoy because of the very nature of these freedoms, such as, "freedom of movement" [Article 19(1)(d)], "freedom to residence and to settle" [Article 19(1)(e)] and "freedom of profession" [Article 19(1)(g)]. But there are other freedoms which can be enjoyed by the prisoners also behind the bars and his imprisonment and sentence has nothing to do with these freedoms, such as, "freedom of speech and expression" [Article 19(1)(a)], "freedom to become a member of an association" [Article 19(1)(b)], etc. These freedoms are very much related to the concept of reformation of prisoners.[10]

The other provisions of the Constitution though directly cannot be called as prisoners' rights but may be relevant are Article 20 (1 and 2), Article 21, and Article 22 (4 to 7) which deals with the rights of any persons. The occasions for judicial intervention in prison matters is so varied and the range of interest covered so vast that, at times, the outcome is rhetorically described as the "prisoners' rights jurisprudence". In no other country of the world has the judiciary played such a key role in evolving a rights touchstone and ultimately contributing to the movement for prison reform itself.

10. *Sunil Batra (II)* v. *Delhi Administration*, AIR 1980 SC 1579.

The trend of judicial activism in this field since the late seventies, was initiated by the series of judicial decisions that ruled out not only what the prisons ought not to do, but also what they ought to do and how they ought to do things. The rationale for such an interventionist approach, a contrast to the 'hands-off' approach adopted by the judiciary till the decision as late as early 1977, in *Bhanudas* v. *Union of India*[11], was that a prisoner is sent to prison as a consequence of a judicial decision, therefore, the judiciary is concerned with how and for what purpose he is imprisoned right till the last day.[12] This was reaffirmed in the landmark case of *Charles Sobraj* v. *Union of India*[13], where it was held that, this Court would intervene even in prison administration when constitutional rights or statutory prescriptions are transgressed to the injury of a prisoner.

Broadly, the judicial control of prisons has arisen from two streams of cases. First, those that focuses on the constitutional rights and human rights of prisoners. Second, those that relate to a wide range of prison conditions and standards of prisonisation. Other significant areas of extension were right not to be handcuffed or leg-fettered unless absolutely necessary, speedy trial, right to counsel, proper condition of detention,[14] dignified prisonisation, undertrials' right to favourable bail release.[15]

The beginning of prisoners' rights can be traced back to the *State of Maharashtra* v. *Prabhakar Pandering,*[16] where the Supreme Court ruled against extinguishing other rights not consistent with the fact of detention. The court included within the purview of prisoners' rights, his freedom to dispatch for publication a manuscript prepared by him while in detention, particularly in the absence of any rules that bar pursuit of such activities. In *D.B.M. Patnaik* v. *State of A.P.*,[17] the Apex

11. AIR 1977 SC 1027.
12. *Giasuddin* v. *State*, AIR 1977 SC 1936.
13. AIR 1978 SC 1514.
14. *Sunil Batra (I)* v. *Delhi Administration*, (1978) 4 SCC 494: 1979 SCC (Cri) 155: AIR 1978 SC 1675.
15. *Prem Shankar* v. *Delhi Administration*, AIR 1980 SC 1535: (1980) 3 SCC 526 and *Citizens for Democracy* v. *State*, (1995) 3 SCC 743.
16. AIR 1966 SC 424.
17. (1975) 3 SCC 185: 1974 SCC (Cri) 803: AIR 1974 SC 2092.

Court asserted even more emphatically that by mere reason of their detention the convicts do not become 'denuded of all the fundamental rights' which they possess. In the case of *Francis Coraile* v. *Union Territory of Delhi,*[18] a challenge was made to a prison rule which permitted only one interview in a month with the members of the family or legal advisor, and was held to be violative of Article 21 of the Constitution. Recently, the Supreme Court in *State of A.P.* v. *Challa Ramkrishna Reddy*[19] speaking through S. Saghir Ahmad (for self and D.P. Wadhwa, J.,) reiterated that, 'a prisoner, being a convict or undertrial or a detainee, does not cease to be a human being.'

In *Hussainara Khatoon* v. *State of Bihar*[20], the court was appalled at the plight of thousands of undertrials languishing in the jails in Bihar for years on end without ever being represented by a lawyer. The court declared that "there can be no doubt that speedy trial, and by speedy trial, we mean reasonably expeditious trial, is an integral and essential part of the fundamental right to life and liberty enshrined in Article 21". The court pointed out that Article 39-A emphasized that free legal service was an inalienable element of 'reasonable, fair and just' procedure and that the right to free legal services was implicit in the guarantee of Article 21.

The recent Supreme Court decision in *State of Gujarat* v. *High Court of Gujarat*[21] represents the high watermark in prisoners' rights field, in as much as the Court in this case for the first time extended Article 23 of the Constitution to prisoners, and created a right not to be put or forced to work unless work is a part of the sentence or with the authority of law. Thus, this view can really constitute the basis for new thinking about prisoners' rights and would mean the end of the prison administration's blanket power over the prisoner. Further, the Supreme Court in *Pathak* v. *State of A.P.*[22] held that the benefit of provision of Article 42 of the Constitution is also applicable to prisoners and extended the dimensions of prisoners' rights making basis for prison reforms.

18. AIR 1981 SC 746.
19. (2000) 5 SCC 712.
20. (1980) 1 SCC 81.
21. (1998) 7 SCC 392.
22. AIR 1994 SC 2092.

In the *Sunil Batra (II) case*[23] the court laid down that prisoners cannot be subjected to deprivations not necessitated except incarceration and sentence of the court, all other freedoms to read and write to exercise and recreation, to meditate and chant, protection from extreme heat and cold, protection against indignities like compulsory nudity, forced sodomy and other forms of vulgarity, joys of self-expression and to acquire skills and techniques are still open to him. In addition visits to prisoners by family members and friends are also to be ensured. In the *Vikram Deo Singh case*[24] the Court ruled that inhuman living conditions in old dilapidated buildings, ill-treatment, insufficient and poor quality food and little medical attention were in derogation of the rights of a detained person. In the *Gurudev Singh case*[25] the Court cast a duty on the State to guarantee basic needs of food, rest, recreation and work and health facilities inside the prison. Finally, in the *Rama Murthy case*[26] the Court considered the issue of standard of prisonisation in the context of overcrowding, delay in trial, torture and ill-treatment, health and hygiene, food and clothing, deficiencies in communication, jail visits and open-air prisons.

Though in the past decades we have witnessed growing control exercised by the judiciary on prison administration, but only a few cases that have contained specific directions such as directions against solitary confinement within prison, bar on minors being detained in adult prisons, etc. have had greater impact on prison administration. However, the growing control of the judiciary has been contested by those who favour prison autonomy. They blame judicial interference both for demotivation of the prison officials as well as the trend of indiscipline among prison inmates. Has the judicial activism done enough to ensure that in future none suffers total denial of fundamental rights and basic human rights, is the question that we need to answer?

23. *Sunil Batra (II)* v. *Delhi Administration*, AIR 1980 SC 1579.
24. *Vikram Deo Singh* v. *State of Bihar*, (1988) Supp. SCC 734.
25. *Gurudev Singh* v. *State of Punjab*, (1992) Supp. (2) SCC 551: (1992) SCC (Cri.) 834.
26. *Rama Murthy* v. *State of Karnataka*, (1997) 2 SCC 642.

Conclusion

Prisons have never been an effective way of responding to serious crimes and/or of protecting the public from crime. Imprisonment is expensive in terms of financial cost and also in terms of the social damage it can cause. It can allow criminal networks to be formed and strengthened, break up families and disrupt prisoners' ties to society such as a home and work. And as such, there is no evidence that the fear of prison as such deters offenders from committing crime.

On the other hand, the open-air prison system has evolved as a very modern and effective alternative to the closed imprisonment system. It plays an important role in the scheme of reformation of a prisoner, which has to be one of the desiderata of prison management. This is in consonance with the reformatory theory of punishment which is essentially the base for the Indian Penal System and more importantly the Criminal Justice Administration. It also represents one of the most successful applications of the principle of individualization of penalties with a view to social re-adjustment. It has been said so because release of offenders on probation, home leave to prisoners, introduction of wage system, release on parole, educational, moral and vocational training of prisoners are some of the features of the open-air prison (camp) system. Furthermore, it is less costly than a closed establishment and also provides employment benefit to the government for the benefit of the public at large, which would have otherwise remained unproductive. The monetary returns are positive, and once put into operation the camps pay for it. For the greater good of the society, which consists in seeing that the inmates of a jail come out, not as a hardened criminal but as a reformed person, no managerial problem is insurmountable.

Centralization of prison administration is one of the important aspects, which needs immediate attention. The prison administration is only under the state list of the respective states' as specified in Schedule VII of the Indian Constitution, which leads to decentralization. The Central Government has been providing financial assistance to State Governments, through the Finance Commission's awards as well as under the Central Scheme for

Modernization of Prison Administration, for strengthening their prison infrastructure. In the gravity of the situation of several thousands languishing and in the wake of deplorable conditions of prisons the administration of prisons should be entrusted to the Central Government. This shall lead to effective centralization of prisons and a setting up of uniform standards to be maintained in all the states. Setting up of a statutory body specifically at the centre for the monitoring of the prisons as well as for allocation of resources or funds for the better upkeep and maintenance of prisons in the states shall be very effective.

One important aspect, which should not be disregarded, is the sympathetic approach and attitude of the prison staff and officers towards the prisoners. Effective and adequate training must be provided to prison officers regarding human rights so as to imbibe in them professional competence and a feeling of social purpose of their activity. The modern theory of prison reformation should focus on the scientific methods of treatment of prisoners like looking into the psychology of the prisoners, being responsive to the need of the prisoners when first offenders are committed to jails and ensuring basic human rights to them. With greater liberties being conferred upon the jail personnel, particularly in a country like India where a bewildering variety of processes goes on; there is ample of scope for abuse of power. Hence, there must be adequate control mechanisms and public accountability so that they are subjected to internal departmental evaluations and control, external monitoring and media scrutiny.

Section 12(c) of the Protection of Human Rights Act 1993, authorizes the National Human Rights Commission (NHRC) to visit, under intimation to the State Government, any jail or any other institution under the control of the State Government, where persons are detained or lodged for purposes of treatment, reformation or protection to study the living conditions of the inmates and make recommendations thereon. Members of State Human Rights Commissions and the National Human Rights Commission being in permanent liaison with the prison administration can have an appropriate external monitoring on prisons and shall be very effective to curb the problem of violation of human rights in prisons. In addition, regular feedback of the prisoners through complaint and feedback boxes in every prison cell, beyond the scrutiny of the prison authorities but under the direct scrutiny of the State Human Rights Commission shall be very effective indeed. This practice shall remove any sort of bias and neglect on behalf of the prison authorities regarding the complaints of prisoners.

Although much has been debated about the reformation of prison system in the country and ensuring basic human rights to prisoners, but practical reality speak otherwise. The legislative, executive and the judiciary have to go hand in hand so as to secure the rights of prisoners through necessary amendments in the existing laws, legislative enactments securing their rights, proper administration of the prison system with proper training and accountability of prison staff and officials and lastly, by appropriate judicial interpretation through judicial activism. At last, emphasizing the exigent need for a humane approach, it is essential that we should create a legal framework so as to ensure legal awareness and change our mindset towards prisoners and take their rights seriously so as to attain our objective of becoming a welfare state in its true sense.

References

African Commission on Human & Peoples Rights. (1999). *Prisons in Mozambique: Report of the special rapporteur on prisons and conditions of detention in Africa* (Series IV, No. 3, p. 26), Paris.

Amnesty International. (2002). *Annual Report 2002* (p. 21), London: International Secretariat. Retrieved September 6, 2005 from http://web.amnesty.org/library/Index/ENGACT530032000?open&of=ENG-MLT

Carney, L.P. (1979). *Introduction to Correctional Science*. Dallas, USA: McGraw-Hill Inc.

Chakraborti, N.K. (1997). *Administration of Criminal Justice: The Correctional Services*. New Delhi: Deep & Deep Publications.

Government of India. (2003). *Report of the committee on reforms of criminal justice system*, pp. 1-298.

Home Office, Prison Disturbances. (1990). *Report of an Inquiry by the Rt. Hon. Lord Justice Woolf (Parts I and II) and his Honour Judge Stephen Tumim (Part II)* (p. 273). London: HMSO. 1991, p. 273.

Human Rights Watch. (2006). *Human Rights Abuses against Prisoners*, Retrieved October 3, 2006 from: http://www.hrw.org/prisons/abuses.html.

Iyer, K.V.R. Justice. (2004). *Legally Speaking*. Delhi: Universal Law Publishing Co. Pvt. Ltd.

Ministry of Home Affairs. (1977). *Committee on Rationalization of Prisoners Classification*. Delhi: Government of India.

——. (1983). *Report of the All-India Committee on Jail Reforms* (1980-83, Vol. 1, Chap. 9). New Delhi: Government of India.

Mohanty, A. (1997). "Correction under Prisons Act Theory and Practice". In N.K. Chakraborty (Ed.), *Administration of Criminal Justice: The Correctional Services* (Vol. II, p. 35). New Delhi: Deep and Deep Publications.

Penal Reform International. (2001). *Making Standards Work: An International Handbook on Good Prison Practice*. London: Penal Reform International.

Radio Free Europe. (1996). *In Search of a Solution—Crime, Criminal Policy and Prison Facilities in the Former Soviet Union*. Moscow: Centre for Prison Reform, Human Rights Publishers.

Stern, V. (1998). *A sin against the future: Imprisonment in the World*. England: Penguin Books.

Vibhute, K.I. (2004). *Criminal Justice (1st Edition)*. Lucknow: Eastern Book Company.

List of Cases

August v. *Electoral Commission*, CCT 8/99 Judgment April 1, 1999, para 18.

Bhanudas v. *Union of India*, AIR 1977 SC 1027.

Charles Sobraj v. *Union of India*, AIR 1978 SC 1514.

Citizens for Democracy v. *State*, (1995) 3 SCC 743.

Communist Party of India, Nagpur v. *State of Maharashtra*, AIR 1989 Bom. 29.

D.B.M. Patnaik v. *State of A.P.*, (1975) 3 SCC 185: 1974 SCC (Cri) 803: AIR 1974 SC 2092.

Francis Coraile v. *Union Territory of Delhi*, AIR 1981 SC 746.

Giasuddin v. *State*, AIR 1977 SC 1936.

Gurudev Singh v. *State of Punjab*, (1992) Supp. (2) SCC 551: (1992) SCC (Cri.) 834.

Hussainara Khatoon v. *State of Bihar*, (1980) 1 SCC 81.

Jennison v. *Baker*, (1972) 1 All ER 997.

Pathak v. *State of A.P.*, AIR 1994 SC 2092.

Prem Shankar v. *Delhi Administration*, AIR 1980 SC 1535: (1980) 3 SCC 526.

Rama Murthy v. *State of Karnataka*, (1997) 2 SCC 642.

Raymond v. *Honey*, (1983) AC 1 (10).

Secretary of State for the Home Department, ex parte Simms ex parte O' Brien, R, (1999) UKHL 33: (2000) 2 AC 115.

State of A.P. v. *Challa Ramkrishna Reddy,* (2000) 5 SCC 712.

State of Gujarat v. *High Court of Gujarat,* (1998) 7 SCC 392.

State of Maharashtra v. *Prabhakar Pandurang,* AIR 1966 SC 424.

Sunil Batra (I) v. *Delhi Administration*, (1978) 4 SCC 494: 1979 SCC (Cri) 155: AIR 1978 SC 1675.

Vikram Deo Singh v. *State of Bihar*, (1988) Supp. SCC 734.

Watchdogs International v. *Union of India*, (1998) 7 SCC 338.

Wolff v. *McDonell*, 418 US 539 (555-56) (1974).

6

Women Prisoners and their Rights

Debarati Halder

Introduction

Some years back, Sun TV, a popular regional channel of southern India telecasted a daily soap named *"Kolangal"*. The immensely popular soap which ran for over a year had couple of slots which showed the prison life of the main protagonist "Abhinaya" played by Actor *Devyani*. The episodes showed how the female inmates are physically and emotionally tortured by supposedly more powerful group including the warden, escorts to the courts and also female prison bullies who are hardcore criminals and who "rule" the female ward under the camouflaged supervision of the warden. The stories thus portrayed are not based on flimsy grounds. In reality, the plight of women prisoners is strongly vouched by recent news reports in *Times of India* (March 8, 2011) which spoke about inhuman treatment of female prisoners in Tamil Nadu jails. Several research reports also advocate the fact that custodial justice is hugely denied to women prisoners in Indian jails (Commonwealth Human Rights Initiative, 1998).

But in reality is the picture so bad? The custodial justice, which originally flows from Article 5 of the universal declaration of human rights, which states "No one shall be subject to torture or cruel, inhuman or degrading treatment of punishment" and Article 10 of the united nation's international covenant on civil and political right, which states "All persons deprived of their liberty shall be treated with humanity and with respect for the inherent dignity of the human person", has been reaffirmed by the Indian Supreme Court in a series of judgments including *D. Bhuvan Mohan Patnaik* v. *State of AP,*[1] *Sunil Batra* v. *Delhi Administration,*[2] *D.K. Basu* v. *State of West Bengal,*[3] *Maneka Gandhi's case,*[4] etc. All these cases highlighted the different nuances of Article 21 which guarantees protection to life and liberty, in the light of prison life or right to life and liberty when it is crippled by procedural pull downs. Apart from Article 21, the Constitution of India further provides rights to the detainees under Article 22 which guarantees four basic rights to the persons who are arrested under an ordinary law. These are: 1. the right to be informed as soon as may be of the grounds of arrest; 2. the right to consult and to be represented by a lawyer of his own choice; 3. the right to be produced before a magistrate within 24 hours; 4. the freedom from detention beyond the said period except by the order of the magistrate. Custodial violence and resultant death was further held as unconstitutional in *Smt. Nilabati Behara* v. *State of Orissa.*[5] The Criminal Procedure Code and the Indian Penal Code also prescribe procedural safeguards against abuse of custodial justice.

From the above, it is apparent that India has strong laws against custodial violence and abuse of custodial rights. But is it a different scenario when it comes to women inmates? In this chapter, I am to research upon this very question. This chapter will follow doctrinal methodology and secondary sources to analyse four typical prison rights for women, namely (i) right against custodial torture including rape; (ii) right to free legal aid, speedy trial and bail; (iii) right to health; and (iv) right to privacy. These issues orbit around the main principle of right to life and liberty as has been guaranteed under Article 21 of the Constitution. I have tested these rights in the back drop of three news reports ranging from 2011 to 2012 which spoke about abuse of custodial justice for women and how the authorities can

1. AIR 1974 SC 2092.
2. AIR 1980 SC 1579.
3. JT 1997 (1) SC 1.
4. (1978) 1 SCC 494.
5. 1993 2 SCC 746.

control such abuse of rights; and also specific provisions of the Criminal Procedure Code and Indian penal code, dealing with rights to bail, appeal, responsibility of the prison management and rape laws. The chapter is limited to the abuse of rights within the four walls of prisons. Further, this chapter will look into the issue of right to privacy not from the perspective of unauthorised search and seizure or unnecessary surveillance as has been settled in the case of *Kharak Singh* v. *The State of U.P. & Others*,[6] but from the aspect of literary meaning of the word "privacy". Also, for the formulation of this chapter, it became obvious that provisions of the Criminal Procedure Code (Cr.P.C.) dealing with court procedures should be discussed in relation to this issue, but this chapter will not extend the discussions on the after-life of women prisoners, especially their rehabilitation, even though this is an important aspect of prison rights. The chapter will offer two phased conclusion; viz., (i) looking into the issue from legal aspects rather than socio-legal aspects; and (ii) shifting the burden to prison authorities and law and justice machinery for the betterment of prison rights.

This chapter is divided into two parts: The first part will speak about the background of the study and the second part will delve into the issue of rights of women prisoners from the perspective of right against custodial torture, right to free legal aid, speedy trial, right to health and right to privacy, etc.

Part I

Background of the Chapter

The Bhopal workshop report on prisons and human rights Commonwealth Human Rights Initiative (CHRI, 1998) had thrown significant light on prison life of individuals, experience of the visitors and the wives of the male prisoners. The workshop not only heard the academicians, activists, lawyers and the judges, but also the former prison inmates who are released. The biggest problem that this workshop highlighted was overcrowding inside the prisons and internal corruption. The workshop thoughtfully portrayed the plight of the dependants of the inmates, mostly wives who had to pay bribes to stretch the visiting hour to a little

6. 1963 AIR 1295, 1964 SCR (1) 332.

longer. The workshop had dedicated a complete paragraph to narrate the plight of women prisoners. It stated that the biggest drawback was bifurcated between absence of proper medical care by women doctors and health care personalities, and proper legal aid to women prisoners. The hard truth is, most of the women inmates came from low social and economic background with nil or very little literacy; majority of them land in prison due to their futile ways to escape from "repressive environment" of their marital homes, brothels and criminal gangs where they are abused hugely. As such, none of them have any awareness about the benefits of Section 437 of the Cr.P.C., which in its first proviso,[7] speaks about granting bail and releasing a convict on bail especially if she is woman. The workshop also highlighted the failure of 1983 Mulla Committee Report which stressed on compulsory availability of lady doctors in prisons with capacity of 25 or more women.

While this CHRI (1998) report spoke mainly about jails in Madhya Pradesh, a report on children of women prisoners in jail in Uttar Pradesh, prepared by Pandit Govind Ballav Pant Institute of Studies in Rural Development, Lucknow (2004), threw more significant light on the plight of women and their children in the jails. This study had beautifully showcased the number of women put up in various jails in India as well as in Uttar Pradesh, the numbers of pregnant, lactating and nursing mothers in the jails and the number of children put up in the jail as they are too young to leave their mothers. Even though this study deals with more child rights for children of women prisoners, it pointed out severe lacunas which make the lives of women prisoners a mockery of justice. Further, a new study by Math, Murthy, Parthasarthy, Naveen Kumar and Madhusudan (2011) had also discussed about prison reforms in India. In this study, it was shown that there are 16 jails all over India (as per 2007 report) made exclusively for women prisoners. The study also highlighted the fact that women prisoners are

7. Section 437, proviso (i) of the Cr.P.C. states that "provided that the court may direct that a person referred to clause (i) or clause (ii) be released on bail if such person is under the age of sixteen years or is a woman, or is sick or infirm".

vulnerable not only to custodial abuse by male officers, but also to numerous physical as well as mental health problems. The abuse of custodial rights for women in India, especially in Tihar jail is very well portrayed by Kiran Bedi (1998) in her book, *It's always Possible: One Woman's Transformation of Tihar Prison.* The chapter dedicated to women prisoners (see Bedi, 1998, pp. 73-90) speak about huge abuse of fundamental rights of women specifically in regard to health, privacy, legal aid and nutrition. Nonetheless, Bedi had done a tremendous work in transforming Tihar jail and thereby reforming the prison administration for the betterment of custodial rights of inmates, including men, women and children.

All of these papers/books/studies showcased abuse of custodial rights for women from three main perspectives; health and nutrition, privacy, and legal aid. All of these studies have given special emphasis on the recommendations made by Justice Krishna Iyer's committee on women prisoners in 1987 and the subsequent amendments made in the Cr.P.C. and the IPC made thereafter to make search and seizure for convicted women more dignified, establishment of separate prisons for women, etc. Apart from these studies, the report of Committee on Empowerment of Women (Government of India, 2001) on the women detainees also needs a special mention here. The report pointed out that prison administration in India still follows colonial provisions like the Police Act, 1861 and Prison Act, 1894. This observation carries high gravity as these provisions gave enormous power to the police and prison authorities to torture the inmates which no longer carry any legal sanction in present days. The committee noted that modern prison manuals prepared by various state governments are now being recommended for every prison. It also noted that basic necessities of women must include clothes, nutritious meal, and sanitary napkins as well. Among the recommendations, the committee laid stress on regrouping the convicts into hardcore criminals and held for petty criminal cases and treat/accommodate such women differently, freedom in letting the inmates wear either *Saree* or *Salwar Kameez*, reformed wage structure, training and courses for rehabilitation for prisoners and compulsory legal aid, sudden surprise visits by the members of parliament, members of national commission for women, etc. for strict vigilance on the prison stuff and their treatment on inmates, relaxing the procedure for letting inmates go in parole, treatment of aged prisoners in more flexible fashion in the issue of bail, etc.

Following these recommendations, considerable changes have been made in the Cr.P.C., specifically in Section 51(2) and Section 100(3) whereby the code lays down that when it is a woman convict who needs to be searched, there must be a woman officer to carry out the necessary procedures. Changes have also been made in the IPC where by Section 376 speak about custodial rape of women and stringent punishment for the same by the officer in charge, who is responsible for the same. However, a minute analysis of the studies above would show that most of them have framed the custodial rights of women in five basic rights, viz., right to health and nutrition, right to proper wage, right against physical and emotional violence, right to legal aid and right to privacy. Each of these studies have given their own recommendations for improving the situation, some of which have been implemented, some have not. But in practice, such implementations have often provided to be scripted lines only. This is evident from a news report (*Times of India*, March 8, 2011). The report spoke about the experience of few ex-female inmates of various jails in Tamil Nadu and showed how their custodial rights have been abused in the prison as well as while in transit custody. This report showed that the issues such as overcrowded jails, poor health and nutrition issues for women and above all, physical violence within the jail premises on the women inmates refuse to go away despite several reports, policy guidelines to this effect and implementation of new laws.

In the light of this particular report, it has become immensely essential to re-examine the custodial rights of women convicts from Indian criminal as well as constitutional law perspectives. The studies that I have referred above and the *Times of India* (2011) news report would test the hypothesis that abuse of custodial rights for women in India have persisted despite several implementations of welfare as well penal laws. The research hitherto in this chapter will therefore proceed as to: what are the basic custodial and post custodial rights of women inmates and whether Indian laws are matured enough to bring a change in the stagnant position of abuse of custodial rights for women?

Part II: Prison Rights for Women in India

Rights and their Sources

The basic prison rights for general adult prisoners irrespective of their gender flow from the International Covenant on Civil and Political Rights, which classifies two basic rights for individuals who have been taken in custody in the prisons and who are either convicts and/or undertrials. These rights are universal irrespective of the inmate's gender (Article 3).[8] These rights are as follows:

(a) Right to humanity and dignity when detained [Article10 (1)]: Article 10 emphasizes three separate rights under this head which are (i) treatment with humanity and dignity [Article 10(1)], which in its broadest sense also includes right against custodial torture; (ii) right to get separate treatment on the basis of stages of prosecution; i.e., an accused person must be kept segregated from and treated separately than a convicted person [Article 10(2a)]; (iii) right to get restorative justice and reformative treatments which will help the inmate for social rehabilitation [Article 10(3)].

(b) Right to free legal aid and fair hearing (Article 14): Article 14 in its opening clause in clause (1) splits the right into three; viz., (i) equal right to be heard; (ii) right to fair hearing before a competent, independent and impartial tribunal; (iii) right to private trial secluded from media and the public, etc. when the situation so needs.[9]

---

8. Article 3 does not directly speak about universal rights of the prisoners though. It states "The States Parties to the present Covenant undertake to ensure the equal right of men and women to the enjoyment of all civil and political rights set forth in the present Covenant." The language of this provision, if taken in the light of Article 10 and subsequent provisions which speak about rights of the individuals under trial would show that women are equally eligible for such rights.
9. See Article 14(1) of the International covenant on civil and political rights. Available @ http://www2.ohchr.org/english/law/ccpr.htm

Article 14 could thus be described as the pivotal provision in formulating rights of the detainees. The philosophy of the clause (1) is further explained and established through the remaining clauses 2-7, which speak about right to be presumed innocent until proved guilty under law (clause 2), to know about the charges framed against him, free legal aid and self-defence and right against self-testimony without consent, etc. (clause 3), right to appeal to higher tribunal (clause 5), right to compensation in case of miscarriage of justice (clause 6) and right against double jeopardy (clause 7). Article 14, further supports right to privacy (Article 17), right to religion (Article 18) and right to speech and expression and opinion (Article 19) with basic restrictions as has been provided under Article 20.[10]

The Situation in India

All of the rights above have been reaffirmed by the Indian constitution especially through Article 14 (which speaks about equality before law), Article 15(3) (special provisions for women), Article 19(1) (freedom of speech and conscience), Article 20 (right against ex-post facto law, double jeopardy and self-incrimination), Article 21 (right to life and liberty), Article 22 (right to fair trial and legal aid), Article 25(1) (right to religion), Articles 32 and 226 (right to constitutional remedies) and finally the groups of provisions embodied in Part IV of the constitution titled directive principles of the state policies, especially Article 39-A (equal justice and free legal aid), Article 42 (state's duty to provide just and human condition for work and for maternity relief) and Article 43 (living wage for workers). Some of these rights have further been tested and also broadened by the Supreme Court.

The landmark cases that have reaffirmed the inmate's rights are as follows: *Hussainara Khatoon & Ors* v. *Home Secretary, State of Bihar 1979*,[11] unfolded different rights of detainees in the Indian prisons, especially emphasising upon the right to life and

10. Article 20 states that any propaganda for war shall be prohibited by law and any advocacy of national, racial or religious hatred that constitutes incitement to discrimination, hostility or violence shall be prohibited by law.
11. AIR 1819, 1979 SCR (3) 1276.

liberty under Article 21 of the constitution. The case established the right to speedy trial and right to free legal aid in the line of Article 39-A of the constitution.[12] Justice Bhagwati, while dealing with this case, had rightly observed that "an unfortunate situation cries aloud for introduction of an adequate and comprehensive legal service programme, but so far these cries do not seem to have revoked any response. It is not possible to reach the benefit of the legal process to the poor to protect them against injustice and to secure to them their constitutional and statutory rights unless there is a nationwide legal service programme to provide free legal service to them." Emphatically, this case also touched upon the issue of overcrowded jails and the right to bail (Andharia, 2011). Further, the case of *Smt. Nilabati Behera Alias Lalit* v. *State of Orissa and Ors*[13] interests me more in relation to this chapter. Nilabati, a mother of her 22-year-old son sought the court's interference vide Article 32 of the Constitution[14] in settling the dispute over the question of custodial torture and subsequent death of her son. Not to forget that the Indian legislation has also prohibited the use of custodial violence in unmistakable terms. Under Sections 330 and 331 of the Indian Penal Code (IPC), 1860, it is an offence to voluntary cause hurt or grievous hurt to extort confession or to compel restoration of property. The punishment is also very severe, in case an offence committed under Section 330, IPC. It is either description for a term which may extend to seven years and also fine. In case offence is committed is covered under Section 331, IPC. The imprisonment is up to ten years Rigorous Imprisonment and fine.

The Code of Criminal Procedure, 1973 has empowered the Magistrate to enquire into the matter where any person dies while in police custody. Section 176 of the Code is relevant. The Indian Evidence Act (1872)[15] also prohibits use of confession made before a police officer or in police custody and the one

12. See http://www.indiankanoon.org/doc/384639/ for better understanding of the case.
13. 1993 AIR 1960, 1993 SCR (2) 581.
14. See http://indiankanoon.org/doc/1628260/
15. The Indian Evidence Act, originally passed by the British Parliament in 1872, contains a set of rules and allied issues governing admissibility of any evidence in the Indian Courts of law.

obtained through inducement, threat or promise, in criminal trials. These provisions are embodied in Sections 24, 25, and 26 of the Evidence Act, 1872. In case of an accused is involved in the erstwhile Prevention of Terrorism Act, 2002, confession before Superintendent of Police may be admissible if certain safeguards are followed. The Supreme Court in this case, not only threw light on the issue of custodial torture and subsequent death as huge abuse of fundamental human rights, but also confirmed the right of the victim/victim's kin for compensation.

The case of *Mrs. Veena Sethi* v. *State of Bihar and Ors*[16] is another case which needs mentioning in this chapter. In this case the Supreme Court took up the issue of right to health, especially mental health of the prisoners, along with the broader question of right to speedy and fair trial. The case portrayed the plight of inmates who have to languish in the jails for years after years due to the stretching judicial process. This was another case which broadened the wings of Article 21, guaranteeing right to life and liberty to cover right to live with a healthy mind, whether with full liberty, or with curtailed liberty. The case of *Nandini Satpathy* v. *Dani (P.L.) and Anr*[17] deserves further mention for this chapter.[18] The case dealt with right against self-testimony as has been guaranteed under Article 20(3) of the Indian constitution, in the light of Section 179 of the Indian Penal Code and Sections 160(1) and 161 of the Criminal Procedure Code of India. While Section 179, IPC compels a person to answer the questions of the investigating officers and prescribes punishment in case of failure of the same, Section 161 of the Cr.P.C. reiterates the same by stating in clause (2) that "such person shall be bound to answer truly all questions relating to such case put to him by such officer other than questions the answers to which would have a tendency to expose him to a criminal charge or a penalty or forfeiture. Section 160(1) of the Cr.P.C. makes the stand of women stronger by relieving them from attending such investigation in some other place other than her residence.

16. AIR 1983 SC 339, 1983 CriLJ 675, 1982 (1) SCALE 793.
17. 1978 AIR 1025, 1978 SCR (3) 608.
18. See http://www.indiankanoon.org/doc/1938988/

Sunil Batra etc v. *Delhi Administration and Ors etc.*[19] was another landmark case which dealt with prisoner's rights to free speech, equality before the law and right to life while being detained in the solitary cell as a convict for death penalty. Justice Krishna Iyer, after a detailed analysis of the laws, especially Sections 30(2) and 56 of the Prison's Act, which speaks about keeping a convict under capital sentence under solitary confinement and huge powers to superintendent of the police in dealing with such convict's rights consecutively; held that solitary confinement itself being a grave punishment, no individual can be expected to go through it in modern times unless it is absolutely needed. Further, he also established that locking up a prisoner in solitary cell does not suspend other basic rights as has been enshrined in Articles 14, 19, 21 specifically. An individual must be allowed to speak, enjoy life through mingling with others and see his relatives and friends even if he is detained.

Lacuna in the Basic Rights for Women Inmates

These are some of the examples as how the courts in India interpreted the fundamental rights of individuals when detained. A minute analysis of the cases above would show that while the Constitution of India enshrined rights in the modern perspective, many jails in India still follow colonial laws such as the Prison Act, the Police Act and also the IPC and the Cr.P.C. in the true colonial meaning of these laws. It must not be forgotten that along with men, women also played vital role in the process of Independence of India and these colonial laws were meant to denude the inmates of all their basic fundamental rights. This was meant for all prisoners irrespective of their gender. However, the principle philosophy on which the courts, especially the Supreme Court relied upon, while interpreting the fundamental rights and the laws meant for inmates, is to give prime importance to the concept of Rule of Law. The court in all the above cases meticulously broke the false mirage that "State can do no wrong". Along with this, the court carefully upheld the right to equality by entertaining the petitions preferred by women for the welfare of men as well as women. This is evident from all of the above cases, except Sunil Batra's. Each of these cases has highlighted

19. 1978 AIR 1675, 1979 SCR (1) 392.

specific rights of inmates that are essential for women prisoners. It must be noted that the inherent philosophy that was established in Hussainara Khatoon's, or Nilabati's or Nandini Satpathy's cases, were either tested earlier or established later in other cases preferred by male detainees themselves or through persons who sympathised with the cause. I have specifically mentioned these cases to show how Supreme Court has dealt with the right of women petitioners, who either were direct victims or had the *locus standi* to fight for the cause. But even though the court did throw light on jail reforms and creation of better jail manuals, several rights of women prisoners are still needed to be addressed properly. These are as follows:

1. Right Against Custodial Torture, Especially Rape

Even though Nilabati Behara's case settled the principle that custodial violence is an abuse of basic fundamental rights to life and liberty as has been guaranteed under Article 21, custodial physical violence against women inmates, especially abuse of human rights through rape, received many strong weathers from the Indian Judiciary. This is evident from the *Mathura Rape case*[20] whereby the Supreme Court acquitted the accused reversing the judgment of the Bombay High Court, on the ground that the victim Mathura did not raise any alarm and hence, it can be presumed that she had consented for the intercourse. Nonetheless, the acquittal created a huge uproar among the people of India and the case called for subsequent amendments for criminal law. It is an unfortunate truth that when a woman is in custody of the police or in the prison, she naturally tends to become submissive in the fear of future torture from the higher authorities (Jagadeesh, 2010). Resultant, she may not immediately prefer a complaint against the same authorities in whose hands she may need to stay back. This was the main issue of concern post Mathura case for the lawmakers and later the criminal law amendment act, 1983 brought in several changes in Indian Penal Code, Criminal Procedure Code and also Indian Evidence Act to make the courts sympathetic towards the women victims of custodial rape and sexual harassment.

20. Tukaram, 1978 Cri.LJ 1864 S.C.

As such, it can be seen that while non-consensual rape is punishable under Section 376 of the Indian Penal Code, clause 2(a) of this section has been made more accurate to deal with custodial rape by officials. This section prescribes punishment for rape by a police officer in the station on a woman in his custody.[21] Further, Section 376-C prohibits and punishes intercourse by superintendent of jail, remand home, etc. This section meticulously maintains a thin line of difference from Section 376(2)(a) by emphasising on the fact that the concerned person, in order to fall under this section must have used his official position and have induced or seduced any female inmate to have sexual intercourse not amounting to rape.[22] Apparently, this section covers consensual sexual activities when the same has been gained by inducing or seducing the victim. The Criminal Law Amendment Act 43 of 1983 also brought in Section 114-A in the Indian Evidence Act to make the position of female victims of custodial rape stronger. This section emphasises on the evidence of the rape victim and the court's liability to accept the same.[23] The Cr.P.C. also supports the victim's stand through Section 164(A), which speaks about medical examination of the rape victim and also the accused in Section 53(A). This has become immensely important provision for dealing with custodial rape victims especially in the light of the observation made by the Supreme Court regarding the necessity of the same by women

21. This section prescribes punishment with rigorous imprisonment for a term which shall not be less than ten years but which may be for life and shall also be liable to fine. The proviso states further that the court may, for adequate and special reasons to be mentioned in the judgment, impose a sentence of imprisonment of either description for a term of less than ten years.
22. This section prescribes punishment with imprisonment of either description for a term which may extend to five years and shall also be liable to fine.
23. Section 114-A of the Indian Evidence Act states that in a prosecution for rape under clause (a) or clause (b) or clause (c) or clause (d) or clause (e) or clause (g) of sub-section (2) of Section 376 of the Indian Penal Code (45 of 1860), where sexual intercourse by the accused is proved and the question is whether it was without the consent of the woman alleged to have been raped and she states in her evidence before the court that she did not consent, the court shall presume that she did not consent.

doctors for general rape victims in the case of *State of Karnataka* v. *Manjanna.*[24] Further, the amended Section 176-(1A) (a, b) of the Cr.P.C. makes it mandatory for investigation by a judicial magistrate in case of custodial rape or death. This provision could be described as the pivotal provision for upholding the detainee's right to fair trial in regard to custodial torture especially rape.

However, in reality, the story could be very different than the written scriptures of law. The *Times of India* report (March 8, 2011) on ex-women prisoner's experience in the Tamil Nadu jails showed the glaring loopholes and hard reality. The story of Parameswari showed the naked abuse of law, especially Section 376-C of the Cr.P.C. If she really musters the courage to prefer the complaint, as has been suggested by the then I.G. Prison, the courts may get enough scope to experiment the strength of this particular section along with Section 114-A of the Evidence Act.

2. Right to Free Legal Aid and Speedy Trial and Right to Bail

All of these three rights have to be seen as a string tied together when in case of a woman detainee. Even though Hussainara Khatoon's case highlighted the need for bail in the light of speedy trial, right to liberty and also the overcrowded jails, very little has been done to this specific prison right for women compared to that of right against custodial violence and rape. Ironically Section 437(1) of the Cr.P.C. speaks about right to bail for women even in non-bailable cases, which the court "may" grant. The language typically runs as follows: "Provided that the court may direct that a person referred to in clause (i) or clause (ii) be released on bail if such person is under the age of sixteen years or is a woman or is sick or infirm: Provided further that the court may also direct that a person referred to in clause (ii) be released on bail if it is satisfied that it is just and proper so to do for any other special reason." While clause (i) speaks about the grounds for denial of bail when there is reasonable belief that the accused has committed an offence punishable with death or imprisonment for life, clause (ii) speaks about the grounds in cases it is a cognizable offence and the person is previously convicted

24. AIR 2000 SC 2231, 2000 (2) ALD Cri 272, 2000 CriLJ 3471. Also see http://indiankanoon.org/doc/1214266/

of non-bailable offence or offence punishable with death or life imprisonment. Hence, read with the second proviso, it could be seen that court's discretion to release a person on bail even in cases of non bailable offences in the first proviso, depends mainly upon the gender of the said person. But it must be noted that the court can deny this right as the section does not make the right for women absolute with the usage of the word "may".[25]

This can be very well noted in the recent 2G scam case, where Kanimozhi, the only woman convict among other "V.I.P." convicts was denied bail by the special CBI judge who was handling the telecom scam case. The judge denied the bail on the foremost grounds that Kanimozhi belongs to "upper echelons of the society", she is a member of the Parliament and she cannot be considered as discriminated on the ground of her gender. Finally after several attempts, the Delhi High Court granted her bail, but not primarily on this very clause on gender, but on principle of parity when the Supreme Court granted bail to five corporate executives in the week earlier than the hearing of Kanimozhi's bail plea (Kumar, 2011). Kanimozhi's six months stay in the prison and journey through the bail applications could find one similarity with the many other women inmates detained in various jails in India as was shown in some studies that I relied upon earlier in this chapter; all these women also stay in prison and they are deprived of the right to bail not because they belong to any upper class or because they hold any position in any prestigious offices like the Parliament, but because they are poor, and they are women detainees whom mostly their families and the societies would have stopped supporting morally and financially and finally they are denied of the basic right of free legal aid and speedy justice.

In *M.H. Hoskot* v. *State of Maharastra*,[26] while explaining the right to appeal, the Supreme Court emphasised the fact that right of appeal is "one component of fair procedure is natural justice". The two ingredient parts of this right is to serve the copy of the judgement at the right time and provision for free legal aid, in case the detainee is incompetent to exercise this right on his own.[27] As settled by this decision, it becomes a prime

25. See Section 437(1) of the Cr.P.C.
26. AIR 1978 SC 1548.
27. See *M.H. Hoskot* v. *State of Maharashtra* AIR 1978 SC 1548.

duty of the jail superintend to hand over the order copy to the detainee without any delay so that he/she can proceed towards appeal if needed. The court further held that it is the duty of the State to see that this right to avail free legal aid is properly exercised by the detainee and this is "the State's duty and not government's charity."[28] It has to be noted that while the court has strongly nodded for presence of female doctors and nurses for checking of women victims of custodial torture and also for treating general women detainees, there is hardly any judgment which makes it mandatory for women lawyers to serve for free legal aid for helping women detainees. But apart from these facts, there is one more hard truth which works as a factor for making women to languish in jails for a longer time and denudes the right to appeal as has been guaranteed under Section 374 of the Cr.P.C.; Section 375 of the Cr.P.C. provides no one can press for an appeal where an accused person has been pleaded guilty and has been convicted. Further, as per the Bhopal workshop (CHRI, 1998) and also as per study of Pandit Ballav Pant institute (2004), many women are arrested and put in jail for petty offences. As per the Criminal Procedure Code, Section 376 especially (b), (c) and (d) state that no appeal shall lie from any order of sessions' judge, or metropolitan magistrate or magistrate of first class for a term of imprisonment not exceeding three months or monetary fine not exceeding ₹ 200 or both, or fine not exceeding ₹ 100. Even though the proviso lays down certain grounds[29] which may enable the concerned persons to go for an appeal, it could be seen that often many women do not get any opportunity to avail these benefits. However, this must not be forgotten that

28. *Ibid.*
29. The proviso says "Provided that an appeal may be brought against any such sentence if any other punishment is combined with it, but such sentence shall not be appealable merely on the round—
    (i) That the person convicted is ordered to furnish security to keep the peace; or
    (ii) That a direction for imprisonment in default of payment of fine is included in the sentence; or
    (iii) That more than one sentence of fine is passed in the case, if the total amount of fine is imposed does not exceed the amount hereinbefore specified in respect of the case."

apart from legal short comings such as these, procedural short comings such as extreme delay in filing charge sheet[30], etc. also aid to the languishment of women.

30. Section 173 of the Cr.P.C. states that "(1) Every investigation under this Chapter shall be completed without unnecessary delay. (2)(i) As soon as it is completed, the officer in charge of the police station shall forward to a Magistrate empowered to take cognizance of the offence on a police report, a report in the form prescribed by the State Government, stating—
    (a) The names of the parties;
    (b) The nature of the information;
    (c) The names of the persons who appear to be acquainted with the circumstances of the case;
    (d) Whether any offence appears to have been committed and, if so, by whom;
    (e) Whether the accused has been arrested;
    (f) Whether he has been released on his bond and, if so, whether with or without sureties;
    (g) Whether he has been forwarded in custody under Section 170.

    (ii) The officer shall also communicate, in such manner as may be prescribed by the State Government, the action taken by him, to the person, if any whom the information relating to the commission of the offence was first given.
    (3) Where a superior officer of police has been appointed under Section 158, the report shall, in any case in which the State Government by general or special order so directs, be submitted through that officer, and he may, pending the orders of the Magistrate, direct the officer in charge of the police station to make further investigation.
    (4) Whenever it appears from a report forwarded under this section that the accused has been released on his bond, the Magistrate shall make such order for the discharge of such bond or otherwise as he thinks fit.
    (5) When such report is in respect of a case to which Section 170 applies, the police officer shall forward to the Magistrate along with the report.
    (6) If the police officer is of opinion that any part of any such statement is not relevant to the sub-matter of the proceeding or that its disclosure to the accused is not essential in the interests of justice and is inexpedient in the public interest, he shall indicate that part of the statement and append a note requesting the Magistrate exclude that part from the copies to be granted to the accused and stating his reasons for making such request.
        (a) All documents or relevant extracts thereof on which the prosecution proposes to rely other than those already sent to the Magistrate during investigation;
        (b) The statements recorded under Section 161 of all the persons whom the prosecution proposes to examine as its witness.

Above all, as these studies have suggested, the poor, illiterate and male dominated background of the female detainees also play a major role in denying of this basic fundamental right to them. Many women come to the jail with their children and as such, their families as well as the men tend to abandon the women in the name of social stigma. Such women can hardly think of any help from their families for moving the courts or even contacting with the lawyers on a regular basis, especially where they are not aware of free legal aid and/or they understand that once freed they would be further denied the basic rights of family, shelter and food due to the hard social customs.

3. Right to Health

Right to health for women prisoners must be read as corollary to the custodial justice as well as a separate basic right. The Supreme Court in *Parmanand Katara* v. *Union of India*,[31] had held that no person, whether innocent or a criminal liable to be punished, can be denied basic medical attention in case he/she needs one. This landmark case has therefore broadly established the principle that right to health is a fundamental right under Article 21 and every individual, including detainees, irrespective of their gender, cannot be denied proper medical care. Relying back to the Bhopal workshop and the report conducted by Pt. Ballabh Pant institute, it could be seen that women detainees from lower income group, poor and illiterate background may suffer from numerous health problem including gynaecological

---

(7) Where the police officer investigating the case finds it convenient so to do, he may furnish to the accused copies of all or any of the documents referred to in sub-section (5).

(8) Notwithstanding in this section shall be deemed to preclude further investigation in respect of an offence after a report under sub-section (2) has been forwarded to the Magistrate and, whereupon such investigation, the officer in charge of the police station obtains further evidence, oral or documentary, he shall forward to the Magistrate a further report or reports regarding such evidence in the form prescribed and the provisions of sub-section (2) to (6) shall, as far as may be, apply in relation to such report or reports as they apply in relation to a report forwarded under sub-section (2)."

31. 1989 AIR 2039, 1989 SCR (3) 997.

problems. However, the issue of pregnancy and childbirth of the female detainees attract my attention more for this chapter.

A series of provisions in the Indian Penal Code speak about punishment for causing miscarriage and subsequently death of the woman. As such, Section 312 states that if anyone voluntarily causes any woman to miscarry and such act is not caused on good faith that he is going to save the woman's life, he will be liable for a punishment for a term which may extend to three years; the section also states that if the woman dies due to this immediately after the miscarriage has occurred, the wrong doer would be liable to imprisonment which may extend to seven years along with monetary fine. Section 313 states that if someone causes miscarriage without the consent of the woman, he would be liable for life imprisonment, or for a prison term extending to ten years along with monetary fine. Section 314 further provides that if the woman dies due to any act done to cause miscarriage, the wrong doer would be liable to prison term which may extend to ten years and also monetary fine. Proviso added to this section further states that if the miscarriage, which caused the death of the woman, was caused without the consent of the victim, the wrong doer would be liable to life imprisonment or prison term for ten years along with fine. Section 315 pronounces punishment of ten years jail term or monetary fine, or both for cases where some one does anything which will cause the death of the unborn child in the mother's womb or immediately after its birth, and the same act is done on false faith of saving the would be mother's health. As such, Sections 312 and 313 speak about punishment for causing miscarriage and Section 314 speak about any act which is done to cause miscarriage. Section 315 on the other hand broadly covers all activities including causing miscarriage, which will cause death to the unborn child on false faith of saving the mother's life.

Broadly seen, these provisions not only speak about the unborn child's right to be born, but also safeguard pregnant woman's right to good health and proper medical care during pre-natal, natal and also post-natal stage. However, I have hardly found any case study where the prison authorities or the concerned doctor was held liable on these very grounds, especially when such cases of medical negligence cannot be ruled out in average Indian prisons. Women prisoners are also vulnerable to severe pre/post-natal critical conditions due to the absence of doctor at the time of need. The provisions discussed above, squarely make the jail authorities liable for any mishap that may occur due to failure in providing medical assistance by registered medical practitioners as well. The studies that are referred to above and case studies such as that of *Mathura rape case* may show that basing on these penal provisions, stricter jail manuals for the purpose of providing proper medical attention to women are prescribed especially for women's cells in various jails in India. But question still larks as to whether these provisions, Supreme Court guidelines and suggestions from the reports are properly being followed in all the jails or not. While Tihar jail had shown some examples of improvements for health care of inmates, including women detainees (Bedi, 1998), other jails may still have to look into this issue especially in the light of the news report published in *Times of India* (March 8, 2011).

4. Right to Privacy

In India, right to privacy for the detainees have been experimented both in negative sense as well as positive senses. While *Sunil Batra* v. *Delhi Administration* had dismissed the thought that prisoners especially with heavy punishments like that of the capital punishment or life imprisonment, should be detained in the private cells secluded from others, the Bombay High Court suggestion in 2010 on the right to private sexual life of the detainee with his wife (PTI, 2010) had broadened the right to life in the light of privacy in the prisons. The Bombay High Court suggestion is further taken by the recent proposal of the Director General of Prisons of Punjab (Prashar, 2012). But this must not be forgotten that right to privacy in the prisons also includes right to covered area while using the toilets and bathrooms also; for this is a corollary right of right to live with dignity as has been enshrined in Article 21 of the constitution. This issue has also been emphasised by the National Human Rights Commission (2007). The *Times of India* report (2011) had been an eye opener to show how this particular right is being abused in many jails in India. This right has been often merged with the basic right to health and nutrition in the jails. Agreeing with the fact that open toilets do create huge health hazards especially for women, I argue that open toilets or shared toilets inside the cell with no divider or cover to separate it from the cell, is also an abuse of right to privacy for prison inmates.

The Supreme Court had recognised right to clean environment including proper sanitation and toilet facility as a basic civil right in Municipal Council, *Ratlam* v. *Shri Vardhichand & Ors*[32] (Singh, 2007). This must be noted that the jail administration is liable for providing basic sanitation, toilet facilities to the inmates. The said administration is also liable to see that right to privacy and basic human dignity are preserved while the detainees avail the sanitation and toilet facilities in the jails.

Conclusion

The discussions above may show that even though the Criminal Procedure Code and the Indian Penal Code had set out several guidelines for well-being of the detainees, including female detainees, and the Supreme Court had paved the way for the same through landmark cases, loopholes still exist to pull down the basic rights of women detainees. The studies that have been relied upon for this chapter, the Supreme Court decisions and news reports may show that in majority of the cases public interest litigations have been filed to attract the attention of the courts towards the plight of the detainees who are poor and unaware of their basic rights. Women are the obvious subjects, but except a few cases, court's as well as general researcher's attentions are drawn for women detainees mainly through academic or NGO's reports. This may be shown as the main example as how the abuse of rights of the women detainees is overlooked in India. The problem may be solved if proper attention is given from criminal and tort law angle, shifting the highlight from sociological perspective of the abuse of rights problems to negligent of the prison authorities and the law and justice administration as a whole.

32. On 29 July, 1980 AIR 1622, 1981 SCR (1). Also see http://indiankanoon.org/doc/440471/

I support my this very argument on the basis of two grounds: (i) the Madhya Pradesh State Women's Commission has constituted a women's panel headed by chairperson of the commission, to study the condition of women prisoners in various jails in the State of Madhya Pradesh on 26th December, 2011 (TNN, 2011). The commission plans to submit its report within six months. Further, the NHRC has ordered the Uttar Pradesh government to provide monetary relief to maltreated prisoners, who were severely beaten up by the concerned prison authorities last year (Balaji, 2012). The commission has reportedly turned down the State Government's plea to suspend the payment of the monetary relief to the victims until the departmental enquiry on the staff was completed. These two above-mentioned moves are commendable as in both the cases, the Commissions have turned the attention towards the responsibility of the prison authorities, and especially in the second case, and the Commission has sought for immediate restoration of justice, making the prison authorities and the government directly liable for the abuse of custodial rights. (ii) I also support my this very argument on the basis of the fact that while courts have made it mandatory for prison doctors/staff nurses in the jail premises, there is hardly any judgment making it compulsory for women lawyers, to provide their services to women detainees. Nonetheless, this may not be acceptable for many as the concept of prisons in India generally portray a den of criminals and hardly any family may allow their women to visit the detainees. But at the same time, if the law schools, NGOs and the government take initiative to make it compulsory for young women advocates, to provide free legal aid to prisons including those situated in interior areas, the problem may be managed.

References

Andharia, P. (2011). Hussainara Khatoon: Overflowing Prisons, Empty Reforms—Sad but True. Let's talk about the law. Retrieved on 15th April 2012 from http://letstalkaboutthelaw.wordpress.com/tag/hussainara-khatoon/

Balaji, J. (January 31, 2012). NHRC orders U.P. to provide relief to maltreated prisoners. *The Hindu*. Retrieved on 23-06-12 from http://www.thehindu.com/news/national/article2845537.ece

Bedi, K. (1998). It always possible: one woman's transformation of Tihar prison. Originally published by Sterling.

Commonwealth Human Rights Initiative (CHRI). (1998). *Prison and Human Rights*. Proceedings on the workshops on 'Prisons and Human Rights' organised at Bhopal by the Commonwealth Human Rights Initiative (CHRI) in collaboration with the Madhya Pradesh Human Rights Commission (MPHRC) conducted on the 25th and 26th of April 1998.

Government of India. (2001). Women in Detention. Committee on empowerment of women. Ministry of Home Affairs and Ministry of Human Resource Development (Department of Women and Child Development). Retrieved on 09-01-2012 from http://164.100.24.208/ls/committeeR/Empowerment/3rd/3rd.htm#contents

Jagadeesh, N. (2010). "Legal changes towards justice for sexual assault victims". *Indian Journal of Medical Ethics*. 7(2), 108-12, April-June.

Kumar, N. (November 28, 2011). Bail for Kanimozhi, four others. *The Hindu*. Retrieved on 23-01-12 from http://www.thehindu.com/news/national/article2668196.ece

Math, S.B., Murthy, P., Parthasarthy, R., Kumar, C.N., & Madhusudhan, S. (2011). *Mental Health and Substance Use Problems in Prisons: Local Lessons for National Action*. Bangalore: National Institute of Mental Health Neuro Sciences, Retrieved on 09-01-2012 from http://www.nimhans.kar.nic.in/prison/chapter_2.pdf

National Human Rights Commission (NHRC) (2007). Human rights manual for district magistrates. Retrieved on 23-01-12 from http://bhrc.bih.nic.in/Docs/HRManual-for-DM.pdf

Pandit Govind Ballabh Pant Institute of Studies in Rural Development. (2004). Final Report: Children of Women Prisoners in Jails: A Study in Uttar Pradesh, Lucknow. Sponsored by: Planning Commission, Government of India, New Delhi. Retrieved on 09-01-12 from http://planningcommission.nic.in/reports/sereport/ser/stdy_jailwm.pdf

Prashar, S. (June 8, 2012). Conjugal visits in Punjab jails soon? *Times of India*. Retrieved on 23-06-12 from http://timesofindia.indiatimes.com/city/chandigarh/Conjugal-visits-in-Punjab-jails-soon/articleshow/13911092.cms

PTI (January 14, 2010). Why can't prisoners have sex in jails, court asks Maharashtra govt. *Times of India*. Retrieved on 23-01-12 from http://articles.timesofindia.indiatimes.com/2010-01-14/india/28134661_1_hiv-positive-prisoners-jail-inmates-medical-officers

Singh, J. (2007). Constitutional safeguards for environment and heritage: an appraisal. Retrieved on 23-01-12 from http://www.nlsenlaw.org/heritage-conservation/articles/constitutional-safeguards-for-environment-and-heritage-an-appraisal/

Times of India. (March 8, 2011). Ex-women prisoners say conditions bad, inmates tortured. Retrieved on 09-01-12 from http://articles.timesofindia.indiatimes.com/2011-03-08/chennai/28667863_1_women-prisoners-tiruchi-jail-wardens.

TNN. (December 27, 2011). Women's panel to study prisons in state. *Times of India*. Retrieved on 23-06-12 from http://articles.timesofindia.indiatimes.com/2011-12-27/bhopal/30560908_1_women-prisoners-jail-reforms-committee-study-problems

7

Rights of Children of Prisoners

T. Lakshmi Narayana

Introduction

The future of the nation depends upon the young generation. Children deserve compassion and bestowal of the best care to protect their burgeoning human resources. As Reddy (2008) states,

> A child is born innocent and if nourished with tender care and attention, he or she would blossom with great physical, mental, moral and spiritual personality. They would become a person of stature and excellence. On the other side, noxious surroundings, neglect of basic needs, bad company and other abuses and temptations would spoil the child, and lead to delinquent behaviour. (p. 32)

Therefore, the adult-child relation, parents in particular, is said to provide 'care and protection', thereby serving in the 'best interests of the child' and meeting their day-to-day 'needs of survival and development'. The adult is presumed to be the guardian and in that respect expected to take the responsibility of the child's welfare and development (Bakri, 2006). Their relationship with the family and the State would create the essential foundation of childhood for all children.

Fundamental Rights and State Duty

The Constitution of India contains provisions for survival, development and protection of children. These are included both in Part III and Part IV of the Constitution pertaining to 'Fundamental Rights' and 'Directive Principles of State Policy'.

These are, Equality before the law,[1] Non-discrimination,[2] Untouchability,[3] Freedom of Speech,[4] Right to Life,[5] Right to Education,[6] Prohibition of Child Labour,[7] Prohibition of human trafficking,[8] etc. The directive principles directs the States to ensure Health, Dignity,[9] Opportunity and non-exploitation of children,[10] Secured human conditions,[11] Care and education[12] and

1. Article 14: provides that the state shall not deny to any person equality before the law or the equal protection of the laws within the territory of India.
2. Article 15: prohibits discrimination on grounds of religion, race, caste, sex or place of birth.
3. Article 17: "Untouchability" is abolished and its practice in any form is forbidden.
4. Article 19: (1) All citizens shall have the right—(a) to freedom of speech and expression; ... (c) to form associations or unions; (d) to move freely throughout the territory of India; (e) to reside and settle in any part of the territory of India.
5. Article 21: No person shall be deprived of his life or personal liberty except according to procedure established by law.
6. Article 21(A), inserted by 86th Constitutional Amendment provides for free and compulsory education to all children of the age of six to fourteen years.
7. Article 24: prohibits employment of children below the age of fourteen years in any factory or mine or engagement in other hazardous employment.
8. Article 23: prohibits trafficking in human beings and all forms of forced labour.
9. Article 39(e) directs the State to ensure that the health and strength of workers, men and women, and the tender age of children are not abused and that citizens are not forced by economic necessity to enter avocations unsuited to their age or strength.
10. Article 39(f) directs the State to ensure that children are given opportunities and facilities to develop in a healthy manner and in conditions of freedom and dignity and that childhood and youth are protected against exploitation and against moral and material abandonment.
11. Article 42: provides that the State shall make provision for securing just and humane conditions of work and maternity relief.
12. Article 45: stipulates that the State shall endeavour to provide early childhood care and education for all children until they complete the age of six years. Article 46 provides that the State shall promote with special care the educational and economic interests of the weaker sections of the people, and, in particular, of the Scheduled Castes and

Standard of living.[13] Besides the Constitution provisions, there are a series of legislations which deal with children issues. These are (Sabharwal, 2006):

- The Guardians and Wards Act, 1890,
- Child Marriage Restraint Act, 1929,
- The Factories Act, 1948,
- Hindu Adoptions and Maintenance Act, 1956,
- Probation of Offenders Act, 1958,
- Orphanages and Other Charitable Homes (Supervision and Control) Act, 1960,
- The Child Labour (Prohibition and Regulation) Act, 1986,
- Juvenile Justice (Care and Protection of Children) Amendment Act, 2006,[14]
- The Infant Milk Substitutes, Feeding Bottles and Infant Foods, (Regulation of Production, Supply and Distribution) Act, 1992,
- Pre-natal Diagnostic Techniques (Regulation and Prevention of Misuse) Act, 1994,
- Persons with Disabilities (Equal Opportunities, Protection of Rights and Full Participation) Act, 1995,
- Immoral Traffic (Prevention) Act, 1986,
- The Commission for Protection of the Child Rights, 2005,[15]

---

the Scheduled Tribes, and shall protect them from social injustice and all forms of exploitation. Article 51A: ... (k) ... parent or guardian to provide opportunities for education to his child or, as the case may be, ward between the age of six and fourteen years (included by 86th Amendment to the constitution, which is not yet notified).

13. Article 47 provides that the State shall regard the raising of the level of nutrition and the standard of living of its people and the improvement of public health as among its primary duty.
14. The Juvenile Justice Act, 2000 was replaced by the Juvenile Justice (Care and Protection) Amendment Act, 2006 to comply with the provisions of the Convention on the Rights of the Child (CRC) which has been acceded to by India in 1992.
15. As envisaged in the Commissions for Protection of Child Rights Act 2005 notified in the Gazette of India on 20th Jan., 2006 as Act No. 4 of 2006 the Government has set up a National Commission

• Prohibition of Child Marriage Act, 2006.

The impact of prison life on the individual is not so much to reform the prisoner but to prevent them from being ruined by the treatment given by the prison authorities as the prison is considered to be a punitive model rather than a treatment model (William & Christopher, 2004). Furthermore, the 'National Charter for Children 2003', "reiterates its commitment to the cause of the children in order to see that no child remains hungry, illiterate or sick" (Government of India, 2004).

The Charter lays down the obligation on States to provide adequate services for children both before and after birth, and during the growing stages for their full physical, mental and social development. The measures suggested include a comprehensive health program, supplementary nutrition for mothers and children, promotion of physical education and recreational activities, special consideration for children of weaker sections and prevention of exploitation of children.

Plight of the Children of Women Prisoners

According to the study on Children of Women Prisoners in Jails (Pandit Govind Ballabh Pant Institute of Studies in Rural Development, 2004):

> Jails are not the space where children should live with mothers. A jail can never provide a family environment in it, which a child very much deserves. In the jail, a woman prisoner faces many problems in respect to her own daily requirements. Her problems are found to increase manifold, in the event of living with their children inside the jail. The jails are neither equipped with adequate infrastructure facilities to accommodate the children of women inmates in a befitting manner, nor is the staffs in jails properly trained to handle the problems arising from children living

for Protection of Child Rights (NCPCR) w.e.f. 5th March, 2007. The Commission's Mandate is to ensure that all Laws, Policies, Programs, and Administrative Mechanisms are in consonance with the Child Rights perspective as enshrined in the Constitution of India and also the UN Convention on the Rights of the Child. The Child is defined as a person in the 0 to 18 years age group.

in jails. Women reported that proper care of their children is not ensured in most of the cases. (p. 109)

Further, the report says jail environment is also negative for the development of children of women prisoners. The quality of food, nutrition, education, health, etc., is also found to be average, which is supposed to hamper the natural growth and development of children in jail. The accommodation facility in the jail is also not suitable for women prisoners. Particularly, for those women who have small kids along with themselves.

States' Practice with Regard to Children of Prisoners

The level and standard of measures vary from state to state in India. It is relevant to observe the study conducted to understand the status of children of prisoners (Chattoraj, et al. 1998; Sabharwal, 2006).

The key observations of the study are as follows (Chattoraj, et al. 1998):

(i) The general impression gathered was that, most of these children were living in really difficult conditions and suffering from diverse deprivations relating to food, healthcare, accommodation, education, recreation, etc.

(ii) No appropriate program was found to be in place in any of the jails, for their proper bio-psycho-social development. Their looking after was mostly left to their mothers. No trained staffs were found in any of the jails to take care of these children.

(iii) It was observed that in many jails, women inmates with children were not given any special or extra meals. In some cases, occasionally, some extra food, mostly in the form of a glass of milk, was available to children. In some jails, separate food was being provided only to grown up children, over the age of five years. But the quality of food would be the same as supplied to adult prisoners.

(iv) No special consideration was given to child bearing women inmates, in matters of food or other facilities. The same food and the same facilities were given to all women inmates, irrespective of the fact whether their children were living with them or not.

(v) No separate or specialised medical facilities were available for children in jails.

(vi) Barring a few, most mother prisoners considered that their stay in jails would have a negative impact on the physical as well as mental development of their children.

(vii) Crowded environment, lack of appropriate food, shelter and above all, deprivation of affection of other members of the family, particularly the father was generally perceived by the mothers as big stumbling blocks for the proper development of their children in the formative years of the child's life.

(viii) Mother prisoners identified six areas where urgent improvement was necessary for proper up bringing of their children. They are related to food, medical facilities, accommodation, education, recreation and separation of their children from habitual offenders.

(ix) No prison office was deployed on the exclusive duty of looking after these children or their mothers. They had to perform this duty alongside many other duties including administrative work, discipline maintenance, security-related jobs, etc. None of them was reported to have undergone any special training in looking after the children in jails.

Based on the affidavits filed by the various States and Union Territories before the Supreme Court of India in *R.D. Upadhyay* v. *State of A.P. & Others* it seems that there were 6,496 undertrial women with 1053 children and 1873 convicted women with 206 children. According to the National Crime Records (Government of India, 2006) there are, 3,904 convicts, 9,455 undertrails, 96 detenues, and 1202 others, bringing it to a total of 14,657. The right to life under the Indian Constitution has been developed extensively which includes, prison rights to the prisoners, but the situation is still unfortunate in context to women prisoners. "The Prison Act and the Prison Rules do not talk about the segregation of the convicts on gender basis and certain rights to women convicts, an area which needs special attention" (Halder & Jaishankar, 2007, p. 17). Conditions of living in most of the prisons are sub-human. Mass approach towards various problems of prisoners is in vogue (Kumar, 2001). Mostly, women with children do not get access to their children after they are six years old. The children are sent to government homes for the remaining period of their mother's conviction, in case the father or the other family members are incapable of taking care.

According to Babita Verma,[16]

> More than 70% of the women prisoners are married and have children. At the time of arrest of the women prisoners having children, indiscriminate arrest is not confined only to women/mother prisoners but such arrest is automatically extended to these children who are of tender age and there is no one to look after or take care of the child without their mother. Such children are subjected to a kind of arrest for no offence committed by them.

The Supreme Court of India on March 20th, 2001 has directed the States and Union Territories to disclose following details on the affidavit in view to frame some guidelines and issue instructions.[17] In response to the directions given by the Supreme Court of India, various State Governments and Union Territories submitted reports with details of asked questions (Sabharwal, 2006).[18]

---

16. Babita Verma is the Program Co-ordinater of "Women's Action Research and Legal Action for Women (WARLAW)" at New Delhi. The WARLAW has filed a petition before the Supreme Court of India to bring the court attention on the problems faced by children of women in Indian prisons. For more detail see *R.D. Upadhyay* v. *State of A.P. & Others*: AIR : 2006 (93) pp. 1946-59.
17. The order of the Supreme Court was issued in response to the letter dated 8th March, 2000 written by a 6 years old girl child from Bangalore addressing to Chief Justice of India, explaining the problems of children in jail with their mothers along with an article published in a news magazine. See for more details, *R.D. Upadhyay* v. *State of A.P. and Others*.
18. The Court directed the States and Union Territories to disclose on affidavit the following: (i) The number of female prisoners (under trial) together with the nature of offence for which they have been detained; (ii) Period of their detention; (iii) Children, if any, who are with the mothers lodged in the jail; (iv) Number of convicted female prisoners and whether any children are also lodged with such convicts in the

Table 1[19]

Name of the State	Measures Provided under State Prison Rules/Manuals
Andaman & Nicobar Islands	Children are allowed to live with their mothers up to the age of 5 years. A special diet is prescribed for children by the Medical Officer. The District Magistrate is empowered to hand over children above 5 years to relatives or any trustworthy person.
Andhra Pradesh	Children are allowed to live with their mothers up to 6 years. Milk with a protein diet is provided along with other special medical facilities like polio vaccines, education, etc.
Assam	Children are allowed to live with their mothers up to the age of 6 years. Literacy training by Lady teachers. The District Magistrate is empowered to hand over children above 5 years to relatives or any trustworthy person.
New Delhi	Children are allowed to live with their mothers up to the age of 6 years. Proper diets and vaccine for popular diseases are adequately provided for the children. Children above 4 years are taught to read and write. They are prepared for admissions in outside schools. Sponsorships for the funding of the children education is provided for by the CASP (Community Aid Sponsorship Program). Two NGO's by the name of Mahila Pratikraksha Mandal and Navjyoti Delhi Police Foundation run crèches and also conduct picnic programs. Admissions for children above 5 years of age, to Government cottage homes and to residential schools are facilitated through NGO's.
Gujarat	Special diet and medical facilities as prescribed by the Medical Officer are available for children. Cradle facilities are provided for infants.

jails; (v) Whether any facilities are available in the jail concerned for taking care of such children and, if so, the type of facilities."

19. For more details on practice of the States with regard to children of women prisoners; see *R.D. Upadhyay* v. *State of A.P. & Others.*

Bihar	Children are allowed to live with their mothers from 2-5 years. Provision is made for ration for children from 12-18 months, and from 18-24 months or as specified by the Medical Officer. Health and clothing facilities are provided by the Government. Toys and other forms of entertainment are also available in some jails.
Goa	The Government provides special dietary facilities for the children. The Medical Officer of the Primary Health Centre visits prisoners and children twice a week.
Haryana	A special diet is provided based on the advice of the Medical Officer. Regular literacy classes are taken by two lady teachers on deputation from the State Education Dept. at Borstal Jail, Hissar. Books and toys are provided.
Mizoram	Children are allowed to live with their mothers up to the age of 6 years. A special diet is prescribed under the Rules of the Jail Manual. However, no proper facilities for education or recreation exist.
Orissa	Children are allowed to live with their mothers up to the age of 4 years or in special cases up to 6 years by the approval of the Superintendent. A special diet is available, as prescribed by the Medical Officer. Children are provided with suitable clothing. On leaving the jail, in consultation with the District Magistrate, the child is handed over to a relative or to some trustworthy person, as selected by the District Magistrate.
Punjab	Children under the age of 1 year are provided with milk and sugar. Provision is also made for ration for children from 12-18 months and from 18-24 months. Extra diet is available on the advice of the Medical Officer. There is a play nursery and one attendant who look after the children from time to time.
Uttar Pradesh	Children are allowed to live with their mothers up to the age of 6 years. A special diet is available under the Rules of the Jail Manual. On leaving prison, in consultation with the District Magistrate, the child is handed over to a relative or to some trustworthy person, as selected by the District Magistrate.

Uttarakhand	Diet is provided as under the Rules of the Jail manual. Education is provided by the Government, which also makes arrangement for extra-curricular activities such as sports.
Meghalaya	Children are allowed to live with their mothers up to the age of 6 years. All aspects of the children's welfare are taken care of according to the Rules under the State Jail Manual.
Nagaland	The provisions of the Assam Jail Manual have been adopted *vis-à-vis* facilities for women and for children living with their mothers.
Puducherry	A special diet is available as prescribed by the Medical Officer. Play things, toys, etc. are provided to the children at Government cost or through NGOs.
Rajasthan	A special diet is available under the rules of the Jail Manual. Special medical facilities are also provided for as prescribed in the manual. Clothing and toys are provided for by NGOs.
West Bengal	Normal facilities are available. In addition the Inner Wheel Club also runs a Homeopathic clinic for children. A non-formal school is run by an NGO for rendering elementary education to children.

The Table 1 (Sabharwal, 2006) indicates that State Practices are not uniform; every State has a different following for providing measures to the children of prisoners due to which the status of children in prisons are more vulnerable. The main problem in Indian prison administration system is the division of powers between the Centre and the States. Prisons, Reformation, Borstal institutions and other institutions of like nature and persons detained in them, as per item 4 of List II of the Lists mentioned in Article 246 of the Constitution, are in sphere of the States (Banerjea, Chatterjee, & Maji, 2001).

To solve this problem the Justice Krishna Iyer Committee (1987) has suggested bringing the Prison administration under the Central Government list for a uniform prison manual. Although some of the states allow children up to 6 years, after 6 years jail authorities are empowered to send them to state homes or rehabilitation centres run by NGO's. There is no monitory mechanism for the welfare of children after 6 or till the end of the conviction period of the parent. It is more difficult to expect the care and protection of children especially a girl child in the absence of monitory mechanism.

The number of such categories of children is increasing day by day, but because of their dispersed character, they have escaped the attention of policy-makers. Response to their needs has been ad hoc and largely in the form of relief. It is important that such categories of children are identified, their problems studied and programs developed, through which these children can be rescued and rehabilitated. We also need to bring about improvement in the standards of service in most State run institutions and those run by voluntary organizations. The best way to reach out to these children would be through non-institutional forms of care and legal measures to protect them.

Supreme Court Guidelines on Children of Women Prisoners

The judiciary and the Supreme Court have played pivotal role in upholding the rights of the child. The jurisprudence of the Supreme Court of India enables an individual or a civil society to intervene in cases relating to violations of fundamental rights even though they may not have been affected personally in the matter. The practice of the Indian judiciary represents an effort to use the legal system to ensure action to enforcement of constitutionally guaranteed rights. These are the most important examples of social action litigation cases for children rights.[20]

20. *Laxmikant Pandey* v. *Union of India* [AIR (1984) SC 469, AIR (1986) SC 276, AIR (1987) SC 232] on Adoption of Children. *Shiela Barse* v. *Union of India* [AIR (1986) SC 1883, AIR (1988) SC 2211] on Trafficking of Children. *M.C. Mehta* v. *State of Tamil Nadu* [JT 1990 SC 263] on Problem of Child Labour. *Vishal Jeet* v. *Union of India* [1990 (3) SCC 318] on Problem of Child Prostitution. *Unni Krishnan* v. *State of Andhra Pradesh* [1993 (1) SC 645] on Education of Children. *Gaurav Jain* v. *Union of India* [1997 (8) SCC 114] on Problems of Prostitution and Children forced into Prostitution. *Gita Hariharan* v. *Reserve Bank of India* [(1999) 2 SC 228] on Guardianship. *Centre for Enquiry into Health and Allied Themes (CEHAT) & Others* v.

Each of these has been a landmark in the process of ensuring children's rights (Bakri, 2006, p. 41).

Though a wide range of statutory laws,[21] constitute the normative basis for the Prison functions, the actual functional level often doubts and controversies arise regarding the ambit and interpretations of the statutory rules, thereby calling for frequent adjudications by the Courts. The Supreme Court of India takes into consideration the various reports and studies conducted by the national institutions (Chattoraj, et al., 1998; Pandit Govind Ballabh Pant Institute of Studies in Rural Development, 2004). All of these studies were in context to the plight of children of Prisoners and recommended various measures for betterment of prison administration. The Supreme Court of India has issued the following guidelines to all states and Union Territories for its incorporation of measures into State prison manuals while amending the provisions of the same. In *R.D. Upadhyay* v. *State of A.P. & Others* (Sabharwal, 2006). The salient features of the Supreme Court Guidelines were (Sabharwal, 2006):

1. A child shall not be treated as an undertrial/convict while in the prison with his/her mother.
2. A pregnant woman if required to be lodged in a jail shall be accommodated in a jail which has the required minimum facilities for child delivery as well as for providing prenatal and post-natal care for both, the mother and the child.
3. Childbirth in Prison:
   (a) As far as possible and provided she has a suitable option, arrangement for temporary release/parole (or suspended sentence in case of minor and casual offender) should be made to enable delivery outside the jail.

Union of India & Others [2000 SC 301] for more case laws refer "Prisons and Law in India" published by BPR&D (2007).

21. The Prison Act, 1894, Prisoners Act, 1900, Laws related to Preventive Detention, Probation of Offenders Act, 1959, Furlough and Parole Rules the State Prison Manuals, the Code of Criminal Procedure, 1973, the Indian Penal Code, 1860, the Protection of Human Rights Act, 1993, etc.

(b) Births in prison while being registered in the local birth registration office shall mention the address as the locality and prison shall not be mentioned and recorded in the certificate of birth that is issued.

4. Female Prisoners and their Children:
   (a) A female prisoner is to be allowed to keep her child with her till the age of six years. Thereafter, the child is to be handed over to a suitable surrogate as per the wishes of the female prisoner or shall be sent to a suitable institution run by the Social Welfare Department.
   (b) Such children are to be kept in protective custody until their mother is released or the child attains such age as to earn his/her own livelihood.
5. Food, Shelter, Clothing:
   (a) Children in jail shall be provided with adequate clothing suiting the local climatic requirement.
   (b) Dietary scale should be laid down. Separate food is to be provided to the children keeping in view their growth needs.
   (c) Separate utensils, clean drinking water, vaccination, medical care, clean and hygienic sleeping facilities, etc. to be provided for children and their prisoner mother.
6. Proper educational and recreational opportunities, crèche and nursery shall be provided in the jail.
7. Women with children shall not be accommodated in Sub-Jails as they are generally not equipped to provide the expected care to them.
8. Children and their mothers shall be separated from the offenders/accused relating to all types of crime.
9. Dietary scale and other food items for children shall be in accordance with the "Dietary Guidelines for Indians —A Manual" published by the National Institute of Nutrition, Council of Medical Research, Hyderabad.

10. Jail Manuals of the States shall be suitably amended to conform to the aforesaid directions.
11. State Legal Service Authorities to inspect jails in order to monitor compliance with these directions.
12. Courts shall give priority to the cases of women prisoners accompanied by children to ensure expeditions disposal of cases pending against them.

The Supreme Court of India disposed of the writ petition with the direction to file compliance report within a period of four months from the date of issue. However, no State has complied the same till date for reasons best known to them.

The Role of the National Human Rights Commission

The 'Rights of Children', is one area on which the National Human Rights Commission (NHRC) has tried to focus continuously ever since it was constituted. It observed from the very beginning that despite there being major provisions in the Constitution of India for the Survival, Development and Protection of Children as well as laws to safeguard their interests including the fact that the Government of India had ratified the UN Convention on Child Rights (CRC) in 2002. Children all over the country, especially those belonging to weaker sections of the society, were found to be vulnerable and their dignity and human rights were often trampled. The Commission mainly concentrated its attention on preventing and eradicating the problems of child labour, child marriage, child trafficking and prostitution, child sexual violence, female foeticide and infanticide, child rape, HIV/AIDS in children and the problem of juveniles.

Majority of the complaints handled by the Commission so far have been on the issue of child labour, child marriage, juvenile justice, child trafficking, child rape, missing children, exploitation of children of varied kinds, deaths in juvenile/observation homes, etc. The Commission till 31st of October 2006 had registered 2,885 cases of children. Out of these, 489 cases pertained to child labour, 266 cases were related to child marriage, 31 cases were of children who were being misused for commercial sexual exploitation, 385 cases were related to different kinds of exploitation and 61 cases pertained to trafficking in children (NHRC, 2007).

The other cases registered were related to disappearance, deaths in juvenile/observation homes, sexual harassment/abuse, rape, etc. While dealing with these cases, the Commission has awarded a total compensation of ₹ 45,20,000 to children who were victims of different kinds of violations (Bakri, 2006, p. 60). Recently on 20th April 2009, The National Human Rights Commission has recommended the Uttar Pradesh government to pay ₹ 1,00,000 as monetary relief to the bereaved mother, who delivered a female child in district jail Agra and lost her due to inadequate medical facilities and lack of nutritious diet (NHRC, 2009).[22] While considering this case the Commission observed that the Supreme Court guidelines on children of women prisoners were not being followed and innocent children continued to be victims of administrative apathy and indifference.

Conclusion

Prisons and Correctional Administration are important components of criminal justice administration. It is that part of the Criminal Justice System that public sees the least of, and knows the least about (Banerjea, Chatterjee, & Maji, 2005, p. 275). Today prisons are said to be in a state of crisis. They are marked by sub-human material conditions, overcrowding, lack of sensitivity, weak motivation and rampant corruption amongst the prison functionaries. "The main reasons for such a state of affairs are, firstly the low priority accorded to prisons at political and social levels, secondly the lack of transparency and visibility of the prison system in public eyes and lastly the inadequate training and orientation of prison officials."

The Supreme Court of India in *Sheela Barse* v. *Secretary, Children's Society*,[23] observed that "children are the citizens of

22. NHRC, Case No. 24687/24/2006-07, date of recommendation 20th April 2009.
23. It further observed that "In recent years, this position has been well realised. In 1959, the Declaration of all the rights of the child was adopted by the General Assembly of the United Nations and in Article 24 of the International Covenant on Civil and Political Rights,

the future era. Proper upbringing of children and giving them appropriate training would help them turn good citizens on whom the future of our country depends." The National Policy for Children (1974) recognized that "Children are the nation's supremely important asset and declared that it is the responsibility of the State to nurture them." It further emphasised that it shall be the duty of the State to "provide adequate services to children, both before and after birth and through the period of growth, to ensure their full physical, mental and social development".

In view of the above-mentioned facts, the present paper would suggest that, the benefits of all schemes for the development of children sponsored by Central Government such as, Balika Samriddi Yojana (BSY),[24] Kishore Shakti Yojana (KSY)[25] Program of Universalisation Elementary Education (UEE),[26] Scheme of

---

1966. The importance of the child has been appropriately recognized. India as a party to these International Charters having ratified the Declaration, it is an obligation of the Government of India as also the State machinery to implement the same in the proper way. The Children's Act, 1948 has made elaborate provisions to cover this and if these provisions are properly translated into action and the authorities created under the Act become cognizant of their role, duties and obligation in the performance of the statutory mechanism created under the Act and they are properly motivated to meet the situations that arise in handling the problems, the situation would certainly be very much eased" *Sheela Barse* v. *Secretary*, *Children's Aid Society*, (1987) 3 SCC 50, Para. 5.

24. To change negative family and community attitudes towards the girl child at birth and her mother. To improve the enrolment and retention of girl children in schools. To rise the age at marriage of girls. To assist the girl to undertake income generating activities. The Balika Samriddhi Yojana will cover both rural and urban areas in all districts in India.
25. The objective of the KSY; to improve the nutritional, health and development status of adolescent girls, promote awareness of health, hygiene, nutrition and family care, link them to opportunities for learning life skills, going back to school, help them gain a better understanding of their social environment and take initiatives to become productive members of the society 11 to 18 years.
26. One of the main objectives of educational development according to Sixth Five-Year Plan 1980-85, is—"to ensure essential minimum education to all children up to the age of 14 years within the next 10 years".

Prevention and Control Juvenile Social Maladjustment (PCJS),[27] Integrated Child Development Services (ICDS),[28] Integrated

---

27. PCJS, is a Centrally Sponsored Scheme was launched in 1986, which was renamed as Program for Juvenile Justice in 1998 under which financial assistance is provided to the State Governments/UT Administrations for establishment and maintenance of various levels of institutions for juveniles in conflict with law as well as children in need of care and protection under the provisions of the Act. The objectives of Program for Juvenile Justice are: (i) To extend help to State Governments to bear the cost of infrastructure and services development under the Juvenile Justice Act. The purpose is to see that in no circumstances the child in conflict with law is lodged in a regular prison; (ii) To ensure minimum quality standards in the juvenile justice services; (iii) To provide adequate services for prevention of social maladjustment and rehabilitation of socially maladjusted juveniles; (iv) To ensure participation of community and other organizations in the care and protection of children in conflict with law who are perhaps more vulnerable than other groups of children.
28. The Integrated Child Development Services (ICDS) launched in 1975 Scheme represents one of the world's largest and most unique programs for early childhood development. ICDS is the foremost symbol of India's commitment to her children—India's response to the challenge of providing pre-school education to children on one hand and breaking the vicious cycle of malnutrition, morbidity, reduced learning capacity and mortality, on the other. ICDS is a centrally sponsored scheme implemented through the State Governments with 100 per cent financial assistance from the Central Government for all inputs other than supplementary food, which the States provide from their own resources. Since 2005-06, grant-in-aid pattern has been modified and the Government of India now provides central assistance to States for supplementary nutrition to the extent of 50% of the cost norms or 50% of the actual expenditure incurred by States, whichever is less. The objectives of the Scheme are multifold: (a) to improve the nutritional and health status of pre-school children in the age-group of 0-6 years; (b) to lay the foundation of proper psychological development of the child; (c) to reduce the incidence of mortality, morbidity, malnutrition and school drop-out; (d) to achieve effective coordination of policy and implementation amongst the various departments to promote child development; and to enhance the capability of the mother to look after the normal health and nutritional needs of the child through proper nutrition and health education. For more details see; Chapter: III, Annual Report; 2007-2008 by Department of Women and Child Development available at http://www.wcd.nic.in/

Child Protection Scheme (ICPS),[29] and Rajiv Gandhi National Crèche Scheme for the Children (RGNC)[30] should extend to the children of prisoners in prison. Secondly, there should be a monitory mechanism to observe the care and protection of the children of prisoners who are above six years old, when they are sent to government homes or NGO centres. Though there are less number of children of male prisoners (where there is no other person in the family than the father) they should also be cared and protected under prison rules/manuals.

The practice of the Indian Administration upholds the 'Doctrine of Precedent' as all the judgments of the Apex court is binding in nature. Accordingly the Supreme Court of India accords the highest precedential value in terms of the Article 141 of the Constitution of India which reads; "The law declared by the Supreme Court shall be binding on all courts within the territory of India". Thus, for all the courts as well as other instrumentalities of the State, the Supreme Court rulings constitute the binding law violation which may entail contempt proceedings. Therefore, it is time to act. The States need to show their concern and commitment to human rights and prisoner's

29. The objectives of the scheme are to contribute to the improvements in the well-being of children in difficult circumstances as well as to the reduction of vulnerabilities to situations and actions that lead to abuse, neglect, exploitation, abandonment and separation of children. These will be achieved by: (i) improved access to and quality of child protection services; (ii) public awareness programs about the reality of child rights, situation and protection in India; (iii) clearly articulated responsibilities and enforced accountability for child protection; (iv) established and functioning structures at all government levels for delivery of statutory and support services to children in difficult circumstances; (v) setting up of an operational evidence based monitoring and evaluation system.

30. Rajiv Gandhi National Crèche Scheme (RGNC) for the Children of Working Mothers was launched with effect from 1st January, 2006 by merging the National Creche Fund with the Scheme of Assistance to Voluntary Organizations for Crèches/Day Care Centres for the Children of Working and Ailing Women. The scheme is being implemented through Central Social Welfare Board and two national level voluntary. The Scheme provides crèche services to the children in age group of 0-6 years, which includes supplementary nutrition, emergency medicines and contingencies.

rights upholding the Apex court guidelines issued for "Care and Protection of Children of Prisoners".

The success in realization of the objectives and goals enshrined in many of the studies and committees which deal with prison reforms and children of prisoners would depend more on attitudinal aspects of the machinery and enforcement agencies involved in implementation, rather than on infrastructure and procedures alone. Finally, the children of prisoners are not criminals but they are victims of circumstances. Therefore, Indian prison administration should reform according to the need of hour, i.e. with the spirit to achieve the solemn task of "National Building Processes" since children are the future of the nation.

References

Bakri, S. (2006). *Children in India and their Rights*. New Delhi: National Human Rights Commission.

Banerjea, D., Chatterjee, D.K., and Maji, P.R. (2001). *Criminal Justice Series. Jharkhand,* Vol. 15. New Delhi: Allied Publishers Private Limited in colloboration with National University of Juridical Sciences, Kolkata. p. 275.

Banerjea, D., Chatterjee, D.K., and Maji, P.R. (2005). *Criminal Justice Series. Chandigarh*. Vol. 17, Part 2. New Delhi: Allied Publishers Private Limited in colloboration with National University of Juridical Sciences, Kolkata. p. 114.

Chattoraj, B.N. et al. (2006). *Children of Women Prisoners in Indian Jail*. New Delhi: Lok Nayak Jayaprakash Narayan National Institute of Criminology and Forensic Science (Ministry of Home Affairs, Government of India).

Government of India (2004). *National Charter for Children, 2003*. New Delhi: Ministry of Human Resource Development, Department of Women and Child Development. Retrieved on June 12, 2009 from wcd.nic.in/nationalcharter2003.doc

Government of India (2006). *Prison Statistics, India 2006*. New Delhi: National Crime Records Bureau, Ministry of Home Affairs, Government of India. Retrieved on June 12, 2009 from http://ncrb.nic.in/PSI2006/prison2006.htm

Halder, D., and Jaishankar, K. (2007). "Rights of Women Prisoners in India: A Legal Analysis". *The Indian Journal of Criminology & Criminalistics,* XXVIII(2), pp. 12-20.

Kumar, M. (2001). Formulating a Pragmatic Prison Policy for India: A Legal Prospective. *Central India Law Quarterly*, *XIV*, pp. 176-211.

Pandit Govind Ballabh Pant Institute of Studies in Rural Development (2004). Children of Women Prisoners in Jails: A Study in Uttar Pradesh. Retrieved on 15th February 2009 from http://planningcommission.nic.in/reports/sereport/ser/stdy_jailwm.pdf

Reddy, S.S. (2008). "Juvenile Justice—Not a Child's Play". *Andhra Law Times*, *15*(6), pp. 32-36.

Sabharwal, Y.K. (13 April 2006). *Judgment of R.D. Upadhyay* v. *State of Andhra Pradesh*. Retrieved on 15th February 2008 from http://www.ipsofactoj.com/international/2006/Part05/int2006(05)-011.htm

William, A.J.T., and Christopher, A.J. (2004). *Women Criminals in India*. New Delhi: Anmol Publications.

8

Rights of Elderly Prisoners: A Study in Tihar Central Prison

Megha Shree and Honey Aggarwal

Introduction

Old age consist of ages nearing or surpassing the average lifespan of human beings, thus ending the human life cycle. Old people have limited regenerative abilities and are more prone to diseases and syndromes than other adults. Old or aged is a relative term and generally used in relation to young. Definition of Elderly varies from society to society. In the Indian context, the age of a senior citizen is considered to be 60 years and above. In Indian society, older people have always been given a place of respect, honour and importance in the society. The traditional culture of India which stands in the matrix of four thousand years old Vedic civilization, considers old age as one of the stages of human development wherein a person attains maturity, wisdom and economic and social stability. This in turn leads to social recognition, emotional fulfilment and ultimately the achievement of salvations which is the supreme aim of human life (Chattoraj, 1997).

Notably, some of the elderly come into conflict with law and languish in the jails or some young people go to prison and stay there to become elderly prisoners. The numbers of elderly individuals breaking the law and being placed in prisons is increasing, and presents a number of problems for correctional facilities in terms of health care and provision as well as mental, social and physical health issues for the inmates themselves (Aday,

1994a & b, 2003). There are various areas of the prison system that could be reformed to address one or more of these problems; older prisoners are unique as they can significantly reduce the threat posed by all the problems. Older prisoners represent a low-risk, high-cost population that can serve as a vital release valve for a system on overload (Turley, 2003).

Elderly Prisoner is also a term than can refer to the concept of an ageing prison population structure, or to the environmental or cultural pressures of being incarcerated accelerating the ageing process. Prisoners who are above the age group of 60 years are called Elderly or Ageing prisoners. The definition of elderly inmates is not standardized (Aday, 1994a & b, 2003). Every country has its own age limit of Elderly, whether it is in the society or in the prison. In India prisoners of and above the age of 60 years are called Elderly prisoners. Thomas, Thomas, and Greenberg (2005) categorize elder inmates into the following three groups:

1. Prisoners who have aged while incarcerated; reflective of a person who was given a long prison sentence at a young age and has served much time.
2. Prisoners sentenced at older ages; individuals who were in their mature years and convicted of a crime and sentenced to prison.
3. Ageing recidivists who have been in and out of prison on numerous occasions (Stojkovic, 2007, Aday, 1994a & b, 2003).

All three groups experience prison in different ways, and stress being the most common problem, which ties them to each other. Elderly prisoners are not given special resources as well as facilities in the prison and they are most often neglected. The challenges associated with an ageing prisoner population are real and growing, yet statistics on the numbers of Elderly inmates are difficult to project (Turner & Trotter, 2010).

As baby boom population is continuously growing, same is the case with the ageing prison population. As a result many problems have associated. Although elderly prisoners constitute a small proportion they are of significant importance. The need to identify and recognize them as a special and vulnerable group and give them certain amount of importance is imperative. While the number of elderly prisoners is growing in the prisons, the current patterns of crime and sentencing remain the same. Their basic needs are substantially different from those of an average offender (Aday, 1994a & b, 2003). Keeping this in mind, it is important to ensure that these needs are not neglected (Turner & Trotter, 2010).

Review of Literature

According to NCRB Prison statistics report (Government of India, 2006), 'total Prisoners in India are estimated about 3,73,271. Out of which, prisoners above the age of 50 are 45,064 (15,761 are convicts and 29,303 are undertrials)'. Elderly population of Indian Prisons is about 12.07 per cent of total population, which is considerably more than other countries (Government of India, 2006). However, in Western countries ageing prisoners are increasing in view of the increase of ageing population compared to India (Aday, 2003; Aleen et al., 2008; Allen, 2003; APCCA, 2001; Australian Institute of Criminology, 2007; Birmingham, 2008; Carlisle, 2006; communitycare.co.uk, 2003; Crawley, 2004; Crawley & Sparks, 2005; Dobson, 2004; Erger, 2002; Evans, 2005; Fazel, Hope, O'Donnell & Jacoby, 2001; Fazel, Hope, O'Donnell, Piper et al., 2001; Grant, 1999; Harrison, M.T., 2006; HM Prison Service [no date]; Jones, 2007; Kempker, 2003; Linder & Meyers, 2007; McCaffrey, 2007; Mitka 2004; Onishi, 2008; Ove, 2005; Prison Reform Trust, 2003a, 2003b, 2003c, 2004, 2006, 2008; Rikard & Rosenberg, 2007; Ruddell & Kuhlmann, 2005; Turner & Trotter, 2010; Valios, 2008; Wahidin, 2003; Wahidin & Aday, 2006; Williams, 2008; Yorston & Taylor, 2006).

United Kingdom saw a great rise in the elderly prisoner population in 2000 (communitycare.co.uk, 2003) and from 1990 to 2004, there was a rise of 216 per cent (Crawley, 2004) and it showed that UK prisons are greying (Valios, 2008). A threefold increase also occurred in prisoners over the age of 60, between 1996 and 2006, in Japan (Birmingham, 2008). A 2006 Japanese National Police Agency report noted that the proportion of people aged 65 and over, arrested or taken into custody for offences (not including traffic offences) rose from 2.2 per cent in 1990 to more than 10 per cent in 2005 (Reynolds, 2008).

In the USA, between 1990 and 1996, the number of prisoners aged 45 to 54 increased by 71 per cent (per 100,000 USA residents) (Gilliard & Beck, 1998). In June 2003, the combined total of people aged 55 or older in US federal, state and local prisons was 66,200 (Harrison & Karberg, 2004). In 2007, this figure for the same age group had increased to 89,400 (West & Sabol, 2009). It is predicted that by 2010, one-third of all prisoners in the United States will be aged 50 or older (Neeley, Addison & Craig-Moreland, 1997) and by 2030, one-third will be over the age of 55 years (Kerbs, 2009). A 1998, Correctional Service of Canada report warned to prepare for the 'graying of Canada' in the prisons and reported that in January 1996, 1,527 people in prison were aged 55 years or more (Uzoaba, 1998). A more recent report indicates that in 2008 this figure increased to 4,109, almost 20 per cent of the federal offender population and it is important to note that the definition of older prisoners expanded to include those 50 years or older (Correctional Service of Canada, 2008).

According to a 2007 prison census report from the New Zealand Department of Corrections, 'Growth in overall numbers has almost entirely been amongst older offenders' (Harpham, 2008). The report classifies 'older prisoners' as those over the age of 30 years and notes that between 1980 and 2007, this age-group increased from comprising 20 per cent of the total prison population to 58 per cent. Moreover, according to a trend graph detailing prison sentencing by age, there appears to be a clear trend since 1987 toward increasing numbers for prisoners aged 50 years and over (Harpham, 2008).

In Australia, the situation mirrors that of these other Western countries. The Australian Institute of Criminology (AIC) (2007) has reported that despite an overall trend towards stabilisation of the prison population; between 1985 and 2006, the numbers continued to increase for prisoners aged 50 years and above. Moreover, while growth varied across older age groups, the highest rate of growth (a mean yearly increase of 16 per cent) was in the group aged 60-64 years (Australian Institute of Criminology, 2007). Between 1995 and 2001, there was a threefold increase in the number of older prisoners serving sentences in the UK of more than four years, an increase from 318 to 966, so that by 2001, of these older prisoners, 80 per cent were serving sentences of four or more years (Dobson, 2004).

There is no clear agreement among researchers, policy-makers and corrections administrators as to what constitutes an 'older offender' and definitions vary substantially throughout the literature, ranging from 45 years and above to 65 years and above (Gallagher, 2001; Her Majesty's Inspectorate of Prisons, 2004; Stojkovic, 2007; Thomas, Thomas & Greenberg, 2005; Turner & Trotter, 2010; Wahidin, 2003; Yorston & Taylor, 2006). Generally, prisoners above the age of 50 in the United States and Australia are defined as 'older prisoners', while in the United Kingdom, this definition applies to those over the ages of 60 or 65 years (United Nations Office on Drugs and Crime, 2009). Canada has a more detailed definition system, using the term 'older prisoners' to refer to those aged between 50 to 64 years, 'elderly prisoners' for those aged 65 or older and 'geriatric offenders' for those aged 70 or more, yet the terms are not used consistently and 'older prisoners'; appears to be the preferred term for all these age-categories (United Nations Office on Drugs and Crime, 2009; Uzoaba, 1998).

The issue of definition is clearly problematic for comparative research and can impede the development of a sound evidence-base around the demographics of older prisoners and making generalisations about related issues, such as offence types, recidivism rates and prison management issues. Definitions can also be arbitrary, unrelated to the 'operational realities of prisons' (Stojkovic, 2007) and the sole reliance on chronological age as an indicator of service need appears misguided (Yorston & Taylor, 2006). Some definitions also clump 'older prisoners' together as a homogenous group without regard for individual characteristics and needs (Heckenberg, 2006). For example, a significant shortcoming to using 60, rather than 50 years to define older prisoners is that this excludes almost all female prisoners in

England and Wales (Dobson, 2004; Her Majesty's Inspectorate of Prisons, 2008).

Despite the variability of definition, most writers and researchers agree that 'older offenders' are at least 50 years of age (Correctional Service of Canada 2008; Gaseau, 2002; Kerbs & Jolley, 2007; Loeb & AbuDagga, 2006; Loeb, Steffensmeier & Lawrence, 2008; London Free Press (Canada), 2003; Martin, 2001, 2002; Mitka, 2004; Oklahoma Department of Corrections, 2008; Stojkovic 2007; Turner & Trotter, 2010; Wahidin, 2003). This tends to vary considerably from the definitions of old age used to refer to people in society generally, where the cut-off age is typically related to the age of retirement from the workforce and eligibility for financial support. In most Western countries, including Australia, 'old age' is considered to start around the age of 60-65 years (Australian Bureau of Statistics, 2009; Department of Health, 2001; Health Canada, 2002).

Many writers suggest that 50 years is used as an appropriate gauge for 'old age' in prison because it is based on research findings that the ageing process is accelerated by approximately 10 years in prison, as the majority of people who end up in prison are already in poor health, due to leading lives involving malnutrition, lack of medical care and substance misuse, and because prison environments escalate age-related illnesses and other conditions [APCCA, 2001; Carlisle, 2006; Charleston Daily Mail, 2006; Correctional Service of Canada, 2008; Dobson, 2004; Erger, 2002; Etter, 2006; Gaseau, 2004; London Free Press (Canada), 2003; Stojkovic, 2007; Turner & Trotter, 2010; United Nations Office on Drugs and Crime, 2009].

As with older people in the wider community, the most immediate and obvious issues facing older prisoners are those related to ageing and associated declines in mental and physical health. However, as noted, considering the advanced gap between the deterioration of prisoners' health and that of the general population, a prisoner who numerically is 50 years of age, biologically, has a body that is much older (up to 10 years), resulting in earlier onset of 'age-related' health concerns (Etter, 2006; Gaseau, 2004; Grant, 1999). These concerns can include, coping with chronic and/or terminal illness, deaths of friends and significant others, social isolation, fear of dying, pain management, reduced levels of mobility, disability, loss of independence, cognitive impairments, depression and suicidal ideation (Aday, 2003; Aleen et al., 2008; Allen, 2003; APCCA, 2001; Caldwell, Jarvis & Rosefield, 2001; Carlisle, 2006; Colsher et al., 1992; communitycare.co.uk, 2003; Crawley, 2004; Crawley & Sparks, 2005; Dobson, 2004; Erger, 2002; Fazel et al., 2001; Fry & Howe, 2005; Gallagher, 2001; Grant, 1999; Harrison, MT 2006; Her Majesty's Inspectorate of Prisons, 2004, 2008; Hobbs et al., 2006; Jones, 2007; Kempker, 2003; Loeb & AbuDagga, 2006; McCaffrey, 2007; Mitka, 2004; Ove, 2005; Prison Reform Trust, 2003a, 2003b, 2006, 2008; Rosefield, 1993; Taylor & Parrott, 1988; Valios, 2008; Turner & Trotter, 2010; Wahidin, 2003; Wahidin & Aday, 2006; Yorston & Taylor, 2006).

A number of researchers also highlight the particular health care needs of older women in prisons and argue for gender-specific responses to address these (Aday, 2003; Bramhall, 2006; Caldwell, Jarvis & Rosefield, 2001; Dobson, 2004; Her Majesty's Inspectorate of Prisons, 2004, 2008; McCaffrey, 2007; Prison Reform Trust, 2003b, 2008; Turner & Trotter, 2010; Valios, 2008; Wahidin, 2003; Wahidin & Aday, 2006). Corresponding with the rise of older prisoners, many researchers and writers point to an increase in health care costs as a concern for policy-makers, prison administrators and the community (Aday, 2003; APCCA, 2001; communitycare. co.uk, 2003; Crawley, 2004; Erger, 2002; Green, 2008; Jones, 2007; Kempker, 2003; McCaffrey, 2007; Ove, 2005; Wahidin & Aday, 2006). Many researchers argue that older prisoners' health concerns are exacerbated, rather than relieved, by most prison environments and regimes (Aleen et al., 2008; Allen, 2003; Australian Institute of Criminology, 2007; Carlisle, 2006; Colsher et al., 1992; Dawes, 2009; Department of Health, 2001; Dobson, 2004; Erger, 2002; Fazel, 2004; Her Majesty's Inspectorate of Prisons, 2004; Prison Reform Trust, 2008; Rikard & Rosenberg, 2007; Turner & Trotter, 2010; Wahidin, 2003).

Many writers point to clear issues of discrimination against such older prisoners, noting difficulties or lack of access to prison facilities (such as libraries, showers, baths, upper bunk beds, stored property), as well as to programs and regimes (such as exercise, crafts, education) (APCCA, 2001; Birmingham, 2008; Dawes, 2009; Her Majesty's Inspectorate of Prisons, 2004, 2008; Turner & Trotter, 2010). Many writers note a lack of appropriate and meaningful programs for older prisoners (Grant, 1999; Harrison, M.T., 2006; Her Majesty's Inspectorate of Prisons, 2004, 2008; HM Prison Service, [no date]; Turner & Trotter, 2010).

The above literature review consists of mostly studies related to ageing offenders and it is found there are very little or sparse studies on Indian ageing offenders. The present study will try to fill the gap in the literature.

The Present Study

No special recognition has been given to the elderly prisoners in the Prison Act, Prisoner's Act, Mullah Committee report, UN Minimum standard rules for the treatment of prisoners as well as the Jail Manual. Therefore, these points explain the main crux on why they need to be focused. There is no relevant study and data in the context to elderly prisoners in Indian Perspective. There is a noticeable lack of intervention initiatives or evaluations in this field. It needs to be focused as this is an important issue and the Elderly are the most vulnerable group. The lack of research in the area of ageing offenders has been described as 'an implicit form of ageism, that implies the problems of this group can be disregarded, or that ageing criminals are simply not worth discussing'. So, this study hopes to re-focus attention on ageing offenders in Indian prisons and by so doing, contribute to a greater understanding of who this group is, what it means to age in prison, what the critical issues are, and how correctional administrators might best respond to their needs. This chapter, an outcome of an extensive literature review and study into some individual prisoners' experience of ageing in various prisons, aims to draw attention to the current situation and what it means to these particular prisoners.

Objectives of the Study

- To study the socio-economic background of elderly prisoners in the Central Prison Tihar.

- To explore the living conditions of elderly prisoners in Central Prison, Tihar, with special reference to UN minimum standard rules.
- To evaluate the problems faced by elderly inmates in protection of their rights.
- To suggest the ways and means for the protection of the rights of elderly prisoners.

Methodology

The main area of the study is Central Prison Tihar. Statistics of the Central Prison, Tihar, is estimated about 491 males and 65 females between the age of 50-65 years and 62 males and 11 females of 65 years above (as on 30 April 2009). This covers about 5.47 per cent of the total Prison population. While it may not be a vast proportion it is not small either. We chose Central Prison, Tihar, for this study because of convenience and also it is considered as a high profile jail and is often called the model jail.

The study proposes to cover the Elderly prisoners of Tihar Prison, Delhi who have been languishing in the jail for a long time. The convicts of both the sexes who are above 60 years of age have been taken into consideration. In addition, the study considered the viewpoints of Prison officials of Tihar Prison. The Study involves the information of the elderly prisoners and Prison Officials as its universe. Sample size of 60 elderly prisoners (60 years and above) are divided into both sexes in the ratio of 2:1 through stratified random sampling and multi-stage sampling. The sample for the study includes 40 male elderly prisoners, 20 female elderly prisoners, and 10 prison officials.

The study includes both primary and secondary data collection. Primary data has been collected through interviews, observations, etc., and secondary data is collected from prison records, journals, books and other documentary evidences. Interview schedules were administered on the elderly prisoners and prison officers. The schedules were prepared covering the demographic details, socio-economic background, their interaction with the prison officials, rights that are violated inside the prison. Interview guide was administered on the Prison staff and Quasi-participant observation was done.

This study is an attempt to check whether the prison follows the UN minimum standard rule for the treatment of prisoners or not? The research design used is exploratory research design with certain basic assumptions. As this is purely a new area to explore, the findings of this research will be helpful in formulating hypothesis for upcoming researches.

Findings

1. Profile of the Elderly Prisoners

The sample consists of the age group of 60 years and above. It consists of a mix age group after 60. Fifty per cent of the respondents belong to 60-70 years of age, 37 per cent belong to 70-80 years, 10 per cent belonged to 80-90 years and 3 per cent belong to 90 years and above. The respondents interviewed consisted of 67 per cent male and 33 per cent female. The number of female elderly prisoners is less as compared to male. All the respondents belong to different religions, 72 per cent of the respondents are Hindu, 10 per cent are Muslim, 15 per cent are Sikh and 3 per cent belong to other groups. Sixty-three per cent were married, 28 per cent were widow/widower, 7 per cent were unmarried and 2 per cent were divorced. It is found that the majority of females present in the jail were undertrials. Twenty-five per cent of the respondents were graduates or above, 22 per cent were illiterate as well as higher secondary, 15 per cent were matric pass, 11 per cent had done primary schooling, while 5 per cent belong to middle school respectively.

Thirty-one per cent of the respondents were languishing in jail from 1-5 years and 28 per cent were in jail from above 10 years respectively. The sample points out that 73 per cent of the respondents have committed crimes against body, 8 per cent have indulged in crime against property, 7 per cent were booked under sexual offences and 12 per cent belong to others. Amongst the elderly prisoners, 26 per cent amongst them have been businessmen, 13 per cent were government officials, and 8 per cent were private employees outside the prison. The data reveals that majority of the prisoners belong to urban and semi-urban section of the society. There is a myth that only rural people indulge in crime but the data shows that 57 per cent of the respondents belong to semi-urban locality, 23 per cent belonged to urban and 12 per cent belonged to the slum areas.

2. Living Conditions and Rights of Prisoners

When one talks about the rights of the prisoners then it is found to be the same for all prisoners. There is always segregation based on sex, type of offences and age as well. However, the worst part is that no one is ready to focus on the elderly prisoners. As such, separate rights and facilities have not been given to them due to their age factor. People are there in the prison not for the punishment but as a punishment. For this, they deserve the basic standard living conditions as per the UN minimum standard rules.

It is found that 40 per cent of the elderly prisoners are found to be unsatisfied with the prison's food quality. As per the unsatisfied respondents, the food given to them is not of bearable standard. Fifty-five per cent of the respondents responded that they are not provided the diet, which is prescribed by the doctors during illness. When the respondents were asked about the mentioned chewable diet in the jail manual, it was found that 100 per cent of the respondents said that boiled gram, boiled cereals and boiled vegetables were not a part of their daily diet. Ninety-three per cent were affirmative for the tea and milk in there diet, while, 7 per cent responded negatively for tea or milk in their diet. This reflects that even during the illness the elderly prisoners do not get the adequate chewable diet. Majority were satisfied with drinking water and clothing. When the respondents were asked whether they get season specific dress? Forty-five per cent strongly responded affirmatively, 47 per cent responded negatively, and 8 per cent were not aware of.

According to UN minimum standard rules, young prisoners and adult prisoners should be segregated. The data shows that there is no segregation in the accommodation on the basis of age in the prison especially in the female jail. Majority pointed out that more than 4 prisoners live in a cell and there is proper supervision by the prison authorities at night.

Jail Manual has a provision that the elderly prisoners can be provided cots or stools due to their immobility for their daily use. When the respondents were asked about the same, all of them responded stating they were not provided with the facility. Along with this, on asking about the mattress facility while sleeping, then 85 per cent responded affirmatively and 15 per cent responded negatively.

When the respondents were asked, whether the jail authorities bear the following commodities of daily use at their own expense, mixed responses were there. It is found that prison authorities never gave them mosquito nets and only 1 toothpaste every two months and 1 toothbrush every 3 months and stool were provided. However, 88 per cent responded that many times, they are given season specific bathing water. Majority responded that they are not even provided with a sweeper or barber at the jail's expense. For such basic amenities, prisoners' have to bear on their own.

When the respondents were asked regarding their medical care satisfaction, almost 85 per cent of the population was unsatisfied and 15 per cent are satisfied as they are given the medical facilities round the clock (whenever required). Sixty per cent responded affirmatively, they are allowed to take rest while illness but on the other hand, 40 per cent responded that they would have to work even during when they were ill. Majority of the respondents suffered from diabetes and were not given adequate diet in the prison. This could be one of the adequate reasons for their consistent illness. Some respondents were also ailing from Cataract, Osteoporosis, Tuberculosis, Lung disorder, Heart problems, and Chest problems, etc. One of the major finding was that there were no HIV patient.

One of the significant outcome of the study is that no one is subjected to handcuffs, etc. and there is complete freedom for spiritual liberty and as well as education of the prisoners. However, corporal punishment still exists in the jail. There is equivalent response for parole that some respondents were satisfied but majority pointed out that they did not get parole. There was discrimination on the basis of age, religion and national origin, however, discrimination on the basis of economic status is rampant.

The respondents were asked regarding prison officials ability to maintain a bound registration book regarding the information which includes informing identifications, reasons for commitment to prison and day hour of release. All the respondents pointed affirmatively, that they maintain the register. But, it is a matter of thought that majority prisoners are unaware about their rights in the prison. Majority prisoners don't have the liberty to make complaints against prison officials. When the respondents were asked whether they receive timely feedbacks on the complaints they register, around 61 per cent responded affirmatively, 27 per cent responded negatively and 12 per cent were neutral in their response. Along with this, majority responded that they don't sign the inventory while entering the prison as well.

Elderly prisoners involve in works like: cleaning of the field, gardening, cleaning of cereals, official work, cutting of vegetables, etc. Majority of the respondent's vision was poor and they were not able to maintain the hygiene. Their poor vision leads to the presence of small insects in the cooked food. Majority are satisfied that they are not forced to perform the work which don't support their health. Majority of the elderly prisoners need to work 6-9 hours but only few were very happy about their very less working hours. When the respondents were asked about the rest day given to them in a week, 72 per cent responded affirmatively while 28 per cent responded negatively.

When the respondents were asked about during their illness or death, whether their relatives or spouse were immediately informed by the jail authorities, 72 per cent responded affirmatively, and 28 per cent responded negatively. When the respondents were asked of the availability of specialists in the prison as per UN minimum standard rules for the prisoners, results showed that there were no interpreters and criminal psychologist/ criminologist in the Central Prison Tihar. It is found that 80 per cent responded positively to psychiatrists, 85 per cent responded positively towards social workers and all reported that there are teachers as well. Eighty-two per cent also responded that a dental officer is present in the prison. On the whole, they are allowed to communicate with their friends and relatives and are even free to spend their earnings on their family.

3. Officials Response

When the prison officials were asked about the problems, which the elderly prisoners face in the prison, 50 per cent of them said there was overcrowding in the prisons, 30 per cent vouched for the importance of good bedding facilities, 10 per cent expressed the need for good medical and toilet facilities. Seventy per cent of the prison officials regularly go and meet them, while 30 per cent of them do not specially visit the prisoners. Most of the prison officials expressed sympathetic treatment towards the elderly prisoners. When the officials were asked whether elderly prisoners were given psychological counselling, 30 per cent of the respondents were affirmative, whereas 70 per cent of them were negative. The respondents enlightened about the fact that elderly prisoners are awarded for their good conduct with different forms of pleasures. For example, 55 per cent of the officials responded that elderly prisoners are given remission, 27 per cent said cash coupons whereas 9 per cent said in the form of wages and 9 per cent said others, respectively. All of them favoured that elderly prisoners are given parole easily.

One of the good factors to know about the prison is that, at the time of death of any elderly prisoner, their family members are informed immediately. If the relatives of the elderly prisoners don't claim the bodies of the prisoners after their death, then prison authorities themselves perform the cremation ceremony with full commitment. This aspect is in line with the protection of human rights by the state and it is appreciated.

It was noted that the responses from the prison officials appear to be very contradictory to the prisoners' responses. For example, 70 per cent of the respondents said that no compensation was given in context to work whereas 20 per cent of the respondents were affirmative and 10 per cent were neutral. All officials replied that elderly prisoners are given special diet and complete rest during illness and corporal punishment does not exist in Tihar prison, and 40 per cent strongly pointed out that no punishment is given to the elderly prisoners. These responses were contradictory to the prisoners' responses.

Discussion

This exploratory study is an attempt to highlight a number of variables that are of major concern to elderly prisoners during their imprisonment. Most importantly, elderly prisoners should be recognized as an entity and should be given separate considerations in the prison programming. For instance, first time elderly prisoner should be integrated into prison life in a different way than the hardened older recidivists who have already been to prison many times. Currently it appears that not many policies, programs, or facilities in Indian prisons exists, that are specifically serving to the needs of older and geriatric inmates. Prisoner's rights are an important issue and are raised by few people. Those who advocate the prisoner's rights, strongly point out those prisoners are often deprived from their very basic rights, with the cooperation of the prison authorities. Justice V. Krishna Iyer in *Sunil Batra* v. *Delhi Administration* stated, "Convicts are not by mere reason of the conviction denuded of all the fundamental rights which they otherwise possess." Indian constitution always favour for the Articles 14 and 21 in respect to everyone except for prisoners. Based on the right to life and right to live life with dignity, here are some proposals to make a change. These basic rights are as discussed in detail in the context of elderly prisoners:

(a) Right to Food and Clothing

Prisoners in the Central Prison, Tihar, are unsatisfied with the food quality due to adulteration in the food, which reveals that it is not of standard. They are not given diet as prescribed by the doctors, which is the duty of the state. Adulterated food especially from insects and from other materials has been reported. According to Delhi Jail manual, on the requirement of the liquid or soft diet, it should be given to the prisoners but boiled grams, vegetables and cereals are never given to the elderly prisoners. It is also found that there is no check by the officials on the food facilities of the prisoners. Prisoners cook their own food. Due to uneven division of labour amongst the prisoners, this problem has been reported. Elderly prisoners are generally given the work of cleaning of cereals, etc. It should be noted that most amongst them suffer from poor eyesight. Due to this, they are unable to see properly and lead to adulteration in the food. It should be noted that out of personal revenge, prisoners might serve each other inadequate and adulterated stuff. There is a lack of quality control check on the prisoner's food. However, as far as clothing is concerned, they are almost satisfied with the clothing but majority pointed out that they don't get season specific dress.

(b) Right to Drinking Water

The prison authorities have protected this basic right. Prisoners are provided adequate tap facilities for drinking water. They are almost satisfied with the drinking water arrangements.

(c) Right to Medical Treatment

Medical facilities are available in the prison. Even though doctors are available round the clock, the prisoners are unsatisfied due to the annoying nature of doctors. It has been reported that the doctors sometimes give medicines to the prisoners without even listening to their complaints. During interviews, this problem has been raised by various prisoners that doctors just repeat the medicines without actually listening to them. It is also found that there were communication gap between the prisoners and doctors.

(d) Right to Freedom of Expression, Reading Materials, and Communication

It has been revealed in this study that the authorities do not respond to complaints frequently and they are not allowed to make the complaints as well. As far as reading materials are concerned, Central Prison Tihar is always in favour of the education and providing the reading materials.

(e) Right to Freedom of Religion

Religion is a social institution and everyone should have the freedom to praise his or her own religion. It is also applicable for the prisoners and this study found that prisoners in the Tihar jail have complete religious freedom.

(f) Right to be Protected by Authorities

Few of the respondents even responded that they are given punishment even at their first disciplinary offence. One of the significant outcomes of the study is that no one is subjected to handcuffs and the prisoners are also not forced by the authorities to work harshly.

Conclusion and Recommendations

Elderly people are the assets of the nation whether they are inside or outside the prison. Making good use of them is the society's responsibility by providing them basic facilities. In turn they will always step forward in helping others. They also work as an agency of social control and bring change in the society by exchanging their culture and experience to young individuals. Therefore, we should understand them and treat them with dignity which they deserve. Following are some of the recommendations to ensure the rights of the elderly prisoners in the Indian prisons:

- Separate basic education classes should be implemented, so that the needs of the elderly prisoners are served. In addition, there should be separate classes to reduce the embarrassment and frustration of elderly offenders, which they might feel in presence of young prisoners. (Fatula, 1977)
- Psychologists and counsellors with special training in geriatrics should be available in the prison to administer rehabilitation programs in order to meet the social, psychological, and emotional needs of these offenders. (Goetting, 1983; Vito & Wilson, 1985)
- Provision for after care services should be available for the orphan people. (whose family members never come to receive them after their removal from the prison)
- Specific training should be offered to custodial staff to reduce the biases and stereotyping regarding ageing. Also they should be given basic information on the ageing process and age-related problems.
- The parole system should be transparent and preference should be given to the elderly prisoners.

Limitations of the Study

All the interviews of the elderly prisoners were conducted in the presence of the Prison staff, so the responses might be biased.

Proper observation and timely follow up were not possible because of the lack of time for data collection. The researchers were given only 2 days permission for data collection from Central Prison Tihar Authorities. This could be a major limitation of the study. Since the data collection was done from only Tihar Prison, Delhi, the findings cannot be generalized for all the prisons. The number of elderly prisoners and prison staff interviewed are less in number; hence we cannot generalize the outcome of the study.

References

Aday, R.H. (1994a). "Aging in Prison: A Case Study of New Elderly Offenders". *International Journal of Offender Therapy and Comparative Criminology*, 38(1), 79-91.

Aday, R.H. (1994b). "Golden years behind bars: Special programs and facilities for older inmates". *Federal Probation*, 58(2), 47-54.

Aday, R.H. (2003). *Aging Prisoners: Crisis in American Corrections*. Westport, CT: Praeger Publishers, Greenwood Press.

Aleen, R.S., et al. (2008). "Religiousness/Spirituality and Mental Health Among Older Male Inmates". *The Gerontologist*, 48, 692-97.

Allen, D. (2003). "Prisoners' health: key concerns: the physical and mental health needs of older people in prison are in urgent need of attention". Nursing Older People, 15(7), 1.

APCCA. (2001). Record of the 21st Asian and Pacific Conference of Correctional Administrators: The Management of Special Groups of Offenders. *Corrections in Asia and the Pacific*, Chiang Mai, Thailand.

Australian Bureau of Statistics. (2008). *Prisoners in Australia*. Cat. no. 4517.0, Canberra, Australia: ABS.

Birmingham, K. (2008). The swelling numbers of older prisoners in Japan's prisons has prompted the government to begin a major revamp of its jails to provide elevators, handrails and wheelchair ramps. *Nursing Older People*, 20(1).

Bramhall, G. (2006). "Older Offenders and Community Penalties: A Framework for Thinking". In A. Wahidin & M.E. Cain (eds.), *Ageing, Crime and Society* (pp. 230-47), Cullumpton: Willan Publishing.

Caldwell, C., Jarvis, M., & Rosefield, H. (2001). "Issues Impacting Today's Geriatric Female Offenders". *Corrections Today*, 63(5), 110-14.

Carlisle, D. (2006). "So far, so bleak: increasing numbers of older prisoners in a prison estate, designed essentially for fit young men, pose a problem for health service providers". *Nursing Older People*, 18(7), 21-23.

Charleston Daily Mail. (2006). *WV inmate medical expenses soaring.* The Corrections Connection News Centre.

Chattoraj, B.N. (1997). "Problems of Senior Citizens in a Changing Society: An Indian Perspective". *Journal of Social Work Research Institute of Japan University*, (One time publication), 105-17.

Colsher, P.L., Wallace, R.B., Loeffelholz, P.L., & Sales, M. (1992). "Health status of older male prisoners: a comprehensive survey". *American Journal of Public Health*, 82(6), 881-84.

communitycare.co.uk. (2003). Poor services put older prisoners at greater risk of ill-health, says report. *Community Care*, Retrieved on 25th November 2010, from http://www.communitycare.co.uk/Articles/2003/09/25/42214/poor-services-put-older-prisoners-at-greater-risk-of-ill-health-says.html.

Correctional Service of Canada. (2008). Speakers Binder: Section 7: CSC Issues and Challenges. Publications. Retrieved on 15th December 2009, from http://www.csc-scc. gc.ca/text/pblct/sb-go/07-eng.shtml.

Crawley, E. (2004). Release and Resettlement: the perspective of older prisoners. Retrieved on August 30, 2009, from http://www.crimeandjustice.org.uk/opus159/cjm56-crawley.pdf

Crawley, E., & Sparks, R. (2005). "Older men in prison: survival, coping and identity". In A. Liebling & S. Maruna (eds.), *The Effects of Imprisonment*, Willan Publishing, Devon.

Dawes, J. (2009). "Ageing Prisoners: Issues for Social Work". *Australian Social Work*, 62(2), 258-71.

Department of Health. (2001). *National Service Framework for Older People: Executive Summary.* UK Government: Department of Health.

Dobson, G. (2004). "Growing old in prison". *Elderly Client Adviser*, 9(5).

Erger, J.S. (2002). "Geriatric nursing in prisons is a growing concern". *Corrections Today*, 64(7).

Etter, S. (2006). *Options for the Elderly.* The Corrections Connection News Centre.

Evans, C. (2005). "Age Concern Leicestershire and Rutland—HMP Gartree Older Prisoner's Advocacy and Support Project". *Prison Service Journal*, 160.

Fatula, B.S. (1977). *Facilitating Adult Learning.* Pennsylvania, USA: Gerontology Centre, Penn. State University.

Fazel, S., Hope, T., O'Donnell, I., Piper, M., & Jacoby, R. (2001). "Health of elderly male prisoners: worse than the general population, worse than younger prisoners". *Age and Ageing*, 30, 403-07.

Fry, D. and Howe, D.H. (2005). Managing Older Prisoners at HMP Wymott. 160.

Gallagher, E.M. (2001). "Elders in prison: health and well-being of older inmates". *International Journal of Psychiatry and Law*, 24(2-3), 325-33.

Gaseau, M. (2002). *The Graying of Prisons: How Corrections is Managing Ageing Prisoners*. The Corrections Connection News Centre.

Gaseau, M. (2004). *Caring for the Ageing Inmate: Solutions for Corrections*. The Corrections Connection News Centre.

Gilliard, D.K., & Beck, A.J. (1998). *Prisoners in 1997*. Washington, D.C.: U.S. Department of Justice, Office of Justice Programs.

Godinez, S.A. (1999). "Managing Juveniles in Adult Facilities: Identifying Population and Institutional Characteristics to Determine Staff Training Needs". *Corrections Today*, 61(2), 86-91.

Goetting, A. (1983). "The Elderly in Prison: Issues and Perspectives". *Journal of Research in Crime and Delinquency*, 20, 291-309.

Grant, A. (1999). *Elderly Inmates: Issues for Australia*. Trends & Issues in Crime and Criminal Justice: 115. Canberra: Australian Institute of Criminology.

Green, F. (2008). *Growing Old Behind Bars*. Richmond Times-Dispatch.

Harpham, D. (2008). *Offender Volumes: Report 2007*. Ara Poutama Aotearoa, Wellington: Department of Corrections.

Harrison, M.T. (2006). "True Grit: an innovative program for elderly inmates". *Corrections Today*, 68(7).

Harrison, P.M., & Karberg, J.C. (2004). *Prison and Jail Inmates at Midyear 2003*. Washington, D.C.: U.S. Department of Justice Office of Justice Programs.

Health Canada. (2002). *Canada's Ageing Population*. Ottawa, Ontario: Public Health Agency of Canada.

Heckenberg, D. (2006). "Ageing Prisoners: Significant cohort or forgotten minority?" Australia, University of Tasmania: Degree of Masters in Criminology and Corrections thesis.

Her Majesty's Inspectorate of Prisons. (2004). 'No problems—old and quiet': Older prisoners in England and Wales: A thematic review by HM Chief Inspector of Prisons. London: Her Majesty's Inspectorate of Prisons for England and Wales (HMI Prisons).

Her Majesty's Inspectorate of Prisons. (2008). Older prisoners in England and Wales: a follow-up to the 2004 thematic review. London: Her Majesty's Inspectorate of Prisons for England and Wales (HMI Prisons).

Hobbs, M., Krazlan, K., Ridout, S., Mai, Q., Knuiman, M., & Chapman, R. (2006). *Mortality and morbidity in prisoners after release from prison in Western Australia 1995–2003, 71, Research and Public Policy Series No. 71*. Canberra: Australian Institute of Criminology.

Jones, B. (ed.). (2007). "Ageing inmates clogging nation's prisons". *USA Today*, 29 September 2007.

Kempker, E. (2003). "Graying of American Prisons: Addressing the Continued Increase in Geriatric Inmates". *Corrections Compendium*, 28(6), 1-2.

Kerbs, J.J. and Jolley, J.M. (2007). "Inmate-on-Inmate Victimization Among Older Male Prisoners". *Crime & Delinquency*, 53(2), 187-218.

Kerbs, J.J. (2009). "A commentary on age segregation for older prisoners: philosophical and pragmatic considerations for correctional systems". *Criminal Justice Review*, 34(1), 119-39.

Krajick, K. (1979). "Growing old in prison". *Corrections Magazine*, 5(1), 32-46.

Linder, J.F., & Meyers, F.J. (2007). "Palliative Care for Prison Inmates: Don't Let Me Die in Prison". *The Journal of the American Medical Association*, 298(9), 894-901.

Loeb, S.J., & AbuDagga, A. (2006). Health¬related research on older inmates: An integrative review. *Research in Nursing and Health*, 29(6), 556-65.

Loeb, S.J., Steffensmeier, D., & Lawrence, F. (2008). "Comparing incarcerated and community-dwelling older men's health". *Western Journal of Nursing Research*, 30(2), 234-49.

London Free Press (Canada). (2003). Ageing Prison Population a Challenge for Canadian System. *The Corrections Connection News Centre.*

Martin, K. (2001). *The POPS Program: Providing a Voice for Older Inmates. The Corrections Connection News Centre.*

Martin, K. (2002). Penn. Program Helps Older Offenders Take a STEP in the Right Direction. *The Corrections Connection News Centre.*

McCaffrey, S. (2007). *Ageing inmate population, clogging nation's prisons.* New York: Associated Press.

Mitka, M. (2004). "Ageing prisoners stressing health care system". *The Journal of the American Medical Association*, 292(4), 423-24.

Neeley, C.L., Addison, L., & Craig-Moreland, D. (1997). Addressing the needs of elderly offenders. *Corrections Today*, 59(4), 120-24.

Oklahoma Department of Corrections. (2008). *Managing Increasing Aging Inmate Populations: A DOC "White Paper"*. Retrieved on August 30, 2009, from http://www.doc.state.ok.us/adminservices/ea/Female%20 Inmate%20Paper.pdf

Onishi, N. (2008). "Japan: Prisons to Adapt To Older Inmates". *New York Times*.

Ove, T. (2005). Pa. prison population growing older, sicker, costlier. *Pittsburgh Post-Gazette*, 6, March, 2005.

Prison Reform Trust. [no date]. *Disabled Prisoners*. London: Prison Reform Trust.

Prison Reform Trust. (2003a). *Double Punishment for Older Prisoners*. London: Prison Reform Trust.

Prison Reform Trust. (2003b). *Elderly Prisoners Neglected*. London: Prison Reform Trust.

Prison Reform Trust. (2003c). *Inspection Report of HMP Frankland*. London: Prison Reform Trust.

Prison Reform Trust. (2004). Statement on Still Life Exhibition: 'Double Punishment For Elderly Prisoners.' London: Prison Reform Trust.

Prison Reform Trust. (2006). Bromley Briefings: Prison Factfile: April 2006. London: Prison Reform Trust.

Prison Reform Trust. (2008). Doing Time: the experiences and needs of older people in prison. London: Prison Reform Trust.

Reynolds, I. (2008). Japan's elderly inmates to get barrier-free jails. Reuters.

Rikard, R.V., & Rosenberg, E. (2007). "Ageing Inmates: A Convergence of Trends in the American Criminal Justice System". *Journal of Correctional Health Care*, 13(3), 150-62.

Rosefield, H.A. (1993). Older Inmate: Where do we go from here? *Journal of Prison and Jail Health*, 12(1), 51-58.

Ruddell, R., & Kuhlmann, R. (2005). "Elderly Jail Inmates: Problems, Prevalence and Public Health". *Californian Journal of Health Promotion*, 3(2), 49-60.

Stojkovic, S. (2007). "Elderly Prisoners: A Growing and Forgotten Group within Correctional Systems Vulnerable to Elder Abuse". *Journal of Elder Abuse & Neglect*, 19(3), 97-117.

Taylor, P., & Parrott, J. (1988). "Elderly offenders. A study of age-related factors among custodially remanded prisoners". *British Journal of Psychiatry*, 152, 340-46.

Thomas, D.L., Thomas, J.A., & Greenberg, S. (2005). "The graying of corrections: The management of older inmates". In S. Stojkovic (ed.), *Managing special populations in jails and prisons* (pp. 11-17), Kingston, NJ: Civic Research Institute.

Turley, J. (2003). California's Ageing Prison Population. Washington, D.C.: George Washington University Law School. Retrieved on June 13, 2009, from http://sinet2.sen.ca.gov/aging/aging_prisoners/turley_testimony.doc

Turner, S., & Trotter, C. (2010). *Growing old in prison? A review of national and international research on ageing offenders*. Corrections Research Paper Series no. 3. Melbourne: Victorian Department of Justice.

UN Office on Drugs and Crime (2009). Handbook on Prisoners with Special Needs. March 2009. Retrieved on 8 January 2012 from http://www.unhcr.org/refworld/docid/4a0969d42.html.

UTS: Nursing Midwifery and Health. (2009). Justice Health Nursing Professorial Unit: Current Practice Improvement Projects.

Uzoaba, J. (1998). Managing Older Offenders: Where do we stand. Ottawa, Ontario: Research Division, Correctional Branch of Canada. Retrieved on May 08, 2010 from http://www.csc-scc.gc.ca/text/rsrch/reports/r70/r70_e.pdf

Valios, N. (2008). *Older People's Plight in Prison*. Community Care.

Vito, G.F., & Wilson, D.G. (1985). Forgotten People: Elderly Inmates. *Federal Probation*, 49, 18-24.

Wahidin, A., & Aday, R.H. (2006). *The Needs of Older Men and Women in the Criminal Justice System: An International Perspective*. European Crime and Employment Briefing.

Wahidin, A. (2003). "We are a significant minority: Old Women in English Prisons". In S. Cottee, C. Smith & E. Wincup (eds.), *British Criminology Conference, Bangor*, 6.

West, H.C., & Sabol, W.J. (2009). Prison Inmates at Midyear 2008—Statistical Tables. Washington, D.C.: U.S. Department of Justice, Office of Justice Programs.

Williams, C. (2008). *PRT: Older prisoners face 'isolation and discrimination'*. Community Care.

Yorston, G.A., & Taylor, P.J. (2006). Commentary: Older Offenders—No Place to Go? *Journal of the American Academy of Psychiatry and Law Online*, 34(3), 333-37.

SECTION THREE

ISSUES OF OFFENDER REHABILITATION

9

Probation: An Appraisal of Community-based Corrections

S. Ramdoss

Introduction

Probation is a system in which a convicted offender is returned to the community under supervision. The most common defense of probation is that it saves the taxpayer money. There are also great social advantages associated with probation. It indicates that society is willing to give the offender another chance. He is not separated from his family or his community. Particularly, he avoids the stigma of prison. However, probation is no panacea and cannot be extended to all offenders. Probation is not likely to eliminate prisons or the need of parole. Where it can be employed it saves the state money and generally affords the offender a better hope of successful rehabilitation (Kane, 1963).

The first and foremost problem in Tamil Nadu Central Prison is overcrowding. The problem of remand prisoners also causes concern to the administration of prisons. Nearly 70-75 per cent are remand prisoners and many of them are loitering in Central Prisons for years together. Even for petty offences, prisoners who are not in a position to get bail are wandering in the prisons (Sambandham, 2006). From these findings one can understand the necessity and significance of the community based correction, i.e. probation. It is felt that in view of the failure of our existing prison system to reform criminals there is a need for increasing application of non-punitive and community-based treatment of offenders such as probation, parole and aftercare (Chakrabarti, 1999). A prevailing belief is that incarceration is ineffective as a deterrent to crime. According to some experts (Walker, 1989), locking up offenders only makes matters worse. Research carried out by criminologists and sociologists around the world has confirmed that imprisonment does not in fact curb criminal behaviour. On the contrary, even a short period of imprisonment is likely to condemn a person who is otherwise law-abiding into a life of criminal conduct. It is known that there are seasoned criminals in any prison. Condemning non-serious offenders to prison carries with it the inherent risk that these persons will also become hardened as a result of their experiences. These people will become a real threat to society on their discharge (Garwe and Andrew, 2000).

Probation is considered as an extramural community based treatment method for offenders and has assumed a great importance in recent years. The futility of incarceration for all types of offenders has been realized by the correctional experts and administrators. Treatment of an offender in the community under the supervision of a professional correctional worker is more effective and cheaper than in institutions. Moreover, community participation in the prevention of crime and the treatment of offenders is ensured through this method of treatment and the problem of rehabilitation of offenders minimized to a considerable extent. In India, the probation program has been implemented in almost all states and Union Territories. However, the progress does not seem to be very encouraging although several years have already elapsed (Bhattacharyya, 1986).

Glueck (1964) opined that the characteristic feature of probation, which distinguishes it from the other crime-treating institutions so far invented, is that it enables the offender to remain in the community but at the same time to be under control and guidance. Custodial treatment removes the offender from his family and community and suspends his social and economic obligations to them. He becomes, indeed, a burden upon society. Probation extracks from the offender a contribution within the limits of his capacity, to the well-being of others, whether it is through his useful employment in the community or through his participation in the life of the family or other social group. In doing so, it minimizes the economic and social disruption caused by the probationer's offence, preserves him from the penal or reformative institution whose constructive work must inevitably be limited by the delinquent community in which the offender is placed, and seeks to avoid the harm to others that follows, for example, the imprisonment of a breadwinner (Report of the Departmental Committee on Probation Services, England, 1962).

Probation reduces crime by rehabilitating offenders. Many offenders become more anti-social by serving a prison term, where they inevitably associate with criminals of many kinds, are infected by anti-social attitudes and in the end, learn more about how to commit crime. Probation protects them from such criminal associations and helps them to lead normal lives in the community. The object of probation, as with all methods of treatment, is the ultimate re-establishment of the offender in the community. The basic idea is that the offender redeems himself and is purged of the offence. The law helps him erase the stigma of conviction and puts him under the guidance of the probation officer. He is not removed from his family and the community and is therefore, compelled to discharge his social and economic obligations to them (Bhattacharyya, 1986). Probation is thus an implied recognition of the limitations of incarceration, and provides a viable sentencing alternative for the judge in the case of selected offenders (Montilla et al., 1977).

Short-term sentences are inadvisable because they seldom deter but frustrate the person. It further punishes the family and there is little possibility of correcting the offender. It is harmful in familiarizing him with the rigours of prison and dangerous potential for contamination. Though this position was realized in all countries, short-term sentences continued, because there were no suitable alternative punishments. Besides, it was an easy disposal for courts. In such a context came the Cambridge Report of 1958. Probation had been in vogue for sometime when the Cambridge Institute of Criminology took up the study of 9000 former probationers and examined if they had made good at least during a period of 3 years after the completion of the period of probation. The result was 74 per cent of the adults and 62 per cent of the juveniles had made good. On the basis of this report, the Streatfield Committee examined the situation, and proposed that probation should be used as an effective alternative for short-term sentences. This was implemented in U.K. from 1960s. As a result, the number of short-term sentences less than 3 months in U.K. was decreased from 12,000 in 1961 to 1,200 in 1971. In India no such study was done, but it is believed that probation has substantially lessened the short-term sentences. Probation is used fairly widely all over India and found useful. But still short-term sentences above 3 months continue (Diaz, 1997).

Probation is not only a more effective method of dealing with sentenced offenders, it is also significantly cheaper. In this connection, the Indian Jails Committee (1919-20) observed that again, great stress is laid on the saving of the community achieved by the system of release on probation. For instance in Massachusetts in 1918 the annual cost of a prisoner in jail is placed at 385 dollars, while that of a case on probation is placed at 19 dollars. The expenditure for maintenance of a prisoner in prison is quite high. Although all convicted offenders cannot be released on probation of good conduct, a good number of offenders, particularly short termers may be granted probation, thereby saving a lot of expenditure from the public exchequer. At present, in India there are about 85 per cent of prisoners whose prison sentence ranges from less than one month to six months. If a majority of such prisoners be released on probation after a careful scrutiny or their antecedents, surroundings and other factors responsible for their anti-social activities, prisons will be relieved of the heavy pressure of the influx of prisoners. The prison authorities will also, in that case, find time and resources to arrange for better treatment of offenders who are in need of the institutional care and treatment (Bhattacharyya, 1986).

To establish the hypothesis that the concept and practice of probation has not found favour with the judiciary leading to the imprisonment of offenders who could be effectively dealt with by the probation method, judges/magistrates of the four states in India were requested to give reasons for sentencing offenders to imprisonment indicating as to how probation was not a better form of disposal. Out of 48 judges/magistrates, 29 (60 per cent) have replied that they have never sentenced to imprisonment any offenders coming within the purview of the Probation of

Offenders Act and have opined that probation is always better form of disposal. The above-mentioned judicial views reveal that judges/magistrates are quite aware of the concept and benefits of probation. In fact, a majority of the judges are favourably inclined towards the concept and practice of probation. It may, therefore, be concluded that the result runs counter to the hypothesis predicted. The above analysis of judicial views broadly confirms the fact that probation as community-based treatment method for offenders is an effective alternative to imprisonment and the judiciary by and large, extends its cooperation in the implementation of the Probation of Offenders Act (Bhattacharyya, 1986).

It is an axiom that expansion of probation services has become possible in view of the growing realization that prison sentence is not the best mode of treatment to ensure the protection of society. Though in specific cases imprisonment may be appropriate to deal with certain classes of offenders, there are several others in whom prison sentence may produce deleterious effects. Instead of becoming a useful citizen, he may become a tough and frustrated individual with a propensity for further crime (Reddi, 1972).

The Concept of Probation

The American Bar Association (1970) defined probation as "A sentence not involving confinement, which imposes conditions and retains authority in the sentencing court to modify the conditions of sentence or to resentence the offender if he violates the conditions." The Report of the Advisory Committee on Penal Institutions, Probation and Parole to the National Commission on Law, Observance and Enforcement defined probation as:

> A process of treatment prescribed by the court for persons convicted of offences against the law, during which the individual on probation lives in the community and regulates his own life under conditions imposed by the court and is subject to supervision by a probation officer. Length of the probation period varies, and is determined by the court. (Bhattacharyya, 1986)

Probation refers to the release of convicted offenders into the community under a conditional suspended sentence, avoiding imprisonment, showing good behaviour, under the supervision of a probation officer (Black, 1990). The word probation derived from the Latin term *probatio*, means a period of proving or trial and forgiveness. Thus, offenders who prove themselves during the trial period by complying with the conditions of their probation are forgiven and released from further involvement with the criminal justice system (Champion, 1996). A generally accepted definition of probation is the supervised release of offenders into the community in lieu of incarceration subject to conditions (Allen et al., 1985).

Community correction refers to any community-based corrections program designed to supervise convicted offenders in lieu of incarceration, either by city, county, state, or federal authority; that provides various services to client offenders; that monitors and furthers client/offender responsibility regarding payment of fines, victim compensation, community service, and restitution orders; and that provides for a continuation of punishment through more controlled supervision and greater accountability (Biles, 1988; Duffee & McGarrell, 1990; Reeves, 1992).

Community-based corrections, essentially refers to a fundamental reorganization of the several aspects of corrections into a new structure. Now limited to probation, institutions and parole, these divisions would loosen their autonomy from each other, and crime prevention activities would be added. The convicted offender now is handled successively by probation institutions and parole as though he essentially had no previous experiences within the system of corrections. Each of these agencies is excessively aloof from the other's activities. Community-based corrections would integrate their several activities to expose the convicted offender to systematic experiences. Instead of dealing with crimes as a discrete problem, community-based correction enters into an active alliance with other agencies responsible for overcoming the various social problems (Johnson, 1973).

The Historical Development of Probation

Probation in the United States was conceived in 1841 by the successful shoemaker and philanthropist, John Augustus, although historical references to this phenomenon may be found in writings as early as 437-422 B.C. John Augustus is most frequently credited with implementing probation on a fairly large scale, even though no local or state statutes were in effect at the time to condone it (Champion, 1996). Parallelly, some work was done by Mathew Davenport Hill in 1841 in the United Kingdom. The practice then spread in a big way to almost all the civilized countries of the world (Diaz, 1979). Strongly influenced by the temperance movement of the period, Augustus made a concerted effort to rehabilitate alcoholics and to assist those arrested for intoxication related offences. Appearing in a Boston municipal court one morning to observe offenders charged and sentenced for various crimes, Augustus intervened on behalf of a man charged with being a "common drunkard" (Augustus, 1852). As an alternative to having the convicted offender placed in the Boston House of Corrections, Augustus offered to supervise the man's behaviour for a three week period and guaranteed his subsequent reappearance in court. Knowing Augustus's reputation for philanthropy and trusting his motives, the judge agreed. When Augustus returned three weeks later with the "reformed" drunkard, the judge was so impressed that he fined the offender only one cent and court costs (which amounted to less than $4) and suspended the usual sentence of incarceration (which was sometimes six months or more). Between 1841 and 1859, the year Augustus died, it is estimated that he saved nearly 2,000 men and women from incarceration by bailing them out and supervising them for a fixed probationary period. He supervised approximately 100 probationers per year and kept detailed records of their progress. In this respect, he compiled what are now called presentence investigation report, although he usually made extensive notes about offenders and their progress, and no doubt many of these probationers were emotionally affected by his kindness and generosity. According to his own assessment of his performance, rehabilitation and reformation were occurring at a significant rate among his clients, and his own efforts were largely responsible (Champion, 1996).

The Advantages of Probation

Probation keeps those convicted of petty crimes from the "criminogenic environment of jails and prisons". Prisons are viewed as colleges of crime where inmates are not rehabilitated but rather learn more effective criminal techniques. One benefit of probation is that it permits offenders to remain in their communities, work at jobs, support their families, make restitution to victims, and perform other useful services (Walker, 1989). Probation helps offenders avoid the stigma of the criminal label. Some authorities believe that once offenders have been labelled as delinquent or criminal, they will act out these roles by committing subsequent offences (Walker, 1985). Although probationers are criminals and their convictions are a matter of public record, they are less obtrusive in their communities compared with ex-convicts who have served time in prison. They often remain in their present jobs as a probation requirement, and they carry on otherwise normal lives. Petersilia (1985) indicates that one per cent of the entire population of California is currently on probation. Unless offenders disclose their probationary status to their neighbours, it is difficult to differentiate former offenders from non-offenders. Probation allows offenders to integrate more easily with non-criminals. Offenders may hold jobs, earn a living for their families and themselves, and develop more positive self-concepts and conforming behaviours not likely acquired if incarcerated. In this respect, "probation is the one correctional treatment program that seems to work" (Walker, 1985). Probation is a practical means by which to ease the problems of prison and jail overcrowding. Increased probation sentences are front-end solutions to overcrowding, meaning that steps are taken to divert certain offenders away from jails and exacerbate the existing overcrowded conditions. Thus, probation serves the purely logistical function of enabling correctional institutions to more effectively manage smaller inmate populations (Champion, 1996). Community-based programs are effective, safer and less costly than incarceration, especially when the right, eligible non-violent clients are targeted (English and Mande, 1991; Eynon, 1989; Hughes, 1990; Tilow, 1989).

A major rationale for the use of community programs is that correctional costs can be considerably reduced by handling in the community a large number of those offenders normally put in institutions. A nationwide survey conducted by NCCD (1966) for the President's Crime Commission found that the daily cost for a juvenile in an institution is ten times the cost of juvenile probation or aftercare. For adults, state institutional costs are about six times that of parole and about fourteen times that of probation.

There is certainly no shortage of literature to document the fact that community-based-corrections functions is largely beneficial in reducing jail and prison populations (Corrections Compendium, 1990; Corrigan, 1990; English and Mande, 1991; Medler, 1985). There are both short- and long-term benefits that accrue to various jurisdictions as the result of establishing community corrections programs (Cohen, 1994). A short-term benefit is reducing jail and prison populations by diverting a substantial number of offenders to community-based supervision. A long-term benefit is that offenders in community-based programmes tend to have lower rates of recidivism compared with paroled offenders who have served some prison time. It may be that "creaming" or selecting the most eligible and least dangerous offenders for community-based-correctional programs accounts for these recidivism differences. In any case, community-based programmes have an ameliorative effect of offender-clients generally (Czajkoski, 1985).

Alternative Methods to Imprisonment in India and Other Countries

In India, the alternatives available to imprisonment are fine, probation and community service order. Of these, probation is most widely used in almost all states in India. Community service order is very rarely used and fine is imposed on the offender for the offence he committed in accordance with Indian Penal Code and other laws.

A prevailing view of sentencing equates punishment and control with incarceration (U.S. Sentencing Commission, 1991). In recent years, however, several proposals have been advanced and adopted in some jurisdictions that favour various alternative sentencing forms or creative sentencing (Klein, 1988; McDonald and Carlson, 1992; Minnesota Sentencing Guidelines Commission, 1991). Alternative sentencing offers offenders, especially those who have committed relatively minor or non-violent offences, an opportunity to serve their sentences outside the prison setting. Usually, alternative sentencing involves some form of community service, some degree of restitution to victims of crimes, becoming actively involved in educational or vocational training programmes, or becoming affiliated with some other "good works" activity (Czajkoski and Wollan, 1986).

The primary goals of alternative sentencing are twofold. First, it is aimed at helping certain types of offenders avoid imprisonment. Imprisonment means associating with other criminals, and labelling theorists consider imprisonment as an important factor in contributing to one's self-concept as a criminal. Second, alternative sentencing is designed as a way of providing needed services and therapy while remaining relatively free within the community. In addition, alternative sentencing tends to reduce overcrowding in prisons and certain correctional operating costs (Klein, 1988; Wallace and Clarke, 1986).

The primary purpose of community-based correctional programmes is to assist probationers in re-integrating into their communities (Racine, Vittitow, and Riggs, 1984). The secondary purpose of community-based programmes is to help alleviate prison overcrowding by accepting probation for those offenders who are not dangerous and pose the least risk to society (Travis, 1985).

A key goal of any offender treatment programmes, whether it is institutional or community-based, is rehabilitation. Thus, community corrections programmes are designed, in part, to rehabilitate offenders. Rehabilitation occurs when community correctional clients, offenders, participate in vocational, educational, and/or counselling programmes that are intended to improve their coping skills (Camp, 1990; Corrigan, 1990). Community-based corrections programmes are particularly beneficial for first time non-violent offenders. Through probation, diversion, halfway houses, and parole, community-based programmes are thought to have considerable success in rehabilitating offenders (Murty et al., 1987).

The following are the alternatives that are used widely in developed countries as well as developing countries like India:

Fines

An integral part of sentencing in an increasing number of cases is the use of fines (Gordon and Glaser, 1991; Wheeler et al., 1990; Zamist, 1986). The use of fines as sanctions can be traced to preindustrialized and non-Western societies (Davis and Lurigio, 1992; Winterfield and Hillsman, 1993). Estimates suggest that over 14 million persons are arrested each year in the United States, and that a significant portion of these receive fines upon conviction (McDonald, Greene, and Worzella, 1992).

Restitution

An increasingly important feature of probation programmes is restitution (Staples, 1986). Restitution is the practice of requiring offenders to compensate crime victims for damages offenders may have inflicted (Davis and Lurigio, 1992). Restitution to victims may be through periodic payments from offender earnings while on work release, probation, or parole. Sometimes, restitution takes non-monetary forms; for example, offenders rebuild or restore property destroyed earlier by their crimes (Champion, 1996).

Community Service

Community service may involve clean up activities in municipal parks, painting projects involving graffiti removal, cutting courthouse lawns, or any other constructive project that can benefit the community (McDonald, 1986). These community service sentences are imposed by judges. Probation officers are largely responsible for overseeing the efforts of convicted offenders in fulfilling their community service obligations. These sentencing provisions are commonly called 'community service orders' (Champion, 1996). Community service is considered a punishment and is court imposed (Galaway, 1988; Maher and Dufour, 1987; Williams, 1986). Community service orders are symbolic restitution, involving redress for victims, less severe sanctions for offenders, offender rehabilitation, reduction of demands on the criminal justice system, and a reduction of the need for vengeance in a society, or a combination of these factors (Donnelly, 1980).

Victim-Offender Mediation

This focuses on victim-offender reconciliation. Alternative dispute resolution is used as a mediating ground for resolving differences or disputes between victims and perpetrators (Patel and Soderlund, 1994). Usually, third party arbiters, such as judges, lawyers, or public appointees, can meet with offenders and their victims and work out mutually satisfactory arrangements whereby victims can be compensated for their losses or injuries (Champion, 1996).

The Legal Provisions in India Relating to Probation

In India, the old composite state of Madras was the first to adopt probation, after the passing of the Madras Probation of Offenders Act, 1936 which was the first Probation of Offenders Act in India (Diaz, 1979). Probation was first introduced under Section 562 of the Code of Criminal Procedure, 1898. It was amended in 1923 and in the thirties; the then provinces of Bombay, Madras and Uttar Pradesh enacted their Probation of Offenders Acts. However, there was no uniformity in the provisions of these acts. After independence, the Government of India realized the importance of the probation law. As a result, the Probation of Offenders Act was passed by the Parliament in 1958 with some progressive provisions. This Act has been enforced by all the States except Nagaland and Sikkim. Section 6 of the Act makes a mandatory provision. In view of this provision, the court must call for a report on an offender below the age of 21 years from the probation officer if his offence is not punishable with death or life imprisonment. The object of the Probation of Offenders Act, 1958 is to treat the offender not as much as a criminal but as a sick man who is capable of being reclaimed and restored to society as a useful and respectable citizen. This Act is a milestone in the progress of the modern trend of reform in the field of penology (Bhattacharyya, 1986). Even in respect of those offenders who are above 21 years, once the Court decides on applying the provisions of the Probation Act, it is bound to call for a report from the probation officer under sub-section (2) of

Section 4, before passing final orders. This was pointed out in the judgment of the Madras High Court in *R. Mahalingam* v. *G. Padmavathy and another* (*L.W. Cri.*, 1978).

Section 360 of the Code of Criminal Procedure, 1973 lays down under what circumstances, and how probation should be freely utilized. Further, Section 361 categorically states that in a case, where probation should have been awarded, it is not given and a short-term sentence passed the reasons for so doing should be clearly stated by the court (Diaz, 1997). Section 15 of the Juvenile Justice (Care and Protection of Children) Act, 2000 enables the Juvenile Justice Board, *inter alia*, to direct the juvenile to be released on probation.

Tamil Nadu Probation Department—A Profile

A Chief Probation Superintendent under the overall administrative control of the Inspector General of Prisons heads the Probation Branch of the Tamil Nadu Prison Department. There are 96 probation officers including 7 leave probation officers and 12 regional probation officers, which also include one research cell officer functioning under this branch throughout Tamil Nadu. Each probation officer exercises jurisdiction of more than one revenue taluk. The main function of the probation officer is sending preliminary enquiry reports to the courts about the offender to whom an order for enquiry is sent. The court will take into consideration of the report of the probation officer. During the period when the offender is released on probation and placed under the supervision of a probation officer (normally for a year), the probation officer makes a visit to the probationer's home at least once a month. Furthermore, the probation officer also makes enquiries on the grant of parole, emergency leave, and premature release of the convicted prisoner lodged in various Central Prisons across Tamil Nadu. Besides, probation officers also take part in the rehabilitative work both for the probationers and ex-convicts.

In the following Table 1 are the details of the total number of cases handled under the Probation of Offenders Act, Juvenile Justice Act and other Acts by the probation branch of Tamil Nadu for the period from 1993 to 2001.

Table 1: Number of Cases Handled by the Probation Branch during 1993-2001

Year	No. of Preliminary Enquiries Conducted	Number of Offenders Placed Under Supervision
1993	6341	3353
1994	6990	3252
1995	5951	2662
1996	5002	3087
1997	4619	2570
1998	5261	2647
1999	5749	2955
2000	4627	2471
2001	4317	2445

(*Source*: Office of the Chief Probation Superintendent, Chennai, Tamil Nadu)

The above Table 1 reveals that the number of offenders placed under the supervision of the Probation Officers in Tamil Nadu decreased from 3353 in 1993 to 2445 in 2001. This is not an encouraging trend considering the number of crimes committed in the State and the problem of overcrowding in central prisons. Measures need to be taken to increase the number of probationers rather than committing them to prison as short-termers. Because it is a proven fact that probation is an effective and viable alternative to imprisonment.

International Documents Pertaining to Community-based Correction

There are several international documents available pertaining to community-based corrections, viz.,

1. United Nations Standard Minimum Rules for Non-Custodial Measures, 1990;
2. The United Nations Standard Minimum Rules for the Administration of Juvenile Justice, 1985; and
3. The United Nations Declaration of the Basic Principles of Justice for Victims of Crime and Abuse of Power, 1985.

The primary international instrument covering sanctions other than imprisonment imposed during the administration of criminal justice is the United Nations Standard Minimum Rules for Non-Custodial Measures, also known as the 'Tokyo Rules'. These rules were adopted by the United Nations General Assembly on 14 December 1990. Rules to govern community-based sanctions were developed because of the increasing use of such sanctions, in a wide variety of cultures and legislations around the world. These sanctions allow offenders to remain with their families and community, along with giving them an opportunity to continue with their employment. However, offenders undergoing such sanctions are still to an extent under the control of authorities. They may be subject to specific restrictions and conditions, and information about their actions and behaviour may be collected by the authorities. Non-compliance with the conditions imposed may lead to serious consequences for the offender, such as imprisonment (Stern, 2000).

The United Nations Standard Minimum Rules for the Administration of Juvenile Justice, 1985 adopted by the UN General Assembly is also known as the 'Beijing Rules'. In the case of the Beijing Rules, member states are urged to develop non-custodial measures to deal with the juvenile offenders both at the pre-trial and the post-conviction stages. This is because it is generally accepted that at this stage of their lives, juveniles are most susceptible to a number of influences, and that given necessary support and encouragement, they will grow out of crime and become normal law abiding citizens (Garwe and Andrew, 2000).

The United Nations Declaration of the Basic Principles of Justice for Victims of Crime and Abuse of Power 1985, adopted by the UN General Assembly. Article 8 of the Declaration requires that "Offenders or third parties responsible for their behaviour should, where appropriate, make fair restitution to victims, their families or dependants. Such restitution should include the return of property or payment for the harm or loss suffered, reimbursement of expenses incurred as a result of the victimization, the provision of services and the restoration of rights."

Measures Suggested for the Betterment of the Probation System in India

Awareness should be created among the judicial officers for the liberal use of the provisions of the laws relating to probation, in accordance with laws. The judiciary needs to be sensitized about the drastic consequences of short-term imprisonment. With regard to the rehabilitation of the probationers, it is felt that the State Governments should establish an exclusive fund to render financial assistance to the deserving probationers and the Central Government could also sanction matching grant to make the programme effective. Besides, as a long-term solution, the State Governments should consider looking for avenues of employment for the probationers. Awareness programmes need to be conducted for the general public to inform them about the benefits of probation. Furthermore, to produce more desirable results, the probation division should be a stand-alone department and should not function under the prison or the social welfare department, as is the current situation.

Conclusion

By considering the positive results of the community-based correction, i.e. probation, it is prudent to follow the probation system which is found to be a viable alternative to short-term imprisonment, as imprisonment is unable to produce the results as intended. At the same time, probation brings about fruitful results in all respects, i.e. correction, rehabilitation, and reintegration of the offender into the community, crime prevention and protection of the society. Therefore, it is an irrefutable fact that probation is a viable alternative to imprisonment.

References

Allen, H.E. et al. (1985). *Probation and Parole in America*. New York: Macmillan.

American Bar Association Project on Standards for Criminal Justice, 1970.

Augustus, J. (1852). *A Report of the Labors of John Augustus for the Last Ten Years: In Aid of the Unfortunate*. New York: Wright and Hasty.

Bhattacharyya, S.K. (1986). *Probation System in India—An Appraisal*. Delhi: Manas Publications.

Biles, D. (1988). *Current International Trends in Corrections*. Washington, DC: Department of Justice, Bureau of Justice Statistics.

Black, H.C. (1990). *Black's Law Dictionary*. 6th ed. St. Paul. MN: West Publishing Company.

Camp, D.D. (1990). *Diversion Center Operations: A Case of Community*. Unpublished paper presented at the annual meetings of the Academy of Criminal Justice Sciences, Denver, CO (April).

Chakrabarti, N.K. (ed.) (1999). *Institutional Corrections—In the Administration of Criminal Justice*. New Delhi: Deep & Deep Publications.

Champion, D.J. (1996). *Probation, Parole, and Community Corrections*. New Jersey: Prentice Hall.

Cohen, F. (1994). "Legal Issues and Community Corrections". *APPA Perspectives*, 18, pp. 28-31.

Corrections Compendium. (1990). "Use of Prison Alternatives Could Save New York Millions". *Corrections Compendium*, 15, p. 14.

Corrigan, M. (1990). *The Use of Community-Based Sentencing Alternatives to Reduce Prison Overcrowding: An Assessment of Policy and Practice*. Unpublished paper presented at the annual meetings of the American Society of Criminology, Baltimore, MD (November).

Czajkoski, E.H., & Laurin, A.W.J. (1985). *Alternatives to Incarceration: The Community Correctional Center*. Washington, DC: U.S. Bureau of Prisons.

——. (1986). "Creative Sentencing: A Critical Analysis". *Justice Quarterly*, 3, pp. 215-29.

Davis, R.C., & Lurigio, A.J. (1992). "Compliance with Court-Ordered Restitution: Who Pays?". *APPA Perspectives*, 16, pp. 25-31.

Diaz, S.M. (1979). *Report of the Tamil Nadu Prison Reforms Commission 1978-79*, Vol. 1. Madras: Government Central Press.

——. (1997). Lecture notes delivered to the postgraduate of students of Criminology, University of Madras during 1997.

Donnelly, S.M. (1980). *Community Service Orders in Federal Probation*. Washington, DC: National Institute of Justice.

Duffee, D.E., & McGarrell, E.F. (1990). *Community Corrections: A Community Field Approach*. Washington, DC: Department of Justice, Bureau of Justice Statistics.

English, K., & Mande, M.J. (1991). *Community Corrections in Colorado: Why Do Some Clients Succeed and Others Fail?* Denver, CO: Department of Public Safety, Colorado Division of Criminal Justice.

Eynon, T.G. (1989). "Building Community Support". *Corrections Today*, 51, pp. 148-52.

Finn, P. (1984). "Judicial Responses to Prison Crowding". *Judicature*, 67, pp. 318-26.

Galaway, B. (1988). "Restitution as Innovation or Unfilled Promise?". *Federal Probation*, 52, pp. 3-14.

Garwe, P., & Msengezi, A. (2000). Exploring Non-Custodial Punishments: Zimbabwe's Community Service Scheme. In R.D. Shankardass (ed.), *Punishment and the Prison—Indian and International Perspectives* (pp. 243-60). New Delhi: Sage Publications.

Glueck, S. (1964). *Ventures in Criminology. Selected Recent Papers*. London: Tavistock Publication.

Gordon, M.A., & Glaser, D. (1991). The Use and Effects of Financial Penalties in Municipal Courts. *Criminology*, 29, pp. 651-76.

Hughes, G.D. (1990). The 90's: A Great Time for Community Corrections? *APPA Perspectives*, 14, pp. 37-38.

Johnson, E.H. (1973). *Social Problems of Urban Man*. New York: Dorsey Press.

Kane, J.J. (1963). *Social Problems*. New Jersey: Prentice-Hall.

Klein, A.R. (1988). *Alternative Sentencing: A Practitioner's Guide*. Cincinnati, OH. Anderson Publishing Company.

Law Weekly Criminal, 24 October, 1978, p. 182.

Maher, R.J., & Dufour, H. (1987). Experimenting with Community Service: A Punitive Alternative to Imprisonment. *Federal Probation*, 51, pp. 22-28.

McDonald, D.C. (1986). *Punishment without Walls: Community Service Sanctions in New York City*. New Brunswick, NJ: Rutgers University.

McDonald, D.C., & Carlson, K.E. (1992). *Federal Sentencing in Transition*, 1990-96. Washington, DC: Bureau of Justice Statistics, BJS Special Report.

McDonald, D.C., Greene, J., & Worzella, C. (1992). *Day Fines in American Courts: The Staten Island and Milwaukee Experiments*. Washington, DC: U.S. Department of Justice, Office of Justice Programs.

Meddler, J.F. (1985). *Oregon Community Corrections: 1977-1984: An Evaluation*. Salem, OR: Oregon Department of Human Resources.

Minnesota Sentencing Guidelines Commission (1991). *Report to the Legislature on the Mandatory Minimum Law for Weapons Offenses*. St. Paul, MN: Author.

Montilla, M.R., & Eugene, M.E. (1977). Corrections in the Community: Success Models in Correctional Reform. Reston: Reston Publishing Co.

Murty, K.S. et al. (1987). *Community-based Programs as an Alternative to Incarceration: The Case of Fulton County, Project Re-Direction.* Unpublished paper presented at the annual meeting of the Academy of Criminal Justice Sciences, St. Louis, MO (April).

NCCD (1996). *Corrections in the United States: A Survey for the President's Commission on Law Enforcement and Administration of Justice*, New York.

Patel, J., & Soderlund, C. (1994). "Greeting a Piece of the Pie: Revenue Sharing with Crime Victims Compensation Programs". *APPA Perspectives,* 18, pp. 22-27.

Petersilia, J.M. (1985). "Rand's Research: A Closer Look". *Corrections Today*, 47, pp. 37-40.

Racine, T., Vittitow, T., & Riggs, R. (1984). *Examining Potential Duplication between Community Corrections Programs and District Court Probation Services*. Topeka, KS: Kansas Legislative Post Audit Committee.

Reddi, O.C. (1972). Place of Probation in Criminal Justice System. *Social Defence*, VII(25), pp. 26-32.

Report of the Departmental Committee on Probation Services, England, 1962.

Reeves, R. (1992). Approaching 2000: Finding Solutions to the Most Pressing Issues Facing the Corrections Community. *Corrections Today*, 54(74), pp. 76-79.

Sambandham, S. (2006). *Recommendations for Prison Reforms*—A Report submitted to the Home Department, Government of Tamil Nadu.

Staples, W.G. (1986). Restitution as a Sanction in Juvenile Court. *Crime and Delinquency*, 32, 177-85.

Stern, V. (2000). Alternatives to Prisons: Reflections and Experiences. In R.D. Shankardass (ed), *Punishment and the Prison—Indian and International Perspectives* (pp. 419-44). New Delhi: Sage Publications.

Tilow, N.F. (1989). Community Facilities: Overcoming Obstacles and Opposition. *Corrections Today*, 51, pp. 88-94.

Travis, L.F. III (1985). *Probation, Parole, and Community Corrections.* Prospect Heights, IL: Waveland Press.

U.S. Sentencing Commission (1991). *The Federal Sentencing Guidelines: A Report on the Operation of the Guidelines System and Short-Term Impacts.* Washington DC: Author.

Walker, S. (1985). *Sense and Nonsense about Crime: A Policy Guide.* Monterey, CA: Brooks/Cole.

——. (1989). *Sense and Nonsense about Crime: A Policy Guide*, 2nd ed. Monterey, CA: Brooks/Cole.

Wallace, W. L., & Clarke, S.H. (1986). *The Sentencing Alternatives Center in Greensboro, NC: An Evaluation of Its Effects on Prison Sentences.* Unpublished paper presented at American Society of Criminology, Atlanta, GA.

Wheeler, G.R. et al. (1990). "Economic Sanctions in Criminal Justice: Dilemma for Human Service?" *Justice System Journal*, 14, pp. 63-77.

Williams, J.R. (1986). *Community Penalties in North Carolina: An Examination of Programs Established by N.C.G.S. 143B-500.* Raleigh, NC: Division of Victim Justice Services, North Carolina Department of Crime Control and Public Safety.

Winterfield, L.A. & Hillsman, S.T. (1993). *The Staten Island Day—Fine Project.* Washington, DC: U.S. Department of Justice.

Zamist, I. (1986). Fines in Sentencing: An Empirical Study of Fine Use, Collection, and Enforcement in New York City Courts. New York: Vera Institute of Justice.

10

Is Parole Rehabilitating Offenders? An Analysis of Criminal Propensity and Psychological Well-being of Convicts

Amit Chaturvedi

Introduction

A small number of prisoners in India are released conditionally, subject to a period of supervision in the community, often called parole. The objectives of parole is to enable an offender live with his family members at the time of marriage, death, harvesting, etc., gratify varied needs, to preserve internal order in prisons, and to motivate inmates to accept the work assignments given to them. Parole also helps the prison administration use the strategy of parole release as the carrot to seek prisoners' conformity to prison rules. Parole is used as both a surveillance tool and a social service mechanism and ideally serves a deterrent role in preventing new crimes from occurring. Parole is effective as a deterrent in that it provides the convict with an opportunity to re-interact with the society outside the prison. In doing so, the convict gets a chance to re-realise the "wrong" committed by him which led to his landing in the jail and in turn leaving the comfort zone of the society outside. Parole can function as a surveillance tool by monitoring and sanctioning those who violate conditions of release, potentially averting more serious re-offending (Solomon, Vera, and Bhati, 2005). Parole can also act as a social service mechanism by using rules and incentives to engage ex-prisoners in positive activities, such as work and drug treatment, and to place ex-prisoners in programs that may help re-entry transitions. While the focus of parole has shifted more toward the surveillance function over the years, the number of people subject to it continues to grow (Solomon et al., 2005).

Parole plays an essential and critical role in the administration of both criminal and juvenile justice in India. They provide a wide variety of services that are critical to the effective and efficient operation of almost every aspect of the justice system, ranging from law enforcement to sentencing to the release of offenders from confinement into the community. While these community corrections agencies conduct investigations to support judicial and parole decision-making, operate residential and secure custodial facilities and provide free labour to local organizations through community service programs, parole is best known for its role in the supervision of offenders in the community.

The provisions relating to parole has been a subject matter of scrutiny since the time they have been incorporated in our penal policy. Probation and Parole have been supposed to represent the humanitarian face of Indian correctional programs these days. In *Suresh Chandra* v. *State of Gujarat,* 1976 (1) SCC 654 saw this court stating about penological innovation in the shape of parole to check recidivism because of which liberal use of the same was recommended. Release on parole also addresses the issue of overcrowding. In *Dharambir* v. *State of U.P.* the Supreme Court gave the rationale for the use of open prison system for reformation and rehabilitation of the offenders and emphasized that the prisoners be released on parole for two weeks, once a year, which should be repeated throughout their period of incarceration provided their conduct, is found to be satisfactory (Dalal, 2005).

In a developing nation like India, where social structure is so uniquely composed of varying components, it becomes very necessary to assess the performance of these "penal innovations" so that the lawmakers and prison authorities improve upon various aspects of punishment and rehabilitation. Talking specifically about parole, it is sad to observe that we are in a position from where we can make little guess as to its success or failure. Not much research has been conducted to assess parole's effectiveness in reforming prisoners; preventing the ill effects of imprisonment; and helping them reintegrate in society. As far as Indian scenario is concerned little or no exercise has been carried out so far to measure the performance of parole. Although various themes related to prisons and rehabilitation has been studied, a study dealing specifically with parole has been hard to locate. International researches have been focusing upon the performance of parole from time to time (Waller, 1974; Petersilia and Turner, 1993; Solomon et al., 2005). A study aimed at finding out the effect of parole on the offender's psychology in India is rare and therefore its analysis was very strongly felt. The present study makes an effort to throw light on the rehabilitative potential of parole.

This chapter is an effort to analyze the impact of parole on the psychology and the social adjustability of an inmate. "Criminal Propensity" and "psychological well-being" were the two parameters studied on a sample of one hundred prisoners (fifty that had been at least once granted parole and fifty others who never had this opportunity). The samples were randomly drawn from District Jail Rohini, Delhi that consisted of inmates sentenced for periods of seven years or more. Questionnaires administered were: The Criminal Propensity Questionnaire (Sanyal and Kathapalia, 1999) and The Psychological Well-Being Scale (Verma and Wig, 1976). Besides these questionnaires each inmate was subjected to a short personal interview. For secondary data, Prison Statistics 2006 (Government of India, 2006) was consulted. The results showed that parole has a definite positive effect on the psychological well-being of the inmate, although, it does not affect his "criminal propensity".

Review of Literature

While no national studies have compared re-arrest rates for Indian prisoners released on parole, a small study investigated the same for prisoners released in Canada in 1968 (Waller, 1974). The study compared the recidivism rates of discretionary parolees [n = 210] to unconditional releases (those who had applied for parole and been denied [n = 100] and those who never applied for parole [n = 113]). Within two years of release, 68 per cent of the unconditional releases were rearrested, compared with 44 per cent of the parolees. When the study controlled for the fact the parole boards select "better risk" individuals, however, the differences in re-arrest rates between parolees and unconditional released offenders were virtually identical.

The most rigorous study of supervision and recidivism in the United States is a nine-state randomized evaluation that compared offenders monitored in Intensive Supervision Programs (ISPs) to those subject to standard supervision. Petersilia and Turner (1993) found little difference in overall re-arrest rates between the ISP treatment group and the control group, although the treatment group had considerably higher levels of technical violations—likely the result of heightened surveillance inherent in ISPs. The study was unable to determine whether intensive monitoring and sanctioning of technical violations actually resulted in improved public safety outcomes. The research did, however, show that intensive supervision was successful at increasing program participation. Importantly, a review of four ISP studies, including the one described above, found that supervision strategies that included some level of rehabilitation or treatment in combination with surveillance techniques were more effective in reducing re-arrest rates than surveillance alone (Sherman, Gottfredson, MacKenzie, Eck, Reuter, and Bushway, 1998). In addition, a small yet relevant study explored the impact of probation on the criminal activity of 125 offenders (MacKenzie, Browning, Skroban, and Smith, 1999). It compared offenders' outcomes while on probation with their outcomes in the year preceding probation. The study found that probation did have an impact on the criminal activities of probationers, particularly among older offenders and property and drug offenders. Probation appeared to reduce the number of offenders who become recidivist; the rate of offending among recidivists; and high-risk behaviour linked to crime. It was not clear, however, whether the arrest and/or sentencing events—and not probation supervision itself—actually affected the offending behaviour.

Grant and Gillis (1999) conducted a study to determine the factors associated with successful sentence completion for offenders who had received day parole. The results of the study indicate that successful completion of day parole is associated with lower readmission and new offence rate. Only 15 per cent of the day parole sample that successfully completed day parole was readmitted after day parole completion, whereas 44 per cent who were unsuccessful on day parole were readmitted. Furthermore, those who were unsuccessful in completing day parole re-offended at three times the rate of offenders who successfully completed day parole (30 per cent compared to 10 per cent). The study also demonstrated that day parole serves the needs of low risk offenders released early in their sentence. Additionally, day parole responds to the needs of higher risk offenders released shortly before their statutory release date, and contributes to community protection. Offenders released on day parole are more likely than the general offender population to be granted full parole. In addition, their success rate on full parole and statutory release is higher compared to the general offender population. The study also looked at risk, needs, motivation, dynamic risk predictors and previous criminal history as factors influencing both day parole and full release outcome. Results confirmed the relationship between release outcome and risk and need, with higher risk and needs associated with higher levels of failure. High-risk offenders were readmitted at nearly three times the rate of low risk offenders (28 per cent compared to 11 per cent) and re-offend at twice the rate (18 per cent versus 8 per cent, respectively). Offenders classified at the high case need level were five times more likely to be readmitted than offenders identified at the low case needs level (35 per cent compared to 7 per cent). Moreover, new offence rates were more than three times greater for high (21 per cent) versus (6 per cent) case needs offenders. In addition, the results indicate those offenders rated as low risk but with high levels of needs are at greater risk to fail on release (29 per cent) than are some high risk offenders (14 per cent for high risk/low needs group). For offenders eligible for day parole, needs may be a more important predictor of outcome than risk.

Solomon et al. (2005) found that parole supervision has little effect on re-arrest rates of released prisoners. Mandatory parolees, who account for the largest share of released prisoners, fare no better on supervision than similar prisoners released without supervision. In fact, in some cases they fare worse. While discretionary parolees are less likely to be rearrested, this difference narrows (to 4 percentage points) after taking into account personal characteristics and criminal histories. Certain prisoners benefit more from supervision—especially discretionary release to supervision—than others. For example, females, individuals with few prior arrests, public order offenders, and technical violators are less likely to be rearrested if supervised after prison. Persons with a combination of these characteristics, representing relatively low-level offenders, exhibit even lower re-arrest rates if supervised. Conversely, supervision does not improve re-arrest outcomes for some of the higher rate, more serious offenders. Of the largest groups of released prisoners—male drug, property, and violent offenders—only property offenders released to discretionary parole benefit from supervision. Violent offenders released to supervision are no less likely to be rearrested than their unsupervised counterparts. For male drug offenders, mandatory release to supervision predicts higher re-arrest rates than for unconditionally released offenders or discretionary parolees.

An Indian study (Khurana and Dhar, 2000) aimed at investigating the effect of Vipassana Meditation (VM) on Quality of Life (QOL), Subjective Well-Being (SWB), and Criminal Propensity (CP) among inmates of Tihar Jail, Delhi. The total sample comprised 262 inmates (males = 232, female = 30). A series of 5 studies were conducted using both before-and-after as well as control group experimental designs. The independent variable was Vipassana meditation. The dependent variables were: Quality of Life (QOL), Subjective Well-Being (SWB), and Criminal Propensity (CP). Life Satisfaction Scale (PGI, Chandigarh), Subjective Well-Being Scale (Nagpal and Sell, 1985), and Criminal Propensity Scale (Sanyal and Kathapalia, 1999) were used to collect data. Student's 't' test was used for data analysis. The results obtained supported the hypotheses to a large extent, though not all the results are significant. Vipassana meditation significantly improved Subjective well-being and reduced Criminal propensity of inmates of Tihar Jail.

Methods

Variables

Parole was selected as the independent variable in the study. Two dependent variables namely 'criminal propensity' and 'psychological well-being' were selected for the research. Criminal propensity is the behavioural tendency of an individual to commit a criminal act provided all other related factors are kept constant. Almost all behaviour of human beings can be categorized and can be measured through psychological tools. The Eysenck Personality Questionnaire measures the various dimensions of a personality such as Neuroticism, Extraversion, etc. Based on this approach the term criminal propensity has been coined. Psychological well-being is the meter of a person's psychological health. It has to deal with such questions as: How "normal" does an individual feel and what are the problematic areas as far as his adjustment to the normal society is concerned?

Hypothesis

The study has been conducted to test the veracity of the following two hypotheses:

1. Granting parole improves the psychological well-being of a convicted inmate.
2. Granting parole affects the criminal propensity of a convicted inmate.

Sampling

Data was collected by simple random sampling method. The total population consisted of one thousand inmates residing in the District Jail Rohini, Delhi. The Jail houses offenders who have been sentenced for a term exceeding seven years. The sample consists of individuals convicted for murder, rape and other such serious crimes. Fifty parolees and fifty non-parolees were randomly selected. Convicts who had at least once been on parole throughout the term of their sentence were termed as 'parolees' and non-parolees consisted of those convicts who had never had this opportunity owing to various reasons. A total of one hundred convicts were selected.

Research Tool

The following two questionnaires were administered to each of the respondents:

1. *Criminal Propensity Questionnaire* (Sanyal and Kathapalia, 1999) consisting of 39 closed ended responses. The more a convict scores on this scale (highest possible score is 39 and lowest 0) the more his criminal propensity is supposed to be.
2. *Psychological Well-Being Scale* (Verma and Wig, 1977) was administered to assess the psychological health of the inmate. The questionnaire consisting of 38 items (Closed ended), measuring two aspects of the respondent's health. The first part (Area A) of the questionnaire dealt with the respondent's physical symptoms of ill health such as headache, fever, indigestion, bowel habits, etc. The next part (Area B) measures the inmate's emotional instability. The lower an inmate scores on this scale the healthier he is psychologically.

Besides the two questionnaires each inmate was also interviewed briefly. The interview focused on their:

- Experiences during confinement; and
- Views regarding the success or failure of parole.

Data Collection and Analysis

The data collected was examined and only significant responses were considered for analysis. The relevant data was statistically analysed. The hypothesis has been tested on a significance level of 5 per cent. The interview responses were studied and relevant conclusions were drawn.

Results

The Criminal Propensity (CP) and the Psychological Well-Being Scores of the two groups, i.e. parolees and non-parolees were compared for their means. CP scores did not vary significantly for the two groups under study. Parolees scored on an average 18.40 whereas the group non-parolees scored an average of 19.78 on the CP scale. A difference emerged when the two groups were analysed for their psychological well-being scores.

Mean psychological well-being score for the parolees was calculated as 13.65. Mean psychological well-being score for the non-parolees was calculated as 17.48. To test the significance of this difference between the mean scores, z test was applied. The value of z obtained was 0.248 which gave a significant difference when corresponding table was referred to. The first hypothesis that parole affects the criminal propensity of the inmate therefore stands disproved and is rejected. The second hypothesis that parole improves the psychological well-being of the inmate stands proved and is accepted.

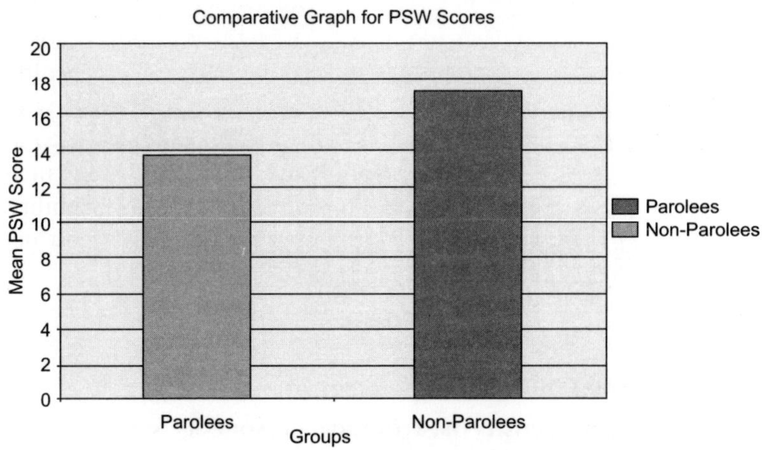

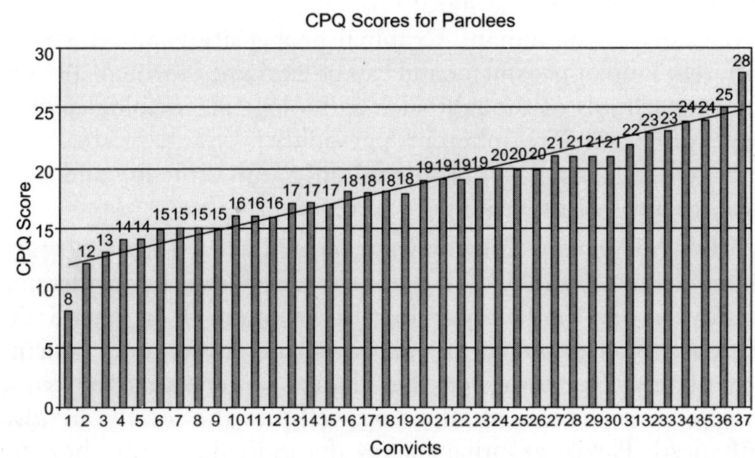

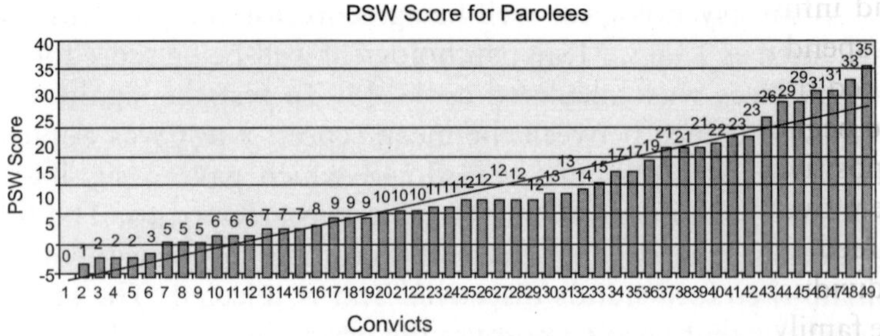

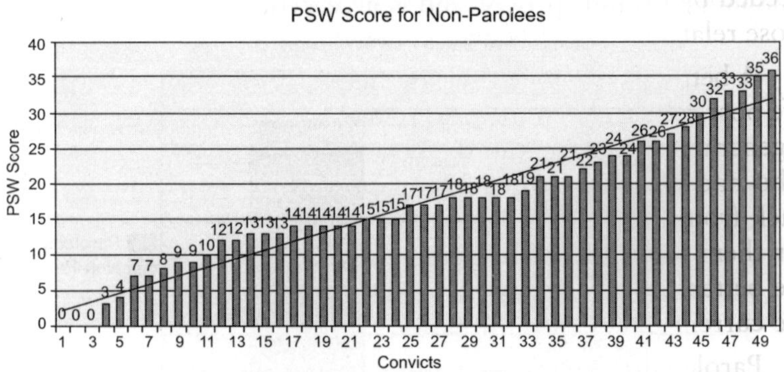

Discussion and Conclusion

Criminal propensity is a unique personality characteristic and does not vary with treatment programmes such as parole. In other words, parole hardly has any impact on the criminal propensity of the inmate. Criminal propensity is an altogether different kind of parameter and can be explained through already existing schools of thought such as biological, sociological and psychological. The inherent personality characteristics like criminal propensity can be altered only with difficulty and with little chances of preventing its recurrence.

Psychological well-being was one area where the two groups differed considerably. This implies that parole has a definite positive impact on the psychology of the inmate. If an inmate gets the chance to go out of the jail on parole, he certainly benefits out of this. Not only does his chance of repeating the crime lowered; his chances of adjusting well into the society are also enhanced. Parole granting makes the individual more hopeful and infuses in him a positive outlook towards life that he has to spend on release outside the prison walls. To a question that asked them "Would you like to die?" the Parolees responded in the negative mostly, whereas the most of the non-parolees gave a positive response. Even the responses in the interview sessions were overwhelming. Majority of participants from both groups agreed that parole is certainly of great help in reforming the individual. Not only it helps at the individual level, it also helps the family members at large. At times, when the individual is most needed by his family such as harvesting, marriage or death of a close relative it is parole that comes to the rescue of the inmate.

A better psychological health means a better reintegration to life post-release. Even the prison inmates agreed to have noticed a general improvement in the behaviour of their fellow inmates who had been on parole. The period when the parolees come back from their parole terms was certainly a very difficult time for them but after a few days of adjustment it all changed for the better. So we can say that parole is completely in tune with the current policy of reformation and reintegration.

Parole granting in Delhi and all other jails of the country is more a haphazard process rather than an organized one. A specific and scientific parole policy is the need of the hour. Ironically, prisoners who genuinely needed parole and were waiting for it since months, while on the other hand there were others who got released on parole within a day or two on account of trivial grounds only because they could hire good lawyers and could spend money easily. In most of the cases where facility of parole was not availed of by the inmate the reason was not anything else but finance. On account of high fees which the advocates took or the amount of security asked for by the judiciary, parole has become a dream for many of the inmates. An average prisoner either spends or expects to spend around twenty to fifty thousand rupees in order to get a parole leave. The jail authority on the other hand had a different story to tell. They claimed of having free legal aid services for the indigent inmates. These findings might seem paradoxical, the truth however emerges that money or the security amount should not be a hindrance in the path of a prisoner getting parole.

The period when an inmate goes back to prison after serving his term of parole, he experiences a lot of grief and frustration and he finds it difficult to readjust (Around 95 per cent of the respondents felt this). Since this is a critical phase for prisoners, extra care should be taken by prison officials. Parole should be a matter of right for the inmate. Only if he violates the conditions of parole or does anything contrary to law he should be denied parole in future. The Prison Statistics (2006) annually published by the National Crime Records Bureau (Government of India, 2006) also points out that the rate of parole violations is very low and parole is granted to a very small population of the jails. Absence of effective supervision during the parole term was also observed. Hardly any parolee agreed to having been subjected to any fruitful or worthy supervision during his parole. The local police should try to actively involve in handling the parolees. Length of parole term was found to be lenient enough.

It was also found that there were prisoners who had been released on parole more than once (6-7 times) and for quite long terms (the longest being 9 months). What is required therefore is a scientific selection of prisoners for granting parole and their effective supervision.

Jail authorities should approach prisoners for parole. The existing process should be revamped. Instead of the inmate approaching the authorities, the authority should approach the eligible inmates and offer them a parole leave. Such a process will help in giving every inmate an equal opportunity of going out on parole. The sample had 6 inmates who were from countries like Pakistan, Nepal, Nigeria and Bangladesh. They had no chance of getting out on parole. Their cases should be either transferred to their respective countries or some arrangement for their meeting with their family members should be made in order to restore their human and conjugal rights.

This study is a micro level analysis and still there is a great void in research on effectiveness of parole. This study throws open new debatable issues such as whether first parole should be a matter of right. Other issues such as financial implications involved with parole need to be analyzed in future researches.

More research needs to be done in order to discover the real rehabilitative potential of parole.

Limitations of the Study

Due to time and money constraints, the study has been conducted on a small sample, i.e. 100 inmates; out of which a few responses were not taken into consideration due to various reasons. Some of the responses were incomplete and others did not contain reliable information. There were others that could not be included for similar reasons. The study fails to account for other factors that can affect the psychology of the inmate other than parole. False responses in the interview sessions cannot be ruled out totally, although every effort was made to extract honest responses from the respondents.

References

Dalal, P. (2005). *Prison Reforms in India.* Retrieved at http://praveen-dalal.blogspot.com/2005/07/prison-reforms-in-india.html on 25th December 2009.

Government of India (2006). *Prison Statistics, India 2006.* New Delhi: National Crime Records Bureau, Ministry of Home Affairs, Government of India. Retrieved on June 12, 2009 from http://ncrb.nic.in/PSI2006/prison2006.htm

Grant, B.A. and Christa, A.G. (1999). *Day Parole Outcome, Criminal History and Other Predictors of Successful Sentence Completion.* Ontario: Research Branch, Corporate Development, Correctional Service of Canada.

Khurana, A. and Dhar, P.L. (2000). *Effect of Vipassana Meditation on Quality of Life, Subjective well-being, and Criminal Propensity among inmates of Tihar Jail, Delhi.* Final report submitted to Vipassana Research Institute.

MacKenzie, D., Browning, K., Skroban, S., and Smith, S. (1999). "The Impact of Probation on the Criminal Activities of Offenders". *Journal of Research in Crime and Delinquency,* 36(4), pp. 423-53.

Nagpal, R. and Sell, H. (1985). "Subjective Well-being", *SEARO Regional Health Paper* No. 7. World Health Organization, New Delhi.

Petersilia, J. and Turner, S. (1993). "Intensive Probation and Parole". In M. Tonry (Ed.), *Crime and Justice: A Review of Research* (vol. 17 pp. 281-335). Chicago: University of Chicago Press.

——. (1993). "Evaluating Intensive Supervision Probation/Parole: Results from a Nationwide Experiment". *NIJ Research in Brief*. Washington, DC: U.S. Department of Justice, Office of Justice Programs.

Sanyal, S. and Kathapalia, V. (1999). Development of the 'C' Scale on the basis of Eyesenckian theory (Criminal Propensity Scale).

Sherman, L.W., et al. (1998). *Preventing Crime: What Works, What Doesn't, What's Promising*. Research in Brief. Washington, DC: National Institute of Justice.

Solomon, A.L., Kachnowski, V. and Bhati, A. (2005). *Does Parole Work? Analyzing the Impact of Post Prison Supervision on Rearrest Outcomes*. Washington D.C.: Urban Institute.

Verma, S.K. and Wig, N.N. (1977). Standardization of a Neuroticism Questionnaire in Hindi. *Indian Journal of Psychiatry*, 19, 67-72.

Waller, I. (1974). *Men Released from Prison*. Toronto, Ontario: University of Toronto Press.

11

Criminality Among Convicted Offenders*

Arvind Verma and Manish Kumar

Introduction

The scientific inquiry into the causes of criminal behaviour is now more than hundred years old. The discipline traces its roots to the growth of the Classical School in Europe around the period of the French Revolution. A series of legal reforms were propounded by social reformers such as Beccaria and Rousseau that established the foundations of modern legal justice system. The reforms that led to the codification of the new laws, creation of the modern police forces and the prison systems were radical innovations that also changed fundamental assumptions about criminal behaviour (Brantingham and Brantingham, 1991; Hall, 1960). The belief that criminals are different from 'normal' changed and criminal behaviour came to be explained in terms of social, economic, political, demographic and psychological factors.

This scientific search for an etiology of crime has contributed an impressive literature to the subject. Criminology has now grown into a major subject of inquiry that is characterized by

* This research project was supported by a grant from Indian Council of Social Science Research (ICSSR), New Delhi. This chapter was originally published as an article in the *International Journal of Criminal Justice Sciences* as: Verma, A. and Kumar, M. (2008). The Etiology of Crime in India. *International Journal of Criminal Justice Sciences*, 3(2), July-December, pp. 138-57. The authors sincerely thank K. Jaishankar, the Editor-in-Chief of IJCJS for providing permission to reprint this article.

an inter-disciplinary approach and is taught on most university campuses. Explanations of criminal behaviour draw concepts from a vast array of social and physical sciences. The reasons why people are motivated to commit crime range from an Ecological perspective (Shaw and McKay, 1942) to Differential Association (Sutherland, 1992), Cultural Conflict (Sellin, 1938), Sub-Cultural influences (Cohen, 1955; Matza, 1969), Anomie and Strain (Durkheim, 1951; Merton, 1968), Lack of Opportunities (Cloward and Ohlin, 1960) to Lack of Self Control (Gottfredson and Hirschi, 1990). However, all these explanations are strongly rooted in the structure, culture and history of the Western (read American) society. The empirical support for most of these theories of crime and deviance has come from the studies of urban growth and social disorganization witnessed in Western societies (Baldwin and Bottoms, 1976; Brantingham and Brantingham, 1991; Fattah, 1991; Voss and Petersen, 1971; Fetchenhauer and Simon, 1998; Indermaur, 1999; Paternoster and Brame, 1998; Wikstrom, 1991).

There has not been a similar development of criminological theorization in India for criminology has yet to emerge as a strong discipline in Indian research institutes. Only a handful of universities in India have an independent criminology department and few institutes offer doctoral programmes in this field. Moreover, the application of some of these theories, such as Social Disorganization, to the Indian situation poses considerable challenges as the Indian cities hardly resemble the Western urban centers. Most Indian cities are hundreds of years old where Mughal period structures, Victorian Villas, modern high rise apartment complexes and thatched huts exist side by side. Almost every residential neighbourhood is surrounded by sprawling slums. There are few exclusive commercial layouts since workers and the Indian business class has traditionally favoured living close to their workplaces (Thakur, 1980; Weinstein, 1974). In most areas the residential areas *near* the centers of the cities have high economic values in contrast to the North American ones. Furthermore, there is little evidence of zonal decay in Indian cities as found in Chicago by Shaw and McKay (1942).

Moreover, the tradition of extended families still persists despite growing urbanization and scarcity of space. An obvious implication of having a large family is that supervision over the young is ubiquitous, social control is extensive and strict. It is no surprise that a careful study found juvenile delinquency to be a *minor* problem in a country of one billion people (Hartjen and Priyadarshini, 1996). Social Control Theory may provide an explanation but the widespread prevalence of child labour in many industries and limited supervision during day by working parents in metropolitan cities will need additional explanations. Similarly, real and perceived social and economic inequalities have been a constant feature of the Indian society for hundreds of years. The caste system continues and people seem to accept their position in the social hierarchy without strong dissent. These disparities too, do not seem to promote strain and be a factor for criminal behaviour. But social conflict and violence against scheduled castes appear to suggest that loss of traditional power amongst the so-called 'higher castes' is causing strain, particularly from positive discrimination policies of the government for the 'backward castes'.

Clearly, the nature of the society, its culture and history are significant variables in understanding criminal behaviour. It follows that the nature of criminality in India must be explained as a consequence of its peculiar social-cultural, political and historical conditions. The texts *Manu Smriti* and *Arthashastra* describe various forms of criminality in ancient Indian society and prescribe various ways of dealing with them (Shamashastry, 1929). However, these explanations were largely rooted in religious beliefs of re-incarnation. Criminal motivation was suggested to be a product of previous life's Karma and influences (Sukla, 1987; Somerville, 2000). During the British period a large section of the people were designated as 'criminal tribes' and were subject to extremely harsh treatment by the regime (Yang, 1985). Nevertheless, studies of these criminal tribes have been limited to the descriptions of social organization, family relationships and economic hardships suffered by these people (Simhadri, 1991). Some other literature books dealing with the concept of criminal behaviour in India (*e.g.*, Nayar, 1975; Upadhyaya, 1978;

Shukla, 1982; Thilagaraj, 1987; Mohanty, 1990; Phulia, 1992), have largely focused upon officials' descriptions of criminality or dealt with the psychological dimensions, comparing 'delinquents' with samples of 'normal'. A large number of police officers have written their memoirs or about policing in which references have been made about certain types of offenders (Lobo, 1992; Shah, 1992). Yet, these efforts have been impressionist rather than based on some careful scientific inquiry. The genesis of dacoity (armed robbery by a gang) in Chambal valley (north-central India) has been a popular theme too (Bhaduri, 1972; Khan, 1981; Jatar, 1980; Katare, 1972). Again, most explanations have simply suggested feudal exploitation as the cause that provoked many people of this region to take to arms. The fact that many gangs operating in this valley were composed of higher castes and wealthy people appears to suggest that feudalism may only be a partial explanation of dacoity in Chambal valley. Clearly, the accounts of criminal behaviour in India remain unsatisfactory. Hartjen and Ketheneni (1996, p. 7) in a review of Indian literature on juvenile delinquency lament that "in contrast to the voluminous literature found for other countries, a coherent body of research and thought relating to delinquency in India is simply not available".

An *empirical* examination and a well formulated theory that provides testable hypotheses about the reasons why people commit crime in India are the objectives of this research. The circumstances that motivate, encourage deviance in the developing state, the economic and social disparities, the rapid urbanization and exposure to new cultural ethos brought about by the new communication systems are factors that may be construed to influence criminality. This paper makes an attempt to explore the causes of criminality amongst a specific set of people and thereby add to the knowledge of criminality in India.

The Research Framework

This exploration of the etiology of crime in the Indian context is based upon an empirical examination of background of those people who have been *recognized* to be deviant by the laws and procedures of the country. The empirical reality that has been sought in this research work is an understanding of the circumstances and motivations that have forced some people to commit acts defined as crime by the law based upon the Positive School of Criminology perspective. For this purpose, the data has been collected from people convicted for their offenses through a well established due process of the law. There is thus little dispute about their legal innocence although one still cannot discount the absence of any kind of false accusations or defective procedures. Clearly, this approach is an unsatisfactory basis of criminality since the notion of criminal behaviour is controversial. Treating officially incarcerated people as criminals and then exploring their reasons for criminality is tautological in one sense. Yet, this process appears to be a good starting point for an exploratory research. Understanding the reasons why people convicted by a due legal process got involved in criminal behaviour is likely to provide some insight about the cause of deviant behaviour in Indian society.

It is nevertheless clear that results of this study cannot be extended to the general population for this method does not differentiate between criminals and non-criminals. People who have been incarcerated through a legal process are an unrepresentative and particular subset of the general population. Their behaviour patterns cannot be ascribed to the people of India. Indeed, the population of interest in this research will simply be the set of convicted offenders—those labeled as 'criminals' by the processes of the criminal justice system. It also needs to be kept in mind that the criminal justice processes and procedures are themselves defective and biased (Verma, 2005). The nature of this study portend that any conclusion be treated with caution. Yet, we believe that this study is important for it does inform about some of the situations and circumstances that have driven a particular set of people towards criminality.

Criminogenic Factors in the Indian Context

India is a heterogeneous society with an ancient culture where diversities stand out. There is a small affluent class that is as rich as any segment of people around the world. On the other hand, the vast majority is impoverished. According to the annual report by the United Nations Development Program, the percentage of population living below $1 per day is an estimated 34.3 in 2005 (UNDP, 2009). The nation has recently acquired nuclear weapons and its Information Technology sector is catching the attention of the world. Yet, illiteracy is widespread and basic schooling is not available to a majority of the children. Women have reached top positions in every sector—politics, business, bureaucracy and academia and still the society remains strongly patriarchal where incidents of female infanticide and the problems of dowry are not uncommon (Madhok, 1998). India has the fourth largest economy in the world and there is rapid industrialization and urban growth. Nevertheless, rural population still accounts for 74.3 per cent of the population (Census of India, 2001). Despite constitutional provisions of equality and one-person one vote, caste remains a dominant factor in social relations. A minority of so-called 'forward castes' continues to occupy the commanding heights of economic and political power in the society. In such a situation, the sociological, economic, political and psychological factors peculiar to the Indian society are likely to play a major role in determining the etiology of crime in the country.

This research project therefore sought information from the convicted offenders about their (i) Sociological factors such as family upbringing, social association, educational and work environment influences, (ii) Economic variables such as income, number of family dependents and unemployment, (iii) Political factors such as group conflict or labeling effect by the official agencies, (iv) Psychological reasons like mental history of the family, etc. Based upon the above-mentioned factors we developed the following hypotheses for criminal behaviour:

1. Large, economically deprived families where parents did not have sufficient education created circumstances that encouraged deviant behaviour.
2. Neglected childhood was a major factor for falling into criminal behaviour.
3. Criminal association developed more for those growing up in low socio-economic status families.

4. Criminal association led to a labeling effect that promoted subsequent criminal behaviour.
5. Failure of the justice system to provide speedy justice was responsible for forcing people to take to criminal acts.
6. Growing consumerism in Indian society tempted the people to adopt illegal short-cuts for making money and led them into criminal activities.
7. The loosening of social bondage due to rapid urbanization, induction of new cultural norms and an independent lifestyle led some people towards deviant behaviour.

Data Collection

Data for this study was collected from Tihar Jail, the largest prison in the country, situated at Delhi, the capital of the country. This city, due to its political and economic importance attracts people (and offenders) from all corners of the nation. Accordingly, the possibility of finding a representative *Indian* sample at Tihar prison appeared to be high. There are some valid grounds for supporting this expectation. Being the capital of the country and also the biggest business center of Northern India, Delhi attracts a large number of persons from all over India in search of employment and better opportunities. All the important institutions are situated here and there is a convenient connecting train from every major city of the country. It may also be pointed out that India has a uniform criminal justice system. Although, some acts are governed by state and municipal laws but the vast majority of crimes against property and body are enshrined in the Indian Penal Code. The procedures of investigation and prosecution are governed by the Code of Criminal Procedure 1973; again applicable to every region. The police and judicial systems are also uniform across the nation. It was hoped that the Tihar prison would be a good starting place for an exploratory study, which may be extended to other parts of the country once the viability and utility of the research design is established. Initially, the plan was to have a sampling frame consisting of the roster or the official records of the prison that contain a list of all the convicted prisoners incarcerated there. However, despite several attempts, the permission to interview prisoners from within the prison premises was denied by the authorities. Accordingly, an arrangement was made to interview offenders who were released after serving their term. There is a turnover of almost 50-75 people every day from this prison. However, majority are undertrials who are arrested as suspects by the police and released on bail by the courts. The proportion of convicted prisoners in this lot would barely be 3-5 per cent. Since our concern was with people whose legal criminality was not in doubt, we attempted to contact convicted prisoners only.

A team of researchers with assistance by the prison guards identified these prisoners as soon as they came out of the prison. These people were then informed about the purpose of the study and assured of their anonymity. The procedure was to contact every second such convicted prisoner walking out of the prison. If he[2] did not agree then the fourth such prisoner was contacted and so on. Through this procedure an attempt was made to be systematic but this was a sample of convenience. Those who agreed were interviewed in one of the teashops scattered around the prison complex. The interview would normally take 25-30 minutes. Some relatives who came to receive the prisoners were also included in the interview to verify or add comments given by the convicted prisoner. A set of survey questions (in Hindi language) was provided to each of the researchers to ensure that the interview was uniform and the variables could be operationalized for statistical analysis.

There were many cases in which the respondents refused participation. Furthermore, the strictness about selecting every second person coming out of prison could not be maintained for various reasons. In some cases, the respondents initially agreed and then refused to continue. All these reasons did vitiate the procedure of selecting a probabilistic sample but nevertheless a quasi-random selection was followed. Considering that the period of data collection was spread over a twenty-month period (1999-2000) we feel confident that the collected sample is fairly representative of convicted prisoners released from Tihar prison during the study period.

2. We have collected data on female offenders also but it is a small sample and its analysis is being done separately.

Data Description

As on 31st December 1999, the population of all the prisoners lodged at Tihar was reported to be 10,625 and the number of convicted male prisoners was 1,835 (Tihar Prison, 2001). We collected data from 424 respondents from Tihar prison but two of the cases were found to be incomplete on some key questions. Accordingly, our sample consists of 422 respondents that roughly form 22.9 per cent of the convict male population. This proportion is a probable estimate only since the numbers of convicted prisoner changes daily.

The following are the descriptive statistics of these respondents. The mean age in the sample was 30.12 with a standard deviation of 12.09. These ages have been recorded on the basis of statements made by the respondents and some of this information seems doubtful. Eleven respondents stated their age to be over 65 years and one said he was 11 years old. There is a possibility that some of them did not know their correct age and spoke in terms of approximate years. This also appears to be supported by the fact that detention above the age of 65 is rare and a child under the age of 12 who has not attained sufficient maturity will also not be detained for criminal behaviour. Either there have been gross violations of these provisions (the possibility cannot be discounted) or else the ages recorded by the officials are different from the ones informed to us. It is also worth pointing out that these respondents were interviewed at the time of their release. Thus, their age at the time of committing the crime and being arrested would have been smaller. Clearly, in at least one of the cases the age appears inaccurate. Since we were denied access to official records we could not verify these statements about age and have retained the information given by the respondents. We aggregated the ages into three groups ranging from <22 years (frequency 114); from 23-30 (frequency 180); and >30 years (frequency 128). Age is everywhere correlated with delinquency and research in the US suggests that the peak age is from 15-25 after which there is a gradual decline in criminal behaviour (Hirschi and Gottfredson, 2000). The Indian data appears to conform to this pattern.

In terms of their residential place, there seems to be a mixed situation: there is somewhat a larger proportion from the city but the number from the rural areas is not insignificant either. There were 64 per cent from urban areas that do not seem to be in accordance with the 25.7 per cent of urban population in the country (Census of India, 2001). Perhaps this is reflective of the adverse impact of industrialization and urban growth being witnessed in the country. The choice of living in an urban or a rural area is likely to offer different opportunities and set of associates. In view of the fact that most educational institutions and employment opportunities lie in urban areas, seems to supplement the sample finding that urban living is being preferred by growing proportion of the population.

In terms of their educational background, an overwhelming majority had less than a High School certificate. A good number of the subjects were illiterate and lacked any formal education. Even for those who had attended some years in school or were beginners, it was clear from the interview that their ability to read and write was severely limited. Education of course plays an important role in criminal behaviour (Crutchfield, Bridges, Weis, and Kubrin, 1999). Education is not only a socializing effect but opens new avenues and imparts skills that can assist in finding jobs and building a stake in conformity. Schooling creates social bonds that may affect delinquent behaviour (Jenkins, 1997). Accordingly, we decided to consider the years of schooling in terms of the likelihood of imparting some skills and opening new avenues. The response category was thus sub-divided into four levels. The first category consists of those who had no schooling and described themselves as illiterates [n = 116]. The next level consists of those who had some formal schooling, till grade VI on the basis that they had some exposure to formal training but it was not complete [n = 61]. The third category is of people who have more schooling, from grade VII to High School [n = 106]. The last category consists of those who have studied beyond High School and have done either their Intermediate (senior high school) or some form of College [n = 139]. This group had a greater exposure to learning, was likely to pick some skills and knowledge and would have undergone greater socialization into conformity. Schooling or education did not appear to have a strong correlation with criminal behaviour.

Although criminologists have long debated about the effects of economic conditions on criminal behaviour but an enduring consensus appears to be that unemployment has positive correlation with crime. Moreover, it has been suggested that juvenile delinquency has correlation with later *adult* unemployment (Robin, 1966). It is a common observation that marginalized groups are over-represented in jobs with low pay, poor benefits and limited prospects for future. Crutchfield and Pittchford (1997) suggest that those who are not confident about retaining their jobs are more likely to have committed crimes. Accordingly, we were interested in determining the employment status of the respondents. From the job descriptions provided by the respondents we determined that 97 were clearly unemployed and jobless, 263 were engaged in jobs that require little formal education and were mostly labour oriented. There were 37 respondents whose jobs required some formal education and training. Unfortunately, not everyone gave sufficient details to determine their employment status and hence the remaining was designated as 'unemployed'.

We decided to classify the job variable into that of Unemployed [n = 110], Manual Worker [n = 144], Skilled Worker [n = 145] and White-Collar Worker [n = 23] since these classes indicate better the nature of work and opportunities associated with it.

The marital status is an important variable in the study of criminal behaviour. An unattached youth is likely to have fewer stakes in the society while a married person is expected to realize greater responsibility towards his family. Marital bonds are also expected to strengthen conformity towards established behaviour and restrict movement in both place and time. Accordingly, for us knowing this factor was important. The status was reported to be as Married [n = 234]; Unmarried [n = 185]. Widower [n = 2] and one did not declare anything. There were no divorcees in the sample.

Not only were most respondents from low socio-economic background but they also came from families where the parents had little or no formal education. We asked questions about the educational qualifications of their parents to probe this matter. It is expected that educated parents are more likely to ensure some education to their children and as we have mentioned above, greater education helps a person develop stake in conformity. Furthermore, educated parents may be more effective in the supervision of their children and perhaps more assertive in controlling their behaviour. Accordingly, the educational level of the parents becomes an important factor in this exploration. The results are as follows:

Educational Qualifications of Parents

	Father	Mother
Illiterate	206	287
Primary	61	59
High School	77	48
College	78	28

We asked one more question to ascertain their socio-economic status. This question concerned the approximate monthly income of the family and whether their imprisonment resulted in some decline in this family income. Clearly, family income plays a decisive role in maintaining the family, in providing educational opportunities, in meeting the basic needs and other wants of the members and even determining the association with other people. We expect income variable to be an important factor in explaining the etiology of crime and categorized it in the following four ordinal levels:

Monthly Family Income

Income	No. of Respondents
Less than ₹ 1000/month	119
Between 1000 and Less than ₹ 3000/month	118
Between 3000 and Less than ₹ 5000/month	76
More than ₹ 5000/month	109

Religious belief and associated practices plays an important role in determining the behaviour of the person in India. It not only places one into a specific mode of conduct but also determines who the associates and acquaintances will be. Furthermore, religion plays an important function in adhering to a moral conduct and in restraining behaviour for fear of divine consequences. In words respondents indicated that they follow the Hindu religion; there were 42 Muslims, 2 Sikhs, 1 Christian and 12 refused to answer. Considering that in India around 85 per cent of the population follows the Hindu religion and Muslims constitute 12 per cent, Sikhs and Christians perhaps 1 per cent each, the above break-up appears to conform to the general population distribution without any one religion having unusually high or low representation. Of course religion may not be an important variable for what is important is the degree of adherence to religious beliefs and practices. However, in such a limited study it was difficult to measure this factor.

We asked one more question regarding the size of the family. This seems to be an important consideration in the etiology of criminal behaviour since large family size may reduce family income and control exercised on the respondents. In words respondents stated their family size to be greater than 9 members including themselves. It is not only the family size but also the influence of family members that perhaps pushes or pulls a person to or away from crime. We were particularly interested to know if there were any family members who had themselves been arrested and prosecuted. We wanted to assess the influence that they may have had upon the criminal activities of the respondents. Criminality of any family member or friend is an important factor in drawing a person into the life of crime. Sutherland's proposition that criminal behaviour is learned within intimate personal groups and that this learning takes place in close association, where not only the tricks of the trade but also the justification for criminal actions are learnt (Sutherland, Cressey and Luckenbill, 1992), was likely to come from close family members and friends. Altogether 278 respondents indicated that they had criminal associates [of which 68 stated they had some family member arrested in a criminal case one time or the other]. This variable was named 'Criminal Associate' and dichotomized in Yes and No categories.

Our last query was about the nature of crime committed by the respondent for which he had been imprisoned. According to the criminal statutes, offenses are categorized as those against the state, the body and property. Indian Penal Code of 1860 is the basic statute covering a majority of the offenses but there are many special laws too that cover areas like demanding dowry, bearing arms and social offenses against the weaker sections. In order to summarize these legal definitions of crime types in more understandable terms, we aggregated them into three classes: of property, physical and miscellaneous crimes. As the labels suggest, property crimes include offenses like theft (all kinds), robbery, extortion, dacoity (or its preparation), pick-pocketing, forgery, cheating and dealing in stolen property. The physical offenses include murder (and its attempt), assaults, rape, kidnapping, affray, rioting, etc. The rest, like the offenses under the arms act, prostitution, smuggling, drug related and such were classified as miscellaneous types. Under such a categorization the frequency of offenders for these three crime types is summarized in table given below:

Property Offenses	=	138
Physical Body Offenses	=	251
Miscellaneous Offenses	=	33

Reasons for Criminal Behaviour

The reasons for committing crimes were not answered directly in a straightforward manner and in many cases the respondents gave more than one explanation. The various reasons mentioned were enmity and association with 'bad-companions'; disputes, domestic problems, anger, feeling of revenge or rivalry; greed, lust or need for money; influence of alcohol, drugs and intoxicants; influence of associates, family members, dispute over land, property, girl, politics, to being dragged into crime by various circumstances. Some acknowledged that an opportunity to commit a crime or such behaviour becoming almost like a profession, or the 'fun' of action had been their reasons. A few also stated the desire for money; involvement with a girl, business interests, and poverty and unemployment problems initiated them into crime. Many stated that they were 'dragged' into the crime. This may have come from situational factors like old enmity or association with disreputable characters that initiated police suspicion towards these respondents. However, in this we need to acknowledge that a good proportion (11.4%) of the respondents resolutely indicated that they were falsely implicated in the incident or charged for a major crime, which was not the true incident. There seems little reason to disbelieve these assertions. The reputation of the police in India to act with probity is not very high (Verma, 2000) and false implications are possible. We noted every reason mentioned by each of the respondents and then determined a main reason under a broader classification that best characterized the situation.

Quite clearly, a desire to *gain* money or property directly or by availing of an opportunity seems a common denominator of some of these statements. Similarly, *dispute* is another important factor that describes reasons such as enmity, rivalry, jealousy, and conflict over property, land, caste and arising from involvement with a girl and even politics. Another common denominator appears to be *lack-of-control* that is underlying the influence of alcohol, drug, peer-pressure, mental problem, and involvement with a gang, fun, etc. There were some statements that suggest *bad association* to be a major reason. This variable covers reasons such as bad company, family influence, gang membership and so on. We also included a factor described as *dragged* that describes the situation wherein the respondent felt he was unintentionally drawn into the act due to fear, friendship, family matters or even false accusation. Clearly, this drag may have come due to one or more of the reasons described above such as bad-company, enmity or rivalry. Nevertheless, the respondents themselves asserted that they were not motivated to commit the act and did not feel guilty of crime. We believe that their belief needs to be mentioned since the Indian criminal justice system has serious defects (Verma, 2005). There is a fair possibility of false accusations and other situations exist that can get an innocent person involved in a criminal case. We decided to honor this situational causality through a separate category. Accordingly, we developed five distinct types of reasons given by the respondents and categorized them based upon the main reason stated by them. These categories and associated numbers are summarized below:

Reasons	Number of Respondents
Bad Association	77
Dispute	147
Dragged	50
Gain	79
Lack-of-Control	69

Since the objective of this research is to explore the reasons why people commit crime this variable 'Reason' is our dependent variable—nominal in five categories.

Analysis

Our interest was in developing a model that could explain the dependent variable in terms of the social-economic and demographic variables described earlier. But before developing our model we examined different forms of association and tested bi-variate relationships to determine and select the most important independent variables.

Inter-variable Correlations

We examined the bi-variate correlations amongst the variables to determine meaningful associations. The analysis suggested that respondents' education, parent's education, marital status and number of family members in the house are not significantly correlated with the 'Reasons' for criminal behaviour. However, father's education has relationship with employment status and family income, which have significant relations with the reasons for crime and hence we decided to retain these variables in the model.

We also explored the bi-variate relations through cross-tabulations. Our interest was in exploring if there is any inter-dependent relationship between the independent variables like age group, income and others with the dependent variable of reasons for criminal behaviour. The following are the statistically significant results of cross-tabulating the variable 'Reasons' with five other variables:

Contingency Table Results

Cross-tab with 'Reasons'

	F Educ.	Place	Employment	Age	Income	Crim. Assoc.	Crime-Type
Chi.sq:	21.97	32.64	33.15	16.56	34.83	59.68	73.964
df	12	4	12	8	12	4	8
p-value	0.038	0.000	0.001	0.035	0.000	0.000	0.000

The above results suggest a close relationship between the 'Reasons' for criminal behaviour and the respondents' family income, employment status, place of residence (urban or rural), age group and quite obviously bad association. We also found that father's educational level is a much better predictor than mother's education level or even a combined variable created to reflect parental educational status. Sarvate (2000) argues that Indian families are strongly patriarchal and the father plays a dominant role in the family. Accordingly, we decided to use this as an independent variable. Naturally, the type of crime committed (body, property or other kinds) adds to the explanation of the dependent variable. These variables can therefore be used as explanatory factors in the multinomial model that we now describe below. Religion and family size (not reported above) did not provide a significant relationship and were dropped from the model.

Accordingly, we decided to model the relationship with age [A], employment [EM], father's education [FE], family income [I], bad association [CA], place of residence [P] and types of crimes committed [T] as the independent variables. Considering that the dependent variable of 'reason for criminal behaviour' [R] is a nominal variable and some of the independent variables are also of nominal category, the best equation to model this relationship is the Multinomial Logit function. Our equation (and model) is of the form

R = f [A, EM, FE, I, CA, P, T].

Multinomial Logit Function [MLF]

MLF is the most generalized probability model to handle explanatory (independent) variables that can range from the highest data type [continuous or interval category] to different categories of the lower types like nominal or ordinal types. The mathematical model is derived as follows:

Let $p_i(x_i)$ denote the probability of response j, j = 1, ..., J, at the ith setting of values of k explanatory variables $x_i = (1, x_{il}, \ldots, x_{ik})$. In terms of the response probabilities, the generalized Multinomial Logit model is given by:

$$p_i(x_i) = [\exp(b_j x_i)] / [\Sigma_1^J \{\exp(b_j x_i)\}] \quad \ldots A$$

This reduces to $\log \{[p_j(x_i)]/[p_J(x_i)]\} = b_j x_i$ for j = 1, ..., J-1.

Here a separate parameter vector applies for each of the J-1 non-redundant Logit equations. To obtain the ML estimates [the b_is] the independent multinomial likelihood is maximized subject to the constraints of equation 'A'. 'The parameter estimates have large sample normal distributions with asymptotic standard errors that are obtained from the inverse of the data matrix. An iterative process like the Newton-Raphson's method is used to determine these estimates' (Agresti, 1990: 313). The computations are quite complex and a computer software program: SPSS was used to estimate them. The results of this Multinomial Logit Regression modeling are as follows:

Results

Model-2	Log Likelihood	Chi-Square	df	Sig.
Intercept Only	1131.309			
Final	887.159	244.150	60	.000

The Pearson value of this goodness of fit measure [1122.033] is also statistically significant at a p-value of 0.002. Cox and Snell's value indicate a variance explanation of 43.9 per cent while Nagelkerke unit suggests it is almost 46.0 per cent. This also indicates that the set of independent variables are able to explain a substantial proportion of the variance of the dependent variable.

Likelihood Ratio Tests

Effect	-2 Log Likelihood of Reduced Model	Chi-Square	df Sig.
Intercept	897.977	.000	0
Employment	902.361	15.202	12.231
F' Education	905.055	17.896	12.119
F' Income	910.300	21.141	12.027*
Bad Association	928.787	41.628	4.000**
Place of residence	908.648	21.489	4.000**
Age	916.149	28.982	8.000**
Types of Crime	928.166	41.007	8.000**
* p < 5% and ** p < 1%			

The Chi-Square statistic is the difference in -2 log-likelihood between the final model and a reduced model. The reduced model is formed by omitting an effect from the final model. The null hypothesis is that all parameters of that effect are 0. From the above table, it is clear that except for the variables of 'Employment' and 'Father's Education' the rest are statistically significant. However, as seen in Table 1 these two variables do provide statistically significant results for some of the sub-categories of the dependent variable.

Interpretation

The derived parameters suggest a clear relationship between the levels of explanatory variables and those of the dependent variable. Table 1 provides the summary of variables, parameter estimates and their significance.

Table 1

Parameter Estimates							
	N = 422	B	Std. Error	Wald	df	Sig.	Exp(B)
Reasons							
Bad Association Intercept	-19.357	1.293	224.152	1	0		
	[EM=1]	17.801	0.659	729.473	1	.000**	5.30E+06
	[EM=2]	17.132	0.556	948.474	1	.000**	2.70E+06
	[EM=3]	16.742	0	.	1	.	1.80E+06
	[EM=4]	0	.	.	0	.	.
	[FE=1]	1.65	0.736	5.031	1	.025*	5.209
	[FE=2]	-0.299	0.868	0.119	1	0.731	0.742
	[FE=3]	0.655	0.761	0.740	1	0.39	1.925
	[FE=4]	0	.	.	0	.	.

	[I=1]	-0.728	0.699	1.083	1	0.298	0.483
	[I=2]	-0.999	0.661	2.282	1	0.131	0.368
	[I=3]	-0.215	0.785	0.075	1	0.784	0.807
	[I=4]	0	.	.	0	.	.
	[CA=1]	3.018	0.558	29.307	1	.000**	20.458
	[CA=2]	0	.	.	0	.	.
	[P=1]	0.381	0.481	0.626	1	0.429	1.464
	[P=2]	0	.	.	0	.	.
	[A=1.00]	1.549	0.59	6.896	1	.009**	4.706
	[A=2.00]	2.052	0.601	11.647	1	.001**	7.78
	[A=3.00]	0	.	.	0	.	.
	[T=1.00]	-1.233	0.959	1.655	1	0.198	0.291
	[T=2.00]	-0.923	0.992	0.867	1	0.352	0.397
	[T=3.00]	0	.	.	0	.	.
Gain	Intercept	-1.134	1.275	0.792	1	0.374	
	[EM=1]	1.596	1.083	2.174	1	0.14	4.935
	[EM=2]	1.027	1.017	1.021	1	0.312	2.794
	[EM=3]	0.768	1.014	0.573	1	0.449	2.155
	[EM=4]	0	.	.	0	.	.
	[FE=1]	1.017	0.686	2.201	1	0.138	2.765
	[FE=2]	-0.499	0.809	0.38	1	0.538	0.607
	[FE=3]	-7.51E-02	0.743	0.01	1	0.92	0.928
	[FE=4]	0	.	.	0	.	.
	[I=1]	-0.466	0.71	0.431	1	0.511	0.627
	[I=2]	-0.452	0.654	0.478	1	0.489	0.636
	[I=3]	0.492	0.757	0.422	1	0.516	1.636
	[I=4]	0	.	.	0	.	.
	[CA=1]	1.606	0.457	12.35	1	.000**	4.985
	[CA=2]	0	.	.	0	.	.
	[P=1]	-1.141	0.496	5.295	1	.021*	0.319
	[P=2]	0	.	.	0	.	.
	[A=1.00]	0.389	0.574	0.459	1	0.498	1.475
	[A=2.00]	1.67	0.584	8.171	1	.004**	5.312
	[A=3.00]	0	.	.	0	.	.
	[T=1.00]	-1.489	0.931	2.555	1	0.11	0.226
	[T=2.00]	-0.197	0.957	0.042	1	0.837	0.821
	[T=3.00]	0	.	.	0	.	.
Lack Control	Intercept	-0.392	1.178	0.111	1	0.739	
	[EM=1]	0.679	0.941	0.52	1	0.471	1.971
	[EM=2]	0.58	0.832	0.486	1	0.486	1.787
	[EM=3]	0.608	0.834	0.531	1	0.466	1.836
	[EM=4]	0	.	.	0	.	.
	[FE=1]	1.363	0.694	3.852	1	.050*	3.907
	[FE=2]	0.453	0.765	0.35	1	0.554	1.573
	[FE=3]	0.698	0.706	0.98	1	0.322	2.01
	[FE=4]	0	.	.	0	.	.
	[I=1]	-1.987	0.693	8.224	1	.004**	0.137
	[I=2]	-2.015	0.647	9.716	1	.002**	0.133

	[I=3]	-0.421	0.725	0.338	1	0.561	0.656
	[I=4]	0	.	.	0	.	.
	[CA=1]	1.206	0.443	7.413	1	.006**	3.341
	[CA=2]	0	.	.	0	.	.
	[P=1]	-1.101	0.487	5.108	1	.024*	0.332
	[P=2]	0	.	.	0	.	.
	[A=1.00]	-4.57E-02	0.57	0.006	1	0.936	0.955
	[A=2.00]	1.341	0.567	5.587	1	.018*	3.824
	[A=3.00]	0	.	.	0	.	.
	[T=1.00]	-0.252	0.967	0.068	1	0.795	0.778
	[T=2.00]	-3.29E-02	1.012	0.001	1	0.974	0.968
	[T=3.00]	0	.	.	0	.	.
Dispute Intercept		-0.28	1.084	0.067	1	0.797	
	[EM=1]	1.189	0.767	2.404	1	0.121	3.283
	[EM=2]	0.302	0.629	0.231	1	0.631	1.353
	[EM=3]	9.93E-02	0.675	0.022	1	0.883	1.104
	[EM=4]	0	.	.	0	.	.
	[FE=1]	0.907	0.614	2.183	1	0.14	2.476
	[FE=2]	0.61	0.65	0.88	1	0.348	1.841
	[FE=3]	0.485	0.641	0.574	1	0.449	1.625
	[FE=4]	0	.	.	0	.	.
	[I=1]	-0.342	0.604	0.321	1	0.571	0.71
	[I=2]	-0.938	0.567	2.735	1	0.098	0.391
	[I=3]	-6.55E-03	0.689	0	1	0.992	0.993
	[I=4]	0	.	.	0	.	.
	[CA=1]	0.911	0.379	5.79	1	.016*	2.486
	[CA=2]	0	.	.	0	.	.
	[P=1]	3.97E-02	0.384	0.011	1	0.918	1.04
	[P=2]	0	.	.	0	.	.
	[A=1.00]	1.16E-03	0.5	0	1	0.998	1.001
	[A=2.00]	1.603	0.506	10.024	1	.002*	4.97
	[A=3.00]	0	.	.	0	.	.
	[T=1.00]	3.13E-02	0.911	0.001	1	0.973	1.032
	[T=2.00]	-0.846	0.966	0.767	1	0.381	0.429
	[T=3.00]	0	.	.	0	.	.
Base: 'Dragged'	* p < 5% and ** p < 1%						

Considering the multinomial Logit model involves categorical data analysis, the results have to be interpreted in terms of probability values. The table uses the last category of each variable as the base for comparison purposes. For instance, in the case of the dependent variable 'Reasons for committing the crime' the category 'Dragged' is used as the base while for the explanatory variables, the highest level is the base with which other levels are compared. We have highlighted the statistically significant results in the table and we will interpret the results for these cases only.

For the category of Bad Association, level 1 of father's education (that he is illiterate) is a significant result in comparison to level 4 (that he is college educated). This implies that the log odds of a person committing crime due to a bad associate in comparison to being dragged into criminal behaviour is greater by a value of 1.65 for the case when the father is illiterate than when he is college educated. This suggests that a more educated father is perhaps able to control his son and prevent him falling into a life of crime even if he has some relatives or friends who are criminals. The other significant results for this category are that of employment, bad association and age. Clearly, being unemployed or engaged only in manual, low paying jobs entices people to commit crimes much more in comparison to those having some kind of white collar job (the base category). It makes sense to also observe that those having bad association are more likely to get involved in criminal behaviour. The age factor also suggests that bad association is more important for those between the ages of 22-30 than the younger ones. Perhaps with growing age a person learns to develop more lasting associations.

For the reason of 'Gain' living in urban areas show significant results. It appears that growing urbanization creates opportunities for crimes that are intensified with criminal association especially for those in the age group of 22-30 years. Most young people of this age are forced to seek jobs in urban areas in view of declining economic opportunities in rural areas. These young men are generally by themselves and face declining family supervision. It is likely that they get involved with criminal associates who induce them to seek illegal gains. All these factors show significant odds for the reason of 'Gain' for committing crimes.

The reason 'Lack Control' has slight significant result for father's low educational status (p-value 0.050). This seems to make sense since an illiterate father (level 1) is unlikely to understand the activities of his children. This lack of supervision may encourage the children to experiment and give vent to their desires. Experimentation with alcohol, drugs and sexual pursuits are some of the more specific reasons within this category and it seems to fit in with the notion that in a family, where the father is unable to provide discipline, children are unlikely to control themselves and will fall into criminal ways. In addition, the significant results of low income (levels 1 & 2) and bad association both point towards the situation where social control is less, the family is in dire circumstances and criminal friends are inducements towards illegal and ill-advised experimentation. That the results are significant for young people between the age group of 22-30, living in urban area as compared to rural regions is again in conformity to the expectations.

Finally, the reason of 'dispute' has largely to do with conflicts of different kinds. The respondents have described these as arising from family problems, land ownership, caste and clan feuds and enmity with some people, especially due to gang affiliations. The significant results for the variables of young age (level 2), bad association and (slightly) for family income (level 2, p-value <1%) appear to draw the respondents into this situation. Disputes are common in any situation, but young age and bad association can get a young person into serious conflicts.

Discussion and Conclusion

Based upon the analysis of the data as described above we are now in a position to empirically comment upon the objectives of the research. Our first hypothesis was that large economically deprived families where parents do not have sufficient education create circumstances that encourage deviant behaviour. Our second hypothesis was that neglected childhood is a major factor in falling into criminal behaviour. This is similar to the assertion that criminal association generally develops for those growing up in low socio-economic status families. Although, the analysis suggests that family size is not a significant factor but income is undoubtedly a major factor in criminal behaviour. Since income is expected to be related to the attainment of higher education it follows that the underlying cause of criminal behaviour of the respondents is definitely linked to their poor educational status. Considering that 283 respondents (67%) had at most, only a few years of schooling, suggests that it pays for the Indian society to educate its children since it provides marketable skills and helps wean them away from a life of crime.

We could also explore these assertions by examining the educational standards of the father of the respondents. Our belief is that uneducated guardians are unlikely to discipline and supervise their children especially if their economic conditions are desperate too. The poverty and absence of any learning initiative would have caused neglect in the upbringing of the children and making them easy prey to delinquent behaviour. This hypothesis appears supported by the fact that the percentage whose parents had at most primary education and whose income was less than ₹ 1000 per month form 16.8 per cent of the sample. In comparison, the group of respondents whose parents were well educated (college level) and had high family income (> ₹ 5000 per month) were only 11, a mere 2.2 per cent of the sample. It is significant that of these 11 respondents, 9 were involved in body type crimes (6 murders) and 5 of them cited dispute or being dragged in the case as their reason for criminal behaviour. Their criminality appears to be related to old standing disputes and questions of family honor. This suggests that better-educated parents are more likely to supervise and prevent their children from getting involved in serious property crimes though not in family related feuds.

Our next set of hypotheses suggested the failure of the criminal justice system in pushing the people into crime. The hypotheses suggest that criminal association leads to labeling effect and the failure of the justice system to provide speedy justice makes it difficult to get out of criminal behaviour and perhaps forces people to take to criminal acts. The survey amply supports these hypotheses since a very large number of respondents have complained about being 'dragged' into the case. Most of these respondents refused to consider themselves as criminal so perhaps the labeling effect had not taken *permanent roots* but they were vociferous in their assertions that they had not committed the crimes for which they were charged. Moreover, the fact that 'dispute' was cited as a major reason seems to suggest that failures of the justice system in resolving conflicts pushed many to indulge in criminal acts. In our discussions the respondents argued that they had to commit the crime (attack or even kill their opponent) or otherwise they (or their family) were themselves at risk of harm. These conflicts appear to have been going on for many years and were related to land, property, rivalries and other kinds of mutual antagonism. The failure of the system to quickly resolve them within the institutional framework appears to have pushed many to find their own solutions with disastrous effects.

It is also noteworthy that only 36 per cent (154 out of 422) reported not having any criminal association. The large majority reported links with family and friends who were engaged in criminal activities and this clearly affected the respondents. Many stated that they were dragged into the case because of their links with these criminal associates. Accordingly, having association with those who act criminally is also a strong reason for criminal behaviour.

Our next hypothesis is suggestive of the weakening of the traditional bonds that hold a person to the norms of the society. The rapid socio-economic and demographic changes that are occurring in the country, especially the culture of consumerism to us appeared to be an important factor in tempting people to act illegally. The artificial desires created by advertisements and the inability of a large number of people to satisfy these desires seemed to drive many towards illegal acquisition of property. The statements about desires for material goods and lack of family supervision suggest to us some of the ill effects of India's economic policies. The ubiquitous advertisements for a consumerist life style, loosening of bonds due to a developing economy appear to have an adverse effect on young impressionable people. Many respondents, especially younger ones expressed clear desires for quick gains. The fact that many were living away from immediate family and developed association with those already engaged in criminal activities seemed to support this conclusion. The desire to acquire money, property or avail an opportunity was frequently mentioned as one the reasons for their crimes. Even in cases where criminal association or being dragged into a case was given as the first reason, the respondents did agree that lure of money was still one of the underlying reasons. The ill effects of alcohol, drugs and sexual drives, especially in combination appear to have been quite devastating. Not surprisingly, in our sample the percentage of respondents whose primary reasons were 'gain' or 'lack-of-control' was seen to be around 40 per cent.

Our final observation from this study has been that severe socio-economic circumstances and failures of the justice system to control social conflicts are important causes that stand beneath a large proportion of deviant behaviours in the country. The acute poverty and the lack of education not only deny entry into legitimate pursuits but it also implies a lack of supervision and discipline during the formative years. Most of the respondents mentioned anger, jealousy, feeling of revenge and enmity as the driving force in their criminal activities. The lack of any institutional system that could deal with these at the initial stage and resolve conflicts appear to be responsible for driving many towards adopting illegal actions. Most of the respondents also displayed extreme anger towards the police and justice officials. A majority did not even contemplate going to the justice officials to seek redress. It seemed clear, and many indeed stated in no uncertain terms that after coming out of the prison they were again going back to a life of crime since their enemies would not let them live otherwise.

The fact that an overwhelming majority of the respondents came from poor, economically disadvantaged background also seems to support the perception that the Indian Criminal Justice System targets only those at the bottom rung of the ladder. The fact that there were only 5 respondents with a postgraduate degree, only 15 who had well established jobs appear to confirm that the vast number of people being processed by the police and judiciary come from low socio-economic background. Obviously, criminal behaviour is not an innate trait of that class of people who find themselves at the bottom. Only 17 respondents (4%) mentioned poverty as one of their reasons for committing the crimes. Clearly, despite the fact that vast majorities of Indian people are poor, they are not contemplating crime as a means of sustenance. Most do believe that this is undesirable and should not be done. Yet, if the jails are filled with people from low socio-economic strata, then it reflects more about official practices than reasons for breaking the law. The Indian authorities need to pay attention to these findings and examine the actions of the police and criminal justice agencies more carefully.

References

Agresti, A. (1990). *Categorical Data Analysis*. New York: John Wiley & Sons.

Baldwin, J. and Bottoms, A.E. (1976). *The Urban Criminal*. London: Tavistock.

Bhaduri, T.C. (1972). *Chambal: The Valley of Terror.* Delhi: Vikas Pub. House.

Brantingham, P.J. and Brantingham, P.L. (1991). *Environmental Criminology.* Prospect Heights, IL: Waveland Press.

Census of India. (2001). http://www.censusindia.net/

Cloward, R.A. and Ohlin, L.E. (1960). *Delinquency and Opportunity: A Theory of Delinquent Gangs*. New York: Free Press.

Cohen, A.K. (1955). *Delinquent Gangs: The Culture of the Gang*. Glencoe Il.: Free Press.

Crutchfield, R.D. and Pittchford, S. (1997). "Work and Crime: The Effects of Labor Stratification". *Social Forces,* 76, 93-118.

Crutchfield, R.D., Bridges, G.S., Weis, J.G. and Kubrin, C. (Eds.) (2000). *Crime Readings*. Thousands Oaks, Ca.: Pine Fore Press.

Durkheim, E. (1951). *Suicide*. Translation by John A. Spaulding and George Simpson edited by George Simpson. New York: The Free Press.

Fetchenhauer, D. and Simon, J. (1998). An experimental test of Gottfredson and Hirschi's 'general theory of crime'. *Monatsschrift fuer Kriminologie und Strafrechtsreform,* 81(5), 301-15.

Hall, J. (1960). *General Principles of Criminal Law* (2nd Ed.) Indianapolis: Bobbs Merrill.

Hartjen, C.A. and Kethineni, S. (1996). *Comparative Delinquency: India and the United States.* New York: Garland Publishing Inc.

Hirschi, T. and Gottfredson, M. (2000). "Age and the Explanation of Crime". In R.D. Crutchfield., G.S. Bridges., J.G. Weis and C. Kubrin. (Eds.), *Crime Readings* (pp. 138-41). Thousands Oaks, Ca.: Pine Fore Press.

Indermaur, D. (1999). "Situational prevention of violent crime: theory and practice in Australia". *Studies on Crime and Crime Prevention,* 8(1), 71-87.

Jatar, D.P. (1980). *The Problem of Dacoity in Bundelkhand and the Chambal Valley.* New Delhi: S. Chand.

Jenkins, P.H. (1997). "School Delinquency and the School Social Bond". *Journal of Research in Crime and Delinquency,* 34(3), 337-67.

Katare, S.S. (1972). *Patterns of Dacoity in India: A Case Study of Madhya Pradesh*. New Delhi: S. Chand.

Khan, M.Z. (1981). *Dacoity in Chambal Valley*. New Delhi: National Publishing House.

Lobo, J. (1992). *Leaves From a Policeman's Diary*. New Delhi: Allied Publishers.

Madhok, S. (1998). "Gender bias, infanticide bane of Indian Women". *The Tribune*, June 19. Retrieved on 28th May 2008 from http://www.tribuneindia.com/50yrs/women.htm#3.

Matza, D. (1969). *Becoming Deviant*. Englewoods Cliffs, NJ: Prentice Hall.

Merton, R.K. (1968). *Social Theory and Social Structure*. Glencoe, Illinois: The Free Press.

Mohanty, S. (1990). *Crimes and Criminals in India: A Socio-Economic Survey*. New Delhi: Ashish Publishing House.

Nayar, B.R. (1975). *Violence and Crime in India: A Quantitative Study*. Delhi: Macmillan.

Paternoster, R. and Brame, R. (1998). "The structural similarity of processes generating criminal and analogous behaviors". *Criminology*, 36(3), 633-69.

Phulia, S.S. (1992). *Criminology: A Psychological and Anthropological Analysis*. Delhi: Friends Publications.

Robin, L.N. (1966). *Deviant Children Grown Up: A Sociological and Psychiatric Study of Sociopathic Personality*. Baltimore: Williams & Wilkins.

Sarvate, S. (2000). "Patriarchy and Landlordism". *Asian Week*, February 24, 21(26). Retrieved on 28th May 2008 from www.asianweek.com/2000_02_24/opinion_voices_sarvate.html.

Sellin, T. (1938). *Culture, Conflict and Crime*. New York: Social Science Research Council.

Shah, G. (1992). *The Indian Police: A Retrospect*. Bombay: Himalayan Publishing House.

Shamashastry, R. (1929). *Kautilya's Arthashastra* (Tr.). Mysore: Wesleyn Press.

Shaw, C. and McKay, H.D. (1942). *Delinquency and Urban Areas*. Chicago: University of Chicago Press.

Shukla, K.S. (1982). "Juvenile Delinquency in India: Research Trends and Priorities". *Indian Journal of Criminology and Criminalistics*, 2, 103-13.

Simhadri, Y.C. (1991). *Denotified Tribes: A Sociological Analysis*. Delhi: Classical Publishing House.

Somerville, A. (2000). *Crime and Religious Beliefs in India.* London: Laurier Books.

Sukla, S. (1987). *Pracina Bharata mem Aparadha aura Danda* [In Hindi]. Kanpur: Praja Prakasana.

Sutherland, E., Cressey, D.R. and Luckenbill, D.F. (1992). *Principles of Criminology* (11th Ed.) New York: General Hall Inc.

Thakur, B. (1980). *Urban Settlements in Eastern India: Entropy Changes and Pattern Analysis.* New Delhi: Concept.

Tihar Prison. (2001). *Prisoner's Profile.* Retrieved on 28th May 2008 from http://tiharprisons.nic.in.

Thilagaraj, R. (1987). "Goal Perceptions of Delinquents and Non-Delinquents: A Comparative Study". *Indian Journal of Criminology,* 2, 145-48.

United Nations Development Fund. (2008). *Human Development Report 2008.* Retrieved on 28th May 2008 from http://www.undp.org/hdro/report.html.

Upadhyaya, V. (1978). *A Study of Hindu Criminology.* Delhi: Chaukhambha Orientalia.

Verma, A. (2000). "Lies, Damn Lies and Police Statistics". *Indian Police Journal,* XLVI (2-3), 29-36.

——. (2005). *Indian Police: A Critical Evaluation.* Delhi: Regency Publications.

Voss, H.L. and Petersen, D.M. (1971). *Ecology, Crime and Delinquency.* New York: Appleton.

Weinstein, J.A. (1974). *Madras: An Analysis of Urban Ecological Structure in India.* Beverly Hills, Calif.: Sage Publications.

Wikstrom, P-O. H. (1991). *Urban Crime, Criminals, and Victims: The Swedish Experience in an Anglo-American Comparative Perspective.* New York: Springer-Verlag.

Yang, A.A. (Ed.). (1985). *Crime and Criminality in British India.* Tucson, Arizona: University of Arizona Press.

SECTION FOUR

INNOVATIONS IN CORRECTIONS

kinds of exploitation and 61 cases pertained to trafficking in children (NHRC, 2007).

The other cases registered were related to disappearance, death in juvenile/observation homes, sexual harassment/abuse, rape etc. While dealing with these cases, the Commission has awarded a total compensation of ₹ 47,20,000 to children who were victims of different kinds of violations (Bakhru, 2006, [illegible] Reddy) on 20th April 2009. The National Human Rights Commission has recommended the Uttar Pradesh government to pay ₹ [illegible],000 as monetary relief to the bereaved mother who [illegible]

[illegible] administrators. Treatment of an offender in the community under the supervision of a professional correctional worker is more effective and cheaper than in institutions. Moreover, community participation in the prevention of crime and the treatment of offenders is ensured through this method of treatment and the problem of rehabilitation of offenders minimized to a considerable extent. In India, the probation program has been implemented in almost all states and Union Territories. However, the progress does not seem to be very encouraging although several years have already elapsed (Bhattacharyya, 1986).

Glueck (1964) opined that the characteristic feature of probation, which distinguishes it from the other crime-treating institutions so far invented, is that it enables the offender to remain in the community but at the same time to be under control and guidance. Custodial treatment removes the offender from his family and community and suspends his social and economic obligations to them. He becomes, indeed, a burden upon society. Probation extracks from the offender a contribution within the limits of his capacity, to the well-being of others, whether it is through his useful employment in the community or through his participation in the life of the family or other social group. In doing so, it minimizes the economic and social disruption causes

12

Open Prisons in India

Tumpa Mukherjee and P. Periakaruppan

Introduction

Open prison, also known as wall-less camps or minimum security prisons are different from the maximum security prisons with respect to administration, relationship structure, role system, normative system, and value system. An open prison is a prison which is open to prisoners, open in organization, open to security, and open to the public (Cole, Smith and Christopher, 2002). Open to prisoners' means that the prisoners are relatively free in the open campus. Open in an organization means that there are no strict rules to be followed by the prisoners regarding work, food, relationships, etc. Instead, they have to determine their own work and have to follow their own rules (Peterson, 1960). This is based on the ideas of self-responsibility and self-discipline. Open in security means that the prisons are so structured that there is complete absence of precautions against escape (Cole, Smith and Christopher, 2002). There are no doors, no windows and no bars and the inmates live freely in a village-type environment. Open to the public means that people from outside can visit the prison freely. They need not seek permission from prison officials for visiting the prisons and to talk to the inmates (Peterson, 1960).

Open prison, for the first time, was discussed in the 12th Penal and Penitentiary Congress held in 1950 at The Hague. Deliberating upon the possibility of replacing the traditional prisons by open prisons, it designed some major broad premises for setting up open penal institutions. The First United Nations Congress on the Prevention of Crime and the Treatment of

Offenders held at Geneva in 1955 deliberated upon the formal and operational structure of the open penal and correctional institutions (United Nations, 1955; Vibhute, 2005). The First UN Congress was convinced that minimum security and self-discipline of inmates of open institution be accepted as the fundamentals of open correctional institutions (Cole, Smith and Christopher, 2002; Vibhute, 2005). Believing that open correctional institutions, by providing inmates better opportunity for interaction with free community, has better potential in achieving the goal of reformation and rehabilitation. The First UN Congress appealed all the Nations to set up open peno-correctional institutions (United Nations, 1955). It also formulated a set of broad guiding principles for the administration of open penal institutions. These principles are still considered highly relevant in the administration of open peno-correctional institutions (Peterson, 1960; Vibhute, 2005).

An open prison differs from a closed prison in its philosophy and administration. The former is based on trust, self-help, constructive work, social usefulness, sense of dignity, and positive attitude of the prisoners towards the free community. The basic justification of open prison as put forward by Sir Alexander Peterson (1960) is: 'You cannot train a man for freedom under conditions of captivity.' An open prison unlike a closed prison emphasizes reformation, social rehabilitation and re-assimilation of its inmates, and relieves its inmates from the constant head-counts, inspections, and discipline. On the other hand, a traditional closed prison is dominated by the 'lock psychosis' and suspicious attitude towards its inmates (Peterson, 1960; Vibhute, 2005).

Since independence, a number of prison reform committees have been appointed by the state governments. There was a report on the prison administration in India by the U.N. expert, Dr. W.C. Reckless in 1951-52. A working group in 1973 suggested that the government should make effective use of alternatives to imprisonment as a policy. Emphasis was placed in starting open prisons. The All India Committee on Prison Reforms (1980 chaired by the Justice A.N. Mulla) popularly known as the Mulla Committee Report states that the camp movement should be developed as a positive measure of correctional treatment (Government of India, 1983). The inmates in open institutions should be granted liberal facilities for functional literacy, recreational and cultural activities, community participation, visit to neighbouring towns for marketing purposes, continued contacts with family, remission leaves and premature release. Before being transferred to an open institution, prisoners should be oriented about the requirements and responsibilities of living in such an institution. Prison offences and punishments for inmates in the open institutions should be separately defined. Inmates not abiding by the rules of the open institution should be sent back to closed prison. Model rules laying down minimum standard for open institutions should be framed (Government of India, 1983).

The open prisons in India have been created with the following manifest and latent objectives: (1) to provide dependable and permanent labour for public projects; (2) to reduce overcrowding in prisons; (3) to reward good behaviour; (4) to give training in self-reliance and self-trust; (5) to examine the suitability of releasing the offenders from the prison; (6) to prevent frustration and create hope in long-termers; and (7) to provide training in agricultural fields which is not possible in the ordinary prisons.

The first open prison in India was established in Uttar Pradesh (U.P.) in October 1952 in Varanasi district under the guidance of the then Chief Minister, Late Dr. Sampuranand. It was established with an idea of providing dependable and permanent labour from the construction of a dam over Chandraprabha River (Ghosh, 1992). About 2,000 prisoners were brought from different districts to Varanasi Prison and from there they were taken by trucks and buses to the site of the dam without any police escort. They were paid wages like ordinary labourers. After the completion of this dam in October 1953, the prisoners were shifted to another camp in the same district for constructing a dam over the Karnasa River. The third open camp was established in Shahbad village in Pillibhit district in U.P. for digging a 13 mile long canal. Some prisoners in U.P. have worked in these open campus or prisons from 1952 till 1985.

After the success of the open prisons in U.P., similar prisons were gradually established in other states too. These States according to the regions are:

1. North India: U.P. (1952), Punjab (1959), Himachal Pradesh (1960), and Bihar (1967).
2. South India: Andhra Pradesh (1954), Tamil Nadu (1982), Kerala (1962), and Karnataka (1968).
3. Central India: Rajasthan (1955, 1963, and 1964), Maharashtra (1955, 1956 and 1972), Gujarat (1968), and Madhya Pradesh (1976).
4. East India: Assam (1964).

At present there are about 40 open prisons in India. In August 1962, Kerala's first open prison was inaugurated. There are fences, but no bars, no surveillance towers. The prison inmates are required to work on the prisons two hundred acre rubber plantation, tapping rubber, preparing rubber sheets or cultivating rice—paddies. Benefits of the open prison include periods of freedom, during which most inmates spends one month out of six with their families. There are also special five-day leaves granted in the event of a family member's death, wedding or other important occasion. Prisoners are also permitted to have family visits during the weekends. The continuing involvement with their home community allows the family to share the burden of reform with the state (Merkel, 1994).

The following tabular information (*Source*: Vibhute, 2005) furnishes State-wise details of open peno-correctional institutions set up in India between 1949 and 2004.

State	Name	Authorised capacity	Year of Establishment
Andhra Pradesh	1. Prisoners' Agricultural Colony, Maula Ali, (now Cherlapalli), Hyderabad.	150	1954
	2. Central Prison-cum-Prisoners' Agricultural Colony, Anantapur.	250	1965
	3. A Semi-open Prison, Rajahmundry.	100	1998
	4. Open Prisoners' Farm, Gachibowli, Hyderabad.	285	2000
Assam	1. Mahendra Nagar Open Air Agricultural-cum-Industrial Colony, Bagbheta, Jorhat.	100	1964

Bihar	1. Open Prison, Mahner	NA	NA
	2. Open Prison, Forbesganj	NA	NA
	3. Open Prison, Harde	NA	NA
Chhattisgarh	1. Open Prison	200	2000
Gujarat	1. Open Prison, Amreli	40	1968
	2. Open Air Prison, Ahmedabad	20	1972
Himachal Pradesh	1. Open Air Prison, Bilaspur	80	1960
Karnataka	1. Open Air Prison, Soundatti	NA	1968
	2. Open Air Prison, Koramangala, Bangalore	150	1971
Kerala	1. Open Prison, Nettukaltheri	250	1962
	2. Open Prison, Thevancode	50	1990
	3. Open Prison, Cheemeni (Kasargod District)	NA	2000
Madhya Pradesh	1. Nav Jiwan Shivir (Open Prison), Mungaoli (Guna District)	150	1973
	2. Nav Jiwan Shivir, Lakhimpur (Panna District)	50	1975
Maharashtra	1. Open Prison, Yeravada, Pune (Attached to the Yervada Central Prison, Pune)	150	1956
	2. Open Prison, Paithan (Aurangabad District)	300	1968
	3. Swatantrapur Open Colony for Temporary Released Prisoners, Atpadi (Sangli District)	21	1972
	4. Open Colony for Temporary Released Prisoners, Kanhergaon (Chandrapur District)	NA	1972
	5. Open Colony for Temporary Released Prisoners, Tondel (Chandrapur District)	NA	1980
Orissa	1. Open Air Prison	NA	NA
Punjab	1. Open Air Prison-cum-Agricultural Prison, Nabha	200	1970
	2. Open Air Prison, Kapurthala	NA	NA
Rajasthan	1. Prisoners' Open Air Camp, Agriculture Research Farm, Durgapura (Jaipur)	15	1955
	2. Semi-Open Prison, Bharatpur (Bharatpur)	50	1962
	3. Sri Sampurnanand Khula Bandi Shivir, (Open Camp), Sanganer (Jaipur)	50	1963
	4. Prisoners' Open Air Camp, Central Mechanised Farm, Suratgarh (Hanumangarh)	150	1964
	5. Open Camp, Mandore (Jodhpur)	20	1974
	6. Open Camp, Jaitsar (Sri Ganganagar)	100	1977
	7. Open Prison, Bichawal (Bikaner)	NA	1996

Tamil Nadu	1. Open Air Prison, Singanallur (Coimbatore District) 2. Open Prison Salem (attached to the Farm Prison in the Central Prison, Salem)	100 12	1956 1966
Uttar Pradesh	1. Open Prison (attached to the Model Prison), Lucknow 2. Sampurnanand Camp, Ghurma, Markundi (Mirzapur District)	24 1,130	1949 1956
Uttarakhand	1. Sampurnanand Agricultural-cum-Industrial Camp, Sitarganj, (Nainital District) (Transferred from Uttar Pradesh after the creation of Uttarakhand as a separate state)	1,000	1960
West Bengal	1. Open Air Prison, Lalgola (Murshidabad District)	70	1987
Total number of States: 17	Total number of Open Institutions reported so far in India: 40	Total capacity: 5,267	1949 to 2004

Source: Vibhute, 2005.

Open Prisons and It's Modalities of Functioning

The open prisons are generally located within 5 kilometres on the outskirts of the town except in Uttar Pradesh, Kerala and Karnataka where they are resituated at a distance of 15 to 35 kilometres from the nearest town. Each prison has an area of 10-20 acres for cultivation except Uttar Pradesh which has an area of 5,800 acres and Andhra Pradesh has an area of 1,425 acres. The Tamil Nadu open prison occupies only 64 acres (Vibhute, 2005).

The inmates are accommodated in huts or *katcha/pucca* barracks. They have electricity as well as pumps or wells. The capacity of an open prison varies from 100 to 3,500 inmates. For example, open prisons in Tamil Nadu, Assam, Gujarat, Madhya Pradesh, and Himachal Pradesh have a capacity of 100 inmates, and those in Maharashtra have a capacity of 1,500 inmates. While Uttar Pradesh accommodates 3,500 inmates, Andhra Pradesh 500 inmates, and Rajasthan, Punjab, Kerala and Karnataka house 200 inmates each.

Open prisons in Tamil Nadu, Rajasthan and Himachal Pradesh permit a remission of one day for each day spent in the open prison but other states do not permit such concession. Sixty per cent of the inmates in the open prisons are those who get more than 10 years' imprisonment and 85 per cent are those who get more than 5 years' imprisonment (Ahuja, 1969). Thus only long-term convicts are kept in open prisons. The average stay of a prisoner in the open prison is 2 to 3 years (Vibhute, 2005).

Certain types of prisoners are not eligible to be kept in the open prisons. For example, those who are less than 20 years or more than 50 years of age, those who are sentenced for less than one year, those who have not served at least one-third of the total sentence in the prison, and those who are convicted for offences like planned murder, dacoity, rape and who have boyish looks (Ghosh, 1992). Generally, the superintendent of the prison submits a list of suitable prisoners to the Inspector-General of Prisons who finally chooses the inmates from the list to be sent to open prisons. In some cases, names are sent by the Minister to the Inspector-General of Prisons to be included in the list. In some States, the Superintendent sends the list through the police or the District Magistrate to the Inspector-General of Prisons (Vibhute, 2005).

The conditions to be fulfilled by the prisoners for being sent to the open prisons are that they should be willing to live in these prisons; they should be physically and mentally fit to work; they should be life convicts, they should have served a minimum number of years in the prison and they should have records of good behaviour. The structure of the open prisons is such that they have no 'inmate system'. The whole system is so organized that inmates freely interact with one another in everyday life situation within the prison. Similarly, the normative system prescribes norms, restrictions and expectations which guide behaviour of the inmates pertaining to work, leisure, sex, clothes, food, etc. Lastly, the value system in the open prison is dominated by a set of values which are neither anti-administrative nor anti-social (Vibhute, 2005).

The structure of remuneration to the prisoners in the open prison varies from state to state. In Rajasthan, in the agricultural farm, prisoners were paid by the employing department ₹ 3 per day plus overtime. In Assam, prisoners were given an annual reward of ₹ 100. In Karnataka where prisoners were employed in digging of a canal, they were paid only ₹ 1 per day. In Tamil Nadu, no wages were paid. In Himachal Pradesh, prisoners received ₹ 4 per day from the employing department, out of which maintenance charges were deducted. In Uttar Pradesh at Churk, prisoners employed in prison services were paid ₹ 0.50 per day, and those working on quarry, received wages on piece work basis, i.e., ₹ 2.12 for an average output of 2.4 tons. The State receives ₹ 1.25 per day towards maintenance charges from the prisoner's wages. At Sitarganj, every prisoner gets ₹ 0.25 per day. In Andhra Pradesh, prisoners received ₹ 0.10 per day and in Maharashtra, they received wages as in the closed prisons (Central Bureau of Correctional Services, 1970; Vibhute, 2005).

In Tamil Nadu no expenditure privilege is available as wages are not paid. In Rajasthan, there is no restriction on expenditure, and prisoners can spend as much as they like. In Assam, prisoners can remit a part of their earnings to their family and a part they can spend on toilet articles. They are encouraged to save money and to deposit it in the Post Office Savings Bank Account. In Karnataka and Andhra Pradesh, prisoners can spend up to 50 per cent of their earnings. In Gujarat two-third earnings, subject to a maximum of ₹ 10 per month, can be spent by a prisoner on himself. In Himachal Pradesh, the maximum limit on personal expenditure is ₹ 7.50 per month, but if one wishes to remit money to his home, he could do it out of the balance at his credit. In Uttar Pradesh while at the Churk Camp, a prisoner could spend ₹ 0.35 per day, at Sitarganj he could spend half of his earnings. They are also encouraged to pay their judicial fines and also remit some money to their home from their earnings. In Kerala, a prisoner can spend up to one-third on him/her and can send home one-third. The remaining one-third he is required to collect at the time of release (Central Bureau of Correctional Services, 1970; Vibhute, 2005).

In West Bengal, the prisoners in an open correctional home shall be permitted to participate in cultural activities such as song, drama, and instrument music. In all types of open correctional homes prisoners may be rewarded for meritorious work at such rate, not exceeding one hundred rupees per year, as may be prescribed. The case of every prisoner accommodated in an open correctional home shall be reviewed once a month by the Superintendent who shall analyze the problems of the prisoner in detail. If the Superintendent is of the opinion that any such prisoner is unfit for being accommodated in the correctional home on grounds of misconduct or unsatisfactory work or for any other cause, he shall, with the approval of the Inspector-General of Correctional Services, transfer such prisoner to correctional home which the Inspector-General of Correctional Services may specify. The Inspector-General of Correctional Services or the Additional Inspector-General of Correctional Services shall inspect every open correctional home once in every six months. The Deputy Inspector-General of Correctional Services shall inspect every open correctional home once in every three months and submit a report to the Inspector-General of Correctional Services (Government of West Bengal, 1992).

Lalgola Open Prison in West Bengal: A Successful Experiment

The State of West Bengal has repealed the old Prison Act and introduced the modern 'West Bengal Correctional Services Act'. With the introduction of this act on 14th April 2000, the Prison Administration in West Bengal ushered a paradigm shift from the colonial legacy of punishment towards the well the thought out new philosophy of correctional approach for the moral reformation and education of the inmates in order to facilitate their reintegration in the society after their release (Government of West Bengal, 1992).

The West Bengal Correctional Services Act, 1992 (Chapter XXVIII) gives a brief description of the Open Correctional Homes. It pointed out that 'the open correctional homes shall be classified as 'A' type, 'B' type, 'C' type correctional homes. In A and B type Open Correctional Homes, the night lockup shall be completed after proper counting at 8 p.m. and shall be opened at such hours as may be prescribed. In C type correctional homes there shall not be any night lockups. There shall not be any day lockup also except in a case where any prisoner violates the rules made under this Act and is found uncontrollable. There shall be constituted for each district a Selection Board for selection of prisoners to be accommodated in different types of correctional homes. The Selection Board should consist of Inspector General of Correctional Services or his nominee not below the rank of Additional Inspector General of Correctional Services as the President, District Magistrate or his nominee, Deputy Inspector General of Correctional Services, each of the Superintendent of Central Correctional Homes, Commissioner of Police, Kolkata or his nominee, Superintendent of Police or his nominee as members.

Every prisoner accommodated in a 'C' type of correctional home shall be:

- Supplied with food, free of cost, for three months from the date of his entry into such home.
- Assisted by the Superintendent in obtaining small trade loan from the State Bank of India or any nationalized bank guaranteed by the State Government for repayment of the loan to the utilized exclusively for the purchase of working implements and raw materials for cottage industry.
- Allowed to go to market or to probable customers for selling of goods produced by him to come back within 7 p.m.
- Allowed to go to a local festival or other congregational amusement as a visitor or to display his products for sale.
- Allowed, on his release, to take with him the implements of work.

After three months from the date of his entry a 'C' type of correctional home, a prisoner shall procure food out of his income from the industry and may live with his family comprising of five members at a time who may contribute to the maintenance of the family, either by participating in such industry or out of the income from any other avocation. After one year from the date of his entry into a 'C' type correctional home, a prisoner shall contribute the income from his industry to the maintenance of the correctional home at such rate as may be prescribed. The provision of sub-sections (2) and (3) shall apply also to a prisoner accommodated in 'A' type or 'B' type Open Correctional home and a prisoner in any type of correctional home shall be permitted to open saving bank account at a nearby post office providing such facility. In every open correctional home there shall be a library for lending books to the prisoners and a reading room provided with the newspapers magazines. Every open correctional home shall be provided with a radio set with speakers installed in different barracks.

In West Bengal, an open air prison was set up at Lalgola in the district of Murshidabad in the year 1987. This is a maiden effort of West Bengal Government to put the ideal of reformation into practice. The open air prison is situated on a hundred acres of land with a large mango garden and a water tank. At present there are around hundred prisoners. Convicts sentenced to 7 years imprisonment or more and who have already served two-third of their sentence and have maintained a good prison record are eligible for getting transferred to the open prison. Thus no inmates in the open prison are a fresh convict. An impartial process of screening takes place where the convicts are personally interviewed by the selection board. In this open air prison there is no system of day lockup. The gates are opened at 0600 hours in the morning and the night lockup is at 2000 hrs and during this time prisoners are free to go anywhere they like and pursue any vocation within and outside the prison premises. Thus inmates here are not kept confined within the high walls like the other prisons for twenty-four hours. The government has started motor driving classes for the prisoners with the help of Don Bosco Institution. The prisoners go to district headquarters, Berhampore, a distance of 50 kilometres from Lalgola, by train unescorted, practice motor driving and come back by 20.00 hrs. Moreover the inmates, even if allowed to move outside the boundary of the prison campus, are not permitted to move beyond the three kilometre radius of the Lalgola police station. Most of the inmates are from the rural Bengal and their prime occupation is in the field of agriculture. Some of them have been engaged in trades like carpentry, blacksmith, repairing works, etc. before their conviction. In rural Bengal most of the disputes are land related factional feuds of the family or village politics. In this system, the inmates have an opportunity to meet their family members for consecutive fifteen days in every six months.

As compared to other central correctional homes this open prison is less crowded. The quality and quantity of food is better than the rest of the correctional homes in the states. The security arrangement and surveillance is also minimal as compared to the rest of the correctional homes in Kolkata. The inmates enjoy comparatively more freedom as they can view cable television (cable line at their own expense) make telephone calls, go to shops and market.

Convicts like Hemant Kole charged for murdering his wife drives van rickshaw, and Randhir Basu another convict is engaged in teaching students (*Anandabazar Patrika*, 2008). He likes to impart moral values to his students. Some prisoners have been allowed to purchase goats and cows with their own money for rearing and selling the milk to the public. In addition prisoners receive vocational training on T.V. repairing, motor mechanism, cane work, electrical wiring, tailoring, horticulture, etc. They are allowed to participate in local festivals and collect orders for their product. A scheme to set up a market with about 100 stalls in the prison campus is being prepared, where prisoners will be able to sell their products to the public. Some of the convicts are working in tea shops, salons, built by the prison authorities.

The Government has proposed to set up a bakery and various small scale industries where prisoners can be gainfully employed. The cottages have been built in the campus where prisoners are staying with their families. These cottages consists of two room flats with separate kitchen and attached bathroom and a small garden. These cottages symbolize halfway homes where prisoners can interact with their families. Such interaction with the family members as well as the general masses at local meals, will facilitates post-release re-integration into the society. With such facilities, the Lalgola Open Prison is proved to be one of the best open prisons in India.

Conclusion

Open prisons and open colonies for prisoners, in the recent past, have emerged as effective institutional reformatory and correctional measures. These institutions, which ostensibly eliminate the 'tensions' and 'barriers' created by the restrictions and physical restraints placed on inmates of a closed prison and provide them better opportunity for re-interaction and re-assimilation with free community and family, strive to bridge the gulf between the traditional closed prison and free community. They in fact furnish a halfway home to their inmates for their smooth and effective socio-psychological rehabilitation and reintegration into the social mainstream. By providing maximum opportunity to their inmates to mould their attitudes and to bring positive changes in their behavioural patterns, these institutions, it is believed, make prisoners fit to lead a law-abiding and self-supporting life after their release. The Indian open prisons have proved to be very successful and we hope that more open prisons will be opened in the near future and it will help in the reformation of prisoners.

References

Ahuja, R. (1969). *Female Offenders in India*. Meerut: Meenakshi Prakashan.

Anandabazar Patrika (20th January, 2008). Dine Baire Uparjan - Rate prison pharen 'Mukto' Bandira.

Central Bureau of Correctional Services (1970). *Open Prisons in India*. New Delhi: Central Bureau of Correctional Services.

Cole, G., Smith, F., & Christopher, E. (2002). *Criminal Justice in America*. 3rd Edition. Belmont: Wordsworth Group. pp. 253-58.

Ghosh, S. (1992). *Open Prisons and the Inmates*. New Delhi: Mittal Publications.

Government of West Bengal. (1992). The West Bengal Correctional Services Act 1992.

Merkel, J. (1994). Prisons Without-Walls. Kerala Open, prison draws on the strength of community life. *The Ecology of Justice*. Spring 1994.

Government of India. (1983). The All India Committee on Prison Reforms (Mulla Committee 1980-83). New Delhi: Ministry of Home Affairs, Government of India.

Peterson, A.W. (1960). "Modern Developments in the Prison System". *The Howard Journal of Criminal Justice*, 10, 167-76.

United Nations. (August 29, 1955). Resolution and Recommendations adopted by the First United Nations Congress on the Prevention of Crime and the Treatment of Offenders.

Vibhute, K.I. (2005). *Open Peno-Correctional Institutions in India: A Review of Fifty-Five Years—Experiences and Expectations*. Frieburg, Germany: Max Planck Institute for Foreign and International Criminal Law.

13

Towards Techno-Corrections: A Frontline View of Hot New Practices and Technologies

P. Madhava Soma Sundaram

Introduction

The field of "techno corrections" can be defined as a correctional infrastructure that takes advantage of all the potentials offered by the new technologies, to reduce the costs of supervising criminal offenders and minimize the risk they pose to society. The recent developments in science and technology will converge with the forces of law and order to create "techno-corrections". The correctional establishment—the managers of the prisons, probation, and other allied systems are seeking more cost-effective ways to increase public safety as the number of people under correctional supervision, continue to grow. A correctional establishment that takes advantage of all the potential offered by the new technologies to reduce the costs of supervising prison inmates and minimizing the risk they pose to society will define the field of techno-corrections, which has emerged elsewhere in the globe, and is likely to catch up in India in the near future.

1. Pharmacological Correctional Methods

The new "wonder" drugs being developed to control behaviour in correctional and non-correctional settings will also help affect techno-corrections. Correctional officials are already familiar with some of these drugs, as many are currently used to treat mentally ill offenders. Yet these drugs could be easily used to control mental conditions affecting behaviours considered undesirable even when the offenders are not mentally ill (Fabelo, 2000). Experiments are now being conducted with drugs that affect the levels of brain neurotransmitters (substances in the body that transmit nerve impulses) and can be used to help treat drug abuse (Fabelo, 2000; Leshner, 1999). On another front, research into the relationship between levels of the neurotransmitter serotonin and violent behaviour continues to be refined. Findings to date seem to indicate that people who have low levels of serotonin are more prone than others to be impulsive, commit violent acts, especially when they abuse alcohol (Fabelo, 2000; Stolberg, 1994).

Reiss and Roth (1993) recommended a new emphasis in biomedical research on violence as a means to understand the biological roots of violent behaviour. Neurobiological processes are the complex electrical and chemical activities in specific brain regions that underlie observable human behaviour. They report that research findings from animal and human studies "point to several features of the nervous system as promising sites" for discovering reliable biological "markers" for violent behaviour and designing preventive therapies.

It is only a matter of time before research findings in this area lead to the development of drugs to control neurobiological processes. By their very nature, these breakthroughs will result in advances (or claims of advances) in early identification of potentially violent individuals. These drugs could become correctional tools to manage violent offenders and perhaps even to prevent violence. Such advances are related to the third area of technology that will affect corrections: genetic and neurobiological risk assessment technologies.

While these are brand new techniques and processes in life sciences, they may not be fully be applicable in the Indian context, as of now, but this is where probably the field of corrections and prison management is likely to move, at least in some countries, in the next few decades and hence becomes vital. It must, however, be added here, that these are methods that are yet to be fully accepted by the scientific community, judicially tested and one cannot rule out the violations of basic Human Rights.

2. Risk Assessment and Corrections

Correctional officials today may be familiar with DNA profiling of offenders, particularly sex offenders, even though it is not adopted in India. This is just the beginning of the application of gene related technologies to corrections. The Human Genome Project was completed in 2003. A map of the 3 billion chemical bases that make up human DNA has been created (Fabelo, 2000). Gene "management" technologies are already widely used in agriculture and are increasingly used in medicine. The progression is likely to continue, with applications in psychiatric and behavioural management. Researchers are investigating the genetic or inherited basis of behaviour, including antisocial and criminal behaviour. Studies of twins, for example, have revealed resemblances in behaviour attributable to a genetic effect (Carey & Goldman, 1997). Eventually, the genetic roots of human behaviour could be profiled. An example of a step in that direction is scientists' search for genetic explanations of variations among individuals in levels of the secretion of serotonin and dopamine (another neurotransmitter, this one playing a major role in addiction). 'Neurobiological research is taking the same path, although thus far no neurobiological patterns specific enough to be reliable biological markers for violent behaviour have been uncovered' (Fabelo, 2000, p. 3).

Is it possible that breakthroughs in these areas will lead to the development of risk assessment tools that use genetic or neurobiological profiles to identify children who have a propensity toward addiction or violence? How about identifying males with a propensity for sex offending? Some researchers working in this field have conducted studies on more than 8,600 children to identify those with high "aggressor" traits and to treat them, through social intervention, to prevent their involvement in violent behaviour (Fabelo, 2000; Stolberg, 1994). What if these children could be more reliably identified with genetic or neurobiological assessments? (Fabelo, 2000, p. 3).

It may be many years away from linking genetic and neurobiological traits with social and environmental factors to reliably predict who is at risk for addiction, sex offending, and violent behaviour, or crime in general. But attempts may be made to develop genetic or neurobiological tests for assessing risks posed by individuals. This is already done for the risk of contracting certain diseases. Demand for risk assessments of individuals will come from correctional officials under pressure to prevent violent recidivism. Once under correctional control, specific offenders could be identified, on the basis of such testing and risk assessment, as likely violent recidivists. The group so classified could be placed under closer surveillance or declared a danger to themselves and society and be civilly committed to special facilities for indeterminate periods. In other words, incarceration could assume a more preventive role. While these methods are not up for adoption in India, for the next decade or so, and may have other repercussions, it still becomes relevant to know what is happening at the field of corrections, in the developed world. "Preventive incarceration" is already a reality for some convicted sex offenders. Many countries commit certain offenders to prisons. This happens today with no clear understanding of the nature of the abnormality, other than that it is an "abnormality of behaviour" detested by society. It is not difficult to imagine what might be done to justify preventive incarceration if this "abnormal" behaviour or criminal behaviour could be explained and predicted by genetic or neurobiological profiling.

3. Tracking and Location Systems: An Aid to Probation Services

While tracking of probationers, under the Probation of Offenders Act, 1956, in India, is done manually by the probation officers, in future home visits, and technologies such as electronic tracking and location systems will assist correctional practitioners.

Electronic monitoring—with either bracelets that communicate through a device connected to telephone lines or more modern versions based on cellular or satellite tracking—are in use in most developed countries. With this technology, correctional officials can continuously track offenders' locations to supervise their movements. Soon some of the current technical glitches in satellite tracking (such as difficulties in urban areas where big buildings block reception) will be removed. The technology will also enable correctional officials to define geographic areas from which offenders are prohibited and to furnish tracking devices to potential victims (such as battered wives). The devices will set "safe zones" that trigger alarms or warning notices upon approach of the offender.

Tiny cameras could be integrated into tracking devices to provide live video of offenders' locations and circumstances. Miniature electronic devices implanted in the body to signal the location of offenders at all times, create unique identifiers that trigger alarms, and monitor key bodily functions that affect unwanted behaviours are underdevelopment and are close to becoming reality (*The Futurist*, 1999). Finally, related technologies that will make it difficult and expensive for offenders to defeat the tracking devices will guarantee their reliability.

4. Prison Management Issues: Monitoring and Surveillance Systems

Monitoring and surveillance systems provide institution personnel with technology that enables them to better control access to off-limits areas within the facility. The major systems being used are closed-circuit TV (CCTV), motion detectors, access-control devices, and audio-monitors.

CCTV

It is probably the only major technological development in an otherwise, underdeveloped prison infrastructure found in most of the prison institutions in India. A casual glance at the reports of the Ministry of Home Affairs, and the schemes of the Bureau of Police Research and Development for modernization of prisons, will reveal that majority of the States in India have adopted this technology, in their prisons. It is an arrangement in which television cameras, placed in potentially vulnerable areas within an institution, can be monitored by staff usually located in a control centre. For institutions, typical camera locations were at entrances and central tower, industries, in visiting areas, and along the prison's perimeter. It must be added here that the CCTV system is comparatively easier to install than to maintain. Also, all parts of the prisons cannot be monitored and there are always dark spots in old Indian prison buildings.

Motion Detectors

This equipment uses infrared light waves, radio frequency transmission, ultrasound, or microwaves to detect changes that occur in a previously empty space when a human body enters it. They detect a change in volumetric pressure or temperature changes as a consequence of radiant body heat (*The Futurist*, 1999).

When radio frequency waves are used, the false alarm rate can be high, because the waves may penetrate walls and respond to motion outside the designated area unless the walls are shielded. Some of these devices can be adjusted by skilled technicians, to tune out motion outside the protected area. Ultrasonic detectors operate in a fashion similar to radio frequency systems; however, they do not penetrate walls. They are not affected by audible noise itself, but such noise can sometimes disturb wave patterns and create false alarms.

Access-control Systems

These systems allow certain designated persons to enter otherwise secured areas. Push-button code systems have keypads installed at the entrance to each controlled-access area. Those authorized to enter are given the combination to be punched into the keypad. There is no keyhole to allow locks to be picked, and locks are easily recoded if prior combinations have been compromised or when there is a staff change.

Card-access-control systems use card readers instead of keypads. Authorized individuals are given programmed cards that allow entrance into a given area. Magnetic key-card systems use a plastic card containing thousands of magnetic bits or particles that are arranged to match the pattern set up in the card reader. When a match is made, the locking system is activated. This system can easily be converted into a total, facility-wide system with the following advantages:

- Key cards can be coded by the facility for use by staff and/or inmates.
- The system can require a coded series of numbers to match the presented card before granting entry.

- The system can generate a printout showing who entered an area, the time and date of entry and exit, and the identity of the areas in which the card was used.
- The system can reject, but record, cards presented for entry into unauthorized areas.
- Additionally, an audio alarm installed at the control centre can be triggered.
- The system can be designed so that key cards will be honored only between designated time periods.
- If necessary, the system can be designed to deny access to a particular card.
- Cards issued to inmates can be tied into data processing for mess arrangements or library use.
- Cards can be coded to prevent them from being used by more than one person (e.g., a card used to enter an area would have to be used to exit the area before it could be used to enter again).

This system is as such practised in many of the multi-national companies in India especially in the Information Technology sector. The flip side of this system is that the equipments are very sensitive, more technology oriented hence requires frequent servicing and the process is dependent on electricity. So, alternative models of management must be put in place, for times of emergency, when the system mal-functions (*The Futurist*, 1999).

Audio-monitors

This technology is similar to the CCTV, but rather than conveying an image, it picks up and transmits sound through a closed-circuit audio system to one or more locations staffed by institution personnel. Existing public address systems, with the speaker turned into a microphone can listen to sounds in the protected area and then trigger an alarm relay when an intrusion takes place. The output of individual audio amplifiers can be adjusted to prevent activation of the alarm by normal noises when the area is unoccupied.

Using two microphones, one within the protected area and one outside it can reduce the false alarm rate. Within the circuit, the noise signals are equalized in relation to a typical noise level for each of the microphones. If an intruder enters the protected area, one microphone will pick up the additional noise and the other microphone will not. The unequal noise levels will set off an alarm.

Another method for reducing audio-monitor false alarms employs complex audio filters. Any recognizable sound has a distinct acoustic spectrum. The audio signal developed by a microphone placed in a protected area is processed through a series of audio-frequency filters tuned to let through signals at certain frequencies and reject others not in the area of interest. Certain band-pass filters can detect a difference between human intrusion noises and other noises of no interest for security purposes.

Management Information Systems

Today managing information is as important as managing people—in fact; information is needed for better management of people. Correction administrators are no exception. While almost all Central Prisons in India have been provided by computers, under the prison modernization schemes, a paradox is caused when staff who were not technically trained, found themselves confronted with an unfamiliar and, therefore, intimidating technology. Also, the district jails and the sub jails, which are more in number, are yet to be provided with computer and are still using age-old practices to compile data.

Managers need accurate and timely data to support a wide variety of administrative decisions. The sheer quantity of data accumulating today cannot be used effectively without technological assistance. Managers have to think short-range about manpower allocation, purchasing, inventories, tracking inmate accounts, bed space, and the state of their current budget. They must think long-range about what caseloads and institution populations will be like, what construction and renovation will be needed, and how much it will all cost in future. If there were no machines to process the numbers, administrators would need more staff; reports processed by hand would contain more errors; institutional data and inmate histories would be harder to obtain and keep current; managers would have more difficulty communicating with other institutions; and agencies could become so inefficient as to be virtually inoperative.

Consequently, Management Information System (MIS) technologies are needed in prisons. For these technologies to function efficiently, staff resistance to change must be overcome, and the difficulties involved in integrating old and new systems must be anticipated and conquered.

Management Information System can be effectively used in the following areas of prison management (*The Futurist*, 1999):

- Accounting applications to track financial matters (e.g., accounts receivable or payable, inmate accounts, or payroll);
- Inventory control programs to monitor what comes into the facility (e.g., equipment, supplies, food) and where it goes, adding items as shipments coming in and subtracting them when used, thereby, keeping a running total of on-hand items;
- Operations applications to track what is done to keep the facility running smoothly (e.g., maintenance, repairs, laundry, medical, and food service);
- Personnel applications to record hires, terminations, scheduling, leave, training, and performance ratings.
- Inmate applications to record and monitor what happens to inmates (e.g., property control, visits, family visit records, and training and work assignments);
- Case management applications to track admission records, and parole decisions, release dates, and records (including prior arrests and convictions); and
- Identification (ID) systems to maintain population statistics and monitor the movements of staff and inmates.

5. Biometric Methods: The Need for Revamping the Contemporary Security Scenario

Keeping track of inmates within a prison or jail is a constant challenge, especially as they move from one part of the facility to another. Monitoring their movements requires corrections officers to accurately identify individual prisoners by sight as they pass through security posts. It also requires frequent oral and radio communications between personnel at two or more security posts, paper passes authorizing inmates' movements, to note when prisoners left one area and entered another. Despite the best precautions and well-thought-out practices, mistakes can be made, officers' attention can be diverted, and late-arriving inmates, who come after 6 P.M., due to transfers, and far of courts are not noticed or searched for promptly. Late-arriving, out-of-place prisoners can cause problems in correctional settings. If nothing else, it means that prison staff does not know where a particular inmate is at any given time. That prisoner may simply have stopped to chat with friends. Or, more seriously, he or she may be engaging in illegal activities. Inmates have committed assaults and even murders as they moved from one part of a prison to another, though not very frequent in India.

The term "biometrics" refers to a variety of methods to verify a person's identity using physiological or behavioural characteristics such as iris, retinal, and facial recognition; hand and finger geometry; fingerprint and voice identification; and dynamic signature (*The Futurist*, 1999). It has the advantage of not requiring a person to remember a user name, password, or series of numbers while confirming that the person is who he or she claims to be. Practical uses of biometrics include allowing person's access to keyless cars, rooms, and buildings; to financial and other personal accounts; and to the departure areas of airport terminals. More broadly, it is used to prevent identity theft, preserve the confidentiality of information, and reduce fraud.

Biometrics has been used previously in some prisons, to track the movement of staff, visitors, and prisoners in and out of correctional facilities. It has also been used to account for staff members in the event of a riot or other prison disturbance. Some prisons in developed countries use biometrics to track prisoner movements within a prison. It is designed to employ computer-based methods of tracking inmates to improve the efficiency of corrections specialists and to demonstrate how advanced technology can make corrections facilities safer (Gonzales, Albert, Schofield, Regina, Schmitt, and Glenn, 2006). Called the Biometric Inmate Tracking System (BITS), it is implemented in phases, elsewhere, to transform the existing manual system into a computer-based system and then into a biometric- and computer-based system (Gonzales, Albert, Schofield, Regina, Schmitt, and Glenn, 2006).

All biometric methods, iris, facial, retinal, finger and hand geometry, voice, and fingerprint were tested over a 3-year period. All had been developed, tested, and used in other settings, mostly by commercial firms. And all were found to have advantages and disadvantages. Facial recognition produced too many false positives on prisoners. Although biometric methods do not have to work every time to be effective, corrections specialists had to visually identify the prisoners too often, thus slowing the process. Iris recognition was the most accurate method tested, but it was similarly judged too slow to work effectively in a prison setting. Voice recognition proved to be the least accurate method tested.

In the end, the fingerprint recognition method, now used in conjunction with hand geometry, was judged to work best. It provided the most accurate and reliable matches at about one-third the cost of iris, facial, and retinal methods. The fingerprint method also moved prisoners through the gates faster than the others. That's a prime consideration when, for example, corrections specialists are moving 100 or more prisoners at once from housing or work areas to the other places at mealtime. Fingerprint readers were also easier to use and more durable than other readers.

Conclusion

Managing crime is everyone's business, and even more so, the correctional wing of the Criminal Justice System. As a developing society, bulk of the resources is spent on the most expensive response: Incarceration. While it may be difficult to predict the future rate of prison population growth, it is comparatively easy to ideate the contribution of 'a la mode' developments in science, technology and management, to the correctional planners and the correctional regimen, of the future. While taking a short retrogressive look at the development of corrections in India, this chapter mainly pivoted on a whole gamut of issues related to the future of corrections based on the technological developments of this modern era. Developments in the field of science and technology, lead human kind to better lives through a complex mesh of growth and progress. The field of corrections too has benefited in the past and is likely to augur more assistance in the future.

References

Carey, G. and Goldman, D. (1997). The Genetics of Antisocial Behaviour. In D.M. Stoff et al. (Ed), *Handbook of Antisocial Behaviour* (pp. 243-54). New York: John Wiley & Sons.

Fabelo, T. (2000). Technocorrections: The Promises, the Uncertain Threats. *Sentencing & Corrections: Issues for the 21st Century*. No. 5 Research in Brief. Papers from the Executive Sessions on Sentencing and Corrections. Washington D.C.: U.S. Department of Justice, Office of Justice Programs, National Institute of Justice.

Gonzales, A.R., Schofield, R.B. and Schmitt, G.R. (2006). *National Institute of Justice Bulletin*, No. 253.

Leshner, A.I. (1999). We can Conquer Drug Addiction. *The Futurist*, 33(9) November: 22-25.

Reiss, A.J. Jr. and Roth, J.A. (eds.) (1993). *Understanding and Preventing Violence*. Washington, DC: National Academy Press.

Stolberg, S. (1994). Scientific Studies are Generating Controversy. *Austin American-Statesman*, January 16.

The Futurist. (1999). Microchip Implants Closer to Reality, 33(8), 9 October.

14

Info-Tech Prisons in the New Millennium: International Perspectives

K. Jaishankar

Introduction

The population explosion in prisons around the world over the last decade has brought new demands for prison administrators. These demands are compounded by many social and technological changes in the contemporary society that have broadened the correctional context. Indeed, prisons are microcosms of society, and confined populations generally require many of the services and amenities that contemporary society offers populations outside of the prison. Consequently, the traditional methods and tools of correctional managers are no longer adequate. Contemporary demands require managers to augment their personal observations and experiences with other sources of information in order to best deal with the new complexity of decision-making (Saylor, 1994). Furthermore, the demand for information has grown along with the confined populations. Before confined populations began to soar, demands for information most frequently came from within an agency (e.g., for management decision support purposes). Subsequently, external information requests (e.g., legislative bodies, the public, or the mass media) have increased in frequency. To achieve better managed prisons, more cost effective operations, and better public accountability in this climate requires quick and efficient analysis of large quantities of valid and reliable information.

Information that is related to the full range of issues required to manage these micro-societies (Saylor, 1994).

Social and technological changes have increased the complexity of decision-making in many contemporary social organizations. This has resulted in many innovations in management of prisons too (Saylor, 1994). The laudable innovation in the management of prisons across the globe is the use of Information Technology (IT). During the last half of the 20th century, IT became a central force in the field of prison management. Information, with its associated technologies, provided a critical support structure for operations (Brown, 2000). Technologies ranging from basic Microsoft application such as MS Word to advanced technologies like electronic monitoring systems, Geographic Information Systems (GIS), Global Positioning Systems (GPS), RFID and Biometrics have now become part and parcel of the prison management all over the world. IT applications have taken firm roots in both institutional as well as community corrections.

In almost all prison systems of the world, there is a flurry of activity to upgrade IT systems. The current situation reflects widespread change in both hardware and software. Furthermore, many correctional agencies are engaged in similar challenges, such as building integrated criminal justice databases; shifting from older mainframes to more current hardware and software; upgrading procedures for data analysis; and report generation. Some of the more popular changes include the introduction of internal classification systems; classification instruments and procedures that are valid for women offenders' re-entry classification and risk and needs instruments; and the automation of classification algorithms (Brennan et al., 2004).

Management of offenders and offender data is a critical issue for every prison's overall operations. With advances in the use of automated computer systems to manage data and the need for better efficiency and more accurate and timely data, IT has become a necessary component of prison management. In recent years, a tremendous amount of information has become available to law enforcement and corrections agencies that could be helpful in managing resources and solving crimes. IT can be applied to connect law enforcement and correctional agencies to one another, thus enabling them to share information. IT can sort, collate, and relate data—in some cases graphically—to assist police and corrections officers in managing scarce resources or indirectly helping them to solve crimes.

Information Technologies in Prisons

Wright (2000) identified IT as the technological advance to have the greatest impact on prison administrative practices. IT has made it possible to manage the burgeoning prisoner populations. Administrators rely on it for time computation, maintaining inmate records, tracking incidence reports, and making decisions about designations based on programming needs, threat levels, and known crime affiliates and enemies. A warden can click on a file and obtain a photograph of the inmates along with his or her entire personal, criminal, and institutional history. Computers are used to manage visits. The use of IT for communication is a key function for many of the wardens and system heads. Electronic mail (e-mail) allows them to know what is going on in other institutions and to discuss matters such as the transfer of difficult inmates. As systems have grown, communication through the computer allows facilities to operate in consistent and integrated ways. Policy and procedures are discussed and can be disseminated quickly. The ability to transfer data electronically supports system wide monitoring and maintenance of accountability systems (Wright, 2000).

The technologies reviewed in this section include those designed to track offenders (electronic supervision technologies and GPS) improve the communications interoperability of law enforcement and corrections jurisdictions so that, when necessary, they can easily work cooperatively (MIS); provide data to a computer so that images can be created or compared with other images in a database to help identify individuals (Biometric Identification); recover and/or enhance data captured on videotape or sound recordings (information sharing and analysis); and to understand the offenders visually by mapping data about crimes (crime mapping and GIS). Though many technologies are used in the prison systems, in this section only advanced technologies are appraised.

1. Electronic Supervision Technologies

The technologies of electronic monitoring have their roots in the work of Ralph Schwitzgebel of the Science Committee on Psychological Experimentation at Harvard University (1968) (Schwitzgebel, 1968; Fox, 1987). In 1964, he developed a one-kilogram Radio Telemetry Device that could be worn by a person. The device transmitted signals to a modified missile-tracking unit up to 400 metres away, which determined the wearer's location on a screen (Black & Smith 2003). In the early 1980s an American judge, supposedly inspired by a Spiderman comic, persuaded a company to develop a monitoring bracelet suitable for offenders to wear (Rondinelli, 1997). In 1983, the first order was made requiring an offender who had breached parole to wear an anklet to monitor his future behaviour (Liverani, 1998). This use of electronic monitoring devices became commonly known as "tagging". These developments took place at a time when community-based sanctions were becoming more prevalent and of greater significance in reducing prison populations (Richardson, 1999). Against a background of stubbornly high prison populations and rapidly developing technology, governments are now reaching a critical point in the use of electronic monitoring as a means of reducing costs and improving the effectiveness of corrections. The aggressive marketing of private companies has been instrumental in the growth of electronic monitoring (Maxfield & Baumer, 1990; Liverani, 1998; Black & Smith, 2004). The use of RFIDs (Radio Frequency Identification Systems) has further enhanced the application of electronic monitoring systems. The following are some of the Electronic Supervision Technologies used in modern prisons across the world.

(i) Automated Reporting Systems

There are currently two types of technology used for automated reporting. One type allows offenders to report from remote locations using a telephone; the other requires them to go to a computerized reporting location. With telephone-based systems, offenders are instructed to call a designated number and respond to verbal questions that are electronically generated. The schedule for the offender to call in can be general, such as during the first week of each month, or specific, such as every Thursday. The calling schedule also can be established for the entire supervision period or specified and changed from time to time. The offender only needs access to a telephone to use this reporting system. The enrolment process includes instructions to the offender about his or her responsibilities for using the system and provision of information to the monitoring service. A means of identifying offenders when they check in is also part of the enrolment process. After that, the offender is responsible for calling at the designated times and correctly answering the required questions. Automated reporting systems can minimize the need to see low-risk, low-need offenders face-to-face and can streamline the collection and processing of offender data, while still holding offenders accountable (Crowe et al., 2002).

(ii) Programmed Contact Systems

Programmed contact systems use various methods to contact and verify the location of an offender in his or her home or in multiple locations. They may be used with offenders who are placed on home monitoring and must stay at home virtually at all times, or they may be used for offenders who are restricted to their homes at various times (e.g., have curfews) but can come and go for approved activities. Programmed contact systems are automated calling systems. The backbone of these systems is a central computer that either receives telephone calls from or makes calls to the offender in one or more locations. The calls may be made either on a scheduled or random timetable, or both scheduled and random calls can be made (Conway, 2001a). Computer-generated calling systems are those in which the central computer makes telephone calls to the offender's number(s) at scheduled or random times. The offender is expected to answer the calls according to a predetermined record of where he or she is to be at given times. Usually, these calls come to the offender's home to ascertain that he or she is at home when required. Random calls can be generated at any time of the day or night to ensure the offender is at home when expected to be and not at home when expected to be at work, treatment, or other obligations. Several systems have the ability to generate calls to other locations or multiple telephone numbers: for example, to ensure the offender's presence at work (Renzema, 1992). Three basic types of verification technology are used (Conway, 2001a):

(a) *Voice Verification*: With these systems, the offender either receives a call from the computer or is signalled to call in. Individuals have unique voice prints just as they have distinctive fingerprints. A voice template is recorded during system enrolment and used for a computerized comparison with future calls. These systems are designed to process the voice sample from any telephone to the centralized computer where it is compared to the original template. (Conway, 2001a)

(b) *Video Verification*: Using a camera installed in the offender's home, a picture is transmitted to the central computer and compared with a photograph on file. (Conway, 2001a)

(c) *Device Verification*: Some systems require that the offender wear a tamper-resistant device, usually on his or her wrist or ankle. When calling in or responding to calls from the central computer, the offender is required to activate the device which then transmits a unique code for that offender over the telephone. The code is then verified by the computer. (Conway, 2001a)

(iii) Continuous Signalling Devices

Continuously signalling devices require the offender to wear a battery-powered transmitting device that emits a radio frequency signal two or more times a minute. These are placed on the offender's wrist or ankle with a tamper-resistant strap, and they must be worn all the time (Conway, 2001b). A receiver is installed in the offender's home and is attached to the telephone. The receiver detects the transmitter's signals and conveys a message via telephone report to a central computer when it either stops receiving the radio frequency or the signal resumes again. Receivers can detect transmitter signals from a range of up to, and in some cases exceeding, 150 feet when installed in a typical home environment. The range on some systems can be programmed for individual offenders from as little as 35 feet to more than 500 feet, depending on the type of equipment used. The range for any setting can vary significantly due to a variety of factors including location and building characteristics. Receivers also have tamper-resistant features to avoid offenders moving or disabling them (Conway, 2001b; Crowe et al., 2002).

(iv) Victim Alert/Notification Systems

A variation of the continuously signalling devices has been developed for victim alert and notification and offender compliance with stay-away orders. It is most often used for domestic violence victims. A receiver is placed in both the victim's and the offender's residences. Both the victim and offender wear transmitters. The victim's transmitter is similar to a pendant and is removable, while the offender wears a tamper-resistant bracelet or anklet that is not removed. The offender's receiver detects his presence in his home to be sure he is there when he is supposed to be there. If he approaches the victim's home, his transmitter signal will be detected by the victim's receiver. The victim also may press a button on the pendant transmitter device she wears and can alert the monitoring staff should the offender approach or enter her home after removing or disabling his transmitter device (NLECTC, 1999).

(v) Group Monitoring Units

Sometimes programs will want to supervise several offenders in the same location using electronic technology. This might be appropriate for tasks such as verifying attendance of multiple offenders in a day-reporting program or monitoring offenders confined in a residential group setting. Each offender in a group setting wears a transmitter, and all transmitters are monitored by one group monitoring unit, much like a field monitoring device. The group monitoring unit reports an exception when an offender's transmitter signal is not picked up (i.e., the offender has left the area) or attempts to tamper with the transmitter. Additional information is received and stored by the group monitoring unit and can be downloaded to a computer to generate reports at a later time (Crowe et al., 2002).

(vi) Biometrics Identification System

Biometric identification technologies use a particular biological aspect of the human body to recognize or confirm that person's identity. The term "biometrics" refers to a variety of methods to verify a person's identity using physiological or behavioural characteristics such as iris, retinal, and facial recognition; hand and finger geometry; fingerprint and voice identification; and dynamic signature. It has the advantage of not requiring a person to remember a user name, password, or series of numbers while confirming that the person is who he or she claims to be. Practical uses of biometrics include allowing person's access to keyless cars, rooms, and buildings; to financial and other personal accounts; and to the departure areas of airport terminals. More broadly, it is used to prevent identity theft, preserve the confidentiality of information, and reduce fraud. These technologies can be applied in the criminal justice system to enhance access control and identity verification in correctional facilities, and as an investigative tool for identifying missing and exploited children as well as criminals captured by surveillance systems. Technologies in the research stage, underdevelopment, and in use in the field include facial recognition technologies and biometrically enhanced smart cards (NIJ, 2001; Crowe et al., 2002; Miles & Cohn, 2006).

2. Geographic Information Systems (GIS)

Geographic Information Systems (GIS) technology is a relative newcomer to the field of criminal justice, having made its debut less than 10 years ago. However, the technology found a niche in crime prevention/reduction and criminal rehabilitation via crime analysis maps (Rose, 1998). As applications of GIS have grown, corrections have begun to explore ways in which computer mapping can expand its analytical repertoire (Cadora, Swartz, & Stoe, 2000; Rich, 1995; Harries, 1999; Harris, Huenke, & O'Connell, 1998; O'Connell & Fleury, 1999). GIS helps the correctional administrators both inside and outside the correctional institutions. GIS plays a significant role in the management of offenders (Jaishankar, 2005). According to the International GIS Dictionary, GIS is a "computer system for capturing, managing, integrating, manipulating, analysing and displaying data which is spatially referenced to the Earth" (McDonnell & Kemp, 1995). GIS has the capability to relate layers of data for the same points in space, combining, analysing and, finally, mapping out the results (Burrough & McDonnell, 1998).

In recent years, U.S. correctional institutions have begun exploring ways GIS can assist their daily operations. California is one of the first states to create a GIS dataset (a part of the database) for corrections. It contains information about the California prison location and youth correctional facilities locations, including addresses, name of the city and the number of prisoners. California adult correctional facilities were mapped using GIS to aid local planning departments by providing the data on prisons and prisoners (Teale GIS Solutions Group, 1997). The Mapping in Corrections Initiative (1999) is a phenomenal effort taken by the U.S. Department of Justice's Crime Mapping Research Center (CMRC) (presently, Mapping and Analysis for Public Safety) to promote the use of GIS for research and practice in community and institutional corrections. Some examples of the utility of GIS for corrections identified by the Mapping in Corrections Initiative include:

- Identifying areas prone to inmate violence in institutional settings;
- Assigning probation and parole officers by geographic location;
- Directing probationers and parolees to services and treatment centers; and
- Making site selection decisions for the placement of new facilities within a community (for a detailed analysis of GIS in Corrections see Jaishankar, 2005).

From tracking the concentration of probationers in a neighbourhood to gang members in an institution, GIS can be a great benefit to the corrections community. Institutional corrections and community corrections are two distinct areas in which GIS can be used (Russo, 2001). Russo (2001) argues that there are more applications of GIS in community corrections than in institutional corrections and he substantiates with the problems related to coordinates, and geo-coding (Geocoding is the process that assigns a latitude-longitude coordinate to an address) (TechBeat, 2002). Mapping tools can help with prison management in numerous ways, including tracking disciplinary incidents, visitation patterns and medical information, managing gangs and escape threats, and identifying personal information about inmates such as contagious diseases (Hart, 2003).

GIS helps correctional officials to determine potential sites for building prisons by examining complex, seemingly unrelated criteria such as demographic characteristics and displaying them all in a graphical, layered, spatial interface or map and in mapping prison expansions (Lawrence & Travis, 2004). It also helps them map inmate populations, fixtures, and equipment to provide for the safety of inmates by separating gang members, identifying high-risk or potentially violent inmates, and identifying hazardous locations in a prison. It reduces the potential for internal violence by providing better command and control. Criminal intelligence information, including photographs, fingerprints, and documents can be included in this interactive graphical interface. Intranet/ Internet capability enables the information to be shared within and between institutions. GIS "live map" (a map which is updated frequently with the help of Global positioning systems, such as movement of persons or vehicles) functions, when combined with capabilities of location identification devices (GPS, personal inertial guidance, etc.), facilitate tracking the movement of high-risk inmates or at-risk personnel throughout any facility or area.

3. Global Positioning Systems (GPS)

For years, the United States has been behind in the development of new prisons. As crime continued to outpace new prison construction, authorities had to develop alternative ways to punish, deter, control, and rehabilitate criminal offenders, while at the same time being pragmatic regarding manpower, budget, and prison space. Over time, electronic monitoring devices were created—the first form was house arrest. People who committed a non-violent crime were often given house arrest to free up space for the more deadly and dangerous criminal.

While house arrest was effective as a starting point, it didn't go far enough because many people were leaving their house and committing crimes, and authorities had no means to track them (Stark, 2003). Furthermore, to help relieve the overcrowding problem, parole was also used for dangerous criminals such as paedophiles. Given their past record, and to increase public safety, authorities have now determined that many paedophiles—and other people with violent track records—are just too dangerous to be left alone. Parole officers are supposed to physically check on parolees, but they're drastically overworked and have more of a caseload than they can handle. With the advent of GPS tracking systems, officers have been given the ability to monitor someone's movement 24 hours a day, seven days a week (Stark, 2003). GPS—rely on 24 satellites that orbit the earth thousands of miles away. These satellites were originally designed by the U.S. military for navigation, mapping, and weapons delivery purposes. However, they are now used in a variety of non-military applications including personal car and boat navigation and electronic supervision of offenders (Rosica, 2000; Crowe et al., 2002).

Subjects under GPS tracking and monitoring wear a removable Personal Tracking Unit (PTU) and a non-removable wireless ankle cuff. The ankle cuff is the size of a large wristwatch. The cuff communicates with the PTU to ensure that both items are always within a close and specific proximity of each other. If communication with the cuff is lost, the PTU assumes that the user has abandoned it and a violation is recorded. The PTU acquires its location from the Department of Defence's GPS satellites, and records this time and location into an Internet-based database system. This information is communicated back to probation, parole, bonding, and court officials. Using a Web browser, authorities are able to look at a detailed map to determine where the person has been. If a violation is detected, that is, if a person was in a place where they were excluded from being, authorities can take action. For instance, a paedophile might be ordered by a court to stay away from schools and the GPS tracking system would indicate if this were being abided. When a crime is committed, law enforcement can also analyze the data from GPS tracking to see if a known criminal was in the general vicinity (Stark, 2003; Crowe et al., 2002).

Candidates for GPS tracking include people at the pre-trial stage (rather than go to jail or get released on their own recognizance, they are sent home with a device), someone on probation, and someone freed on parole. Other users might include people being released to a halfway house or furloughs. The largest group of individuals who can benefit from GPS tracking systems is the non-violent offender whose detention in prison will only worsen their economic and social situation. For example, a person who has been convicted of a non-violent crime, and who is a full-time employee, and full-time parent. Sending this individual to prison would cause a loss of employment, reduction in taxes, increase in correctional spending, and deterioration in their family structure. Granted, this person broke the law and deserves some form of punishment, but prison does not rehabilitate offenders, it is simply a warehouse to remove individuals from society. With GPS tracking, these non-violent offenders can remain employed, continue to pay taxes, and maintain their status as a family member, while at the same time being punished by the restriction in movement. While imprisonment costs thousands of dollars per month, the cost for GPS tracking per person is significantly lower, about one-tenth the cost (Stark, 2003; Crowe et al., 2002).

Info-Tech Prisons in the Developed Countries

The Corrections Departments of United States are the pioneers in the application of IT for all their day-to-day activities. In U.S., in the mid-1970s, correctional operations, which lacked financial capital for computerization, remained largely manual in nature. A study (Brown, 2000) revealed that no more than 15 per cent of county correctional systems had automated arrest records and only 12 per cent had automated jail population records. Although counties appeared slow to innovate, cities were making a bit more progress. Thirty per cent of the cities had automated arrest records and 9 per cent had automated jail population records. Overall, by 1975 only approximately 23 per cent of local government agencies had computerized arrest records and only 10 per cent had automated jail population records. In 1980's too correctional agencies continued to lag in their technology adoption efforts. Although nearly one-third of the agencies reported automated wants and warrants, only a small percentage (12 per cent) reported automated jail management records (Brown, 2000).

By the mid-1990s, concern about underutilization of IT in corrections led to National Institute of Justice (NIJ) and the National Institute of Corrections (NIC) sponsoring several studies on the adoption rate of technology in corrections. A survey of 49 correctional institutions concluded, 'Correctional officials were unanimous in describing management information systems as essential to their work. However, their biggest complaint was that their systems were underutilized' (Kichen, Murphy & Levinson, 1993). The survey suggested that the underutilization resulted from poorly designed information systems and a lack of sufficient equipment and adequate training. Although IT had become an integral support mechanism in many daily operations, systems were not well managed, negating many potential benefits. A second correctional survey released in 1995 examined 148 federal, state, and local correctional agencies comprising of 48 state and federal adult prisons, 44 large prisons and prison systems, and 56 community correctional agencies. By this time, IT was in use in numerous corrections operations. Approximately 80 per cent of adult facilities, nearly 70 per cent of community correctional agencies, and approximately 60 per cent of large jails had access to a local area network with electronic mail capability. The majority of the facilities also had access to NCIC and local or the state's online offender information. Interestingly, even though the vast majority of the facilities were satisfied with their technology, negative comments such as 'minimally adequate', 'slow' and 'cumbersome' surfaced.

A third survey of state and federal correctional information systems, released in 1998, focused not on hardware access but rather on the extent to which electronic data were available to support correctional operations in all 50 state-level institutions. Respondents identified the data collected and maintained in electronic format the data available for computation. The survey asked if the state correctional departments maintained a database of 207 specific items deemed critical by the researchers. The data categories included offender profiles, behaviours, and release information. It turned out that no department collected all of the data elements. Collection rates ranged from 16 to 85 per cent and 32 departments captured at least 50 per cent of the critical data elements. Only 40 departments maintained data on offender behaviour and only 38 maintained data on crimes committed by offenders under some form of supervision. Unfortunately, the study failed to evaluate data quality (Brown, 2000). Today U.S. is the major user of IT in prison systems and most of the technologies reviewed in this chapter are the ones which are currently adapted successfully in their prison systems (Brown, 2000).

In Canada, the Corrections Offender Management System (COMS) has been installed in three Canadian provinces and territories, including the province of Manitoba, running on province/territory-wide networks, supporting the offender and case management activities of corrections personnel at all locations. This product was first installed in 1998, and these projects are in the middle stages of a multiyear modular development process. COMS is a versatile, easy-to-use tool that improves both the efficiency and the effectiveness of corrections record-keeping and information sharing. It improves communications by providing a common database for youth, adult, custody, and community corrections data, reduces paperwork, particularly the redundant entry of information, improves record keeping; program evaluation; statistical analysis; and management information integration with other justice initiatives to provide data exchange among police, courts, and corrections, within and between jurisdictions (Niche, 2006).

In the United Kingdom over 50 prisons are now using state-of-the-art Prison Video Links (PVLs) improving security, and saving time and public money. Video link technology has been installed in 54 prisons in England and Wales, allowing them to link directly to 30 Crown Courts and 153 Magistrate Courts across England and Wales. PVLs allow offenders to appear in court via a live video link from prison, reducing the cost of transporting prisoners between prisons and courts. Other benefits include the protection of witnesses and victims in court and improved security. PVLs were introduced across the country after being successfully piloted between Manchester Crown Court (Crown Square) and Manchester Prison in 1999 (Crown, 2004a). Apart from the PVLs a satellite tracking system to keep close tabs on offenders has been launched in three areas of the U.K. Offenders will be tracked following their release from custody or as part of their compliance with a new community penalty called the exclusion order, which prevents an offender going to specific locations. The tracking technology uses a satellite Global Positioning System (GPS), backed up by mobile phone technology to monitor offenders' movements and ensure they are complying with the restrictions placed on them. Satellite tracking will also be used as part of the ongoing intensive supervision of persistent juvenile offenders in the community, which combines close surveillance and strict curfews with mentoring and support programmes to keep young offenders out of prison (Crown, 2004b).

Inmates' movements are monitored remotely by prison staff in The Netherlands. The hi-tech jail in the central city of Lelystad opens and locks its doors to low-risk inmates. Electronic bracelets track their moves while emotion recognition software monitors tempers—with good behaviour rewarded with privileges. The tags and touch-screen computers at the end of their beds allow them to organise their own daily schedules—with a choice of sports, recreation, personal development, education and outdoor activities. The tag sends a signal every two seconds, so if a prisoner is not where he should be, an alarm will sound and he will lose out on credits for good behaviour. These can be used towards privileges such as extra phone calls, visiting time or the chance to swap cells. The prison is also equipped with monitoring systems that detect aggression—as used by police in various districts in the northern town of Groningen. The prison will be run on an experimental basis for six months, with offenders being given the option of serving time at Lelystad. Hardened criminals, people with heavy drug dependency or psychological problems are not admitted in these prisons (*BBC News*, 2006).

The New Zealand Corrections Department became responsible for its own IT resources in 1995, and initially it was found that the IT systems were unreliable, had been badly managed, contained poor information, and provided little support to enhance business capability or capacity. The existing IT systems did not match the then current business needs, and there was no IT direction to align IT systems to future needs. In the first IT Strategic Plan 1996-99, outdated stand-alone systems were replaced with a modern integrated technology platform built around new core business systems and these systems became the building blocks for more advanced information management and analytical tools. Central to corrections information management is the Integrated Offender Management System (IOMS). It is highly networked and supports at least 1,500 concurrent users at peak time, to exchange information about 20,000 people on probation and 6,000 in prisons. IOMS can be accessed from 230 sites using desktops and remotely if required. Only incremental changes to IOMS are planned in the next few years.

Dubai is one country which has started the implementation of IT in the correctional system with the help of Microsoft. Microsoft South Gulf inaugurated the first two Microsoft training centres in correctional facilities in Dubai as part of its unlimited potential initiative in 2006. The training centres were recently opened in Dubai's Drug Rehabilitation Programme Centre in *Al Awir* and at the Central Prison in *Jumeira*. Both centres will provide prisoners with the equipment to undertake technology training courses, allowing them to enhance their professional skills and provide them with better opportunities to become productive members of the community once they are released. The Microsoft initiative is being implemented in coordination with Dubai police and Dubai eGovernment as well as New Horizons-Human (Bink.nu, 2006).

In Singapore, a Housing Unit (HU) Management System implemented in 1999 to enable prison officers to perform the dual roles of effective safe custody and rehabilitation of inmates through teamwork and purposeful interaction. The commissioning of the Prison Management System (PMS) in 2000 heralded a new era in (Singapore Prison Service) SPS and was a significant start to the new millennium. The PMS is an integrated electronic database which supports prison operation, tracks all information of inmates and is the first amongst Prison and Correctional Services in the world to be equipped with digital imaging technology. Tele-visit facilities are provided in certain institutions to help inmates maintain contact with their families from a remote location, via the Prisons Link Centre. Also SPS was awarded the inaugural e-Society Excellence Award in 2005 for its application of information-communication technology in internet home tele-visit project (SPS, 2006).

Info-Tech Prisons in Less Developed Countries

The less developed countries still use the term 'computerization' which has become obsolete in developed countries and the level of usage of IT is less than developed countries. In India, a "Prisoners Information System", was made by NIC (National Informatics Centre). This is purely a MIS based system and not equivalent to advanced systems in developed countries. All the Central Prisons in Tamil Nadu and Kerala have been provided with computers and the "Prisoners Information System". The NIC is also developing software, for computerization of prison records. In Tamil Nadu, a computer centre has been started in each central prison and special prison for women, at a cost of ₹ 155 lakhs to provide computer training to prisoners. A similar training (named Akshya) is available in Kerala Kannur prison (IT Kerala, 2006). To promote transparency in administration, and to enable the public awareness about the activities of this department, a website designed and hosted by NIC was launched by the Prison Department (Tamil Nadu prison policy note, 2005). The West Bengal government has taken up an ₹ 2 crore computerisation program in central jails to simplify access to prisoner records and improve security. According to the plan, the case histories, court orders, duty rosters of jailers and the security details will be stored in computers once the system is in place. NIC has also developed a software for this purpose. In addition, all the central jails will be connected with Writers' Buildings by a network. Six central jails, including Presidency, Alipore and Dum Dum, will initially be made a part of the network (*The Telegraph*, Feb. 8, 2006).

All the jails in *Tihar* have been computerised way back in 1994. There are eight NIC computer centres in Tihar Jail Complex, one in each of the seven jails and one in Prison Head Quarters. All these Computer Centres are connected to each other through Fiber Optic LAN. Each centre is equipped with a Pentium Pro Server and different nodes have been given to different sections. There is a computer centre at the Tihar Jail Reception for Public Inquiry. The Tihar Prison Department is shortly introducing Biometric Finger Identification System wherein every newly admitted prisoner and escort staff of Delhi Police would be photographed along with their finger prints. Also going in the way of advance technology like use of CCTV, DFMD's and HHMD's etc. NIC is giving all the hardware and software support. An engineer from NIC is permanently posted in Tihar Jail for the hardware and software maintenance and software development. Upgradation of the prison inmates' information system has been proposed to the government incorporating finger prints and photographs of prisoners to enhance security. The proposed upgradation also aims at fully computerising systems of visitors' management, hospital management, personnel management, inventory management, etc. This will immensely help jail administration in proper management of prisons (Tihar Prisons, 2006).

Olsen (2003) in a study on computerization of legal institutions in Zambia has analysed the situation of usage of computers in Zambian Prison Service (ZPS). In ZPS, the outcome of computerisation has been relatively successful; the computerised system has led to more reliable information being distributed throughout the legal system, and it has resulted in prisoners having their trials scheduled in a better manner. In Zambia, the existing records of prisoners are in the electronic format, but they have not installed or make use of any advanced application (Olsen, 2003). Video conferencing technology has now played a role in Thailand corrections. Everyday, the Department of Corrections has to transport a number of inmates to and from criminal courts. Such burden consumes both correctional manpower and time. At present, some prisons have installed video conference system with the courts to operate regular trial warrants procedure. This innovation has helped in lessening the daily number of inmate transportation to the court, and the use of limited manpower. It also enhances the security system for the courts as well as the prisons. So as to improve the management on corrections to catch up with the world's technological progress, the Thailand Department of Corrections is now operating the on-line computer system. This on-line computer system provide network among the headquarters and 148 prisons across the country. Prisoner's fingerprint shall be kept and accessed to by digital system, and the past, present or future information of inmates and concerned data shall be computerized. This is considered as an important step of bringing technology to develop correctional management in Thailand (TDOC, 2004).

The Mauritius Prison Administration, being aware of the importance of computers in management, and of the rapid developments taking place in this sector, set out in April 1994, to introduce computerisation of its services. This program, being the fruit of a study effected by the "State Informatics Limited"—spread over different phases, was laid down as follows:

Phase 1: Computerisation of the administrative block and the central prison;

Phase 2: Computerisation of other penal institutions;

Phase 3: Linking up the computer system of the prison department to that of the judiciary and the police in view of a common action, thus being more effective; For the time being, Phase 1 is nearly complete and the prison administration is seriously contemplating to start Phase 2 by the beginning of next year. Moreover, the service is connected to the internet since March 1996 (Mauritius Prisons Service, 2006).

Conclusion

This chapter has provided an overview of how IT may support the decision-making processes in prisons. It focused on the use of appropriate IT tools used in the prison administration and three major types of IT tools were described. The increasing use of technology is an important aspect in addressing the needs of correctional administration. Predicting the future of IT in prisons is very problematic. How the prison systems will respond to technological change is also unknown at this point. The prison system appears to lag behind other areas of society in the adoption of new technologies. Nevertheless, some trends appear certain. Prison administration has become more and more dependent on computers and networked data sources. IT skills have become essential. Systems such as these are likely to receive widespread adoption in the developed as well as less developed countries. Particularly as budgets for correctional institutions continue to grow, the public may demand shifting towards effective and safe community alternatives. As the technology becomes more sophisticated and less expensive, and a greater number of correctional databases are made available via secure networks, the implementation of systems approaching real time integration may be possible. Rather than waiting for overnight data, correctional officials will be tracking monitored offenders in real time and getting access to crime report data as soon as it is filed.

Even though IT has occupied the top place in the prisons systems, Wright (2000) argues that it is only a tool and not a panacea. Wright (2000) also warns that an administrator who relies on technology alone to maintain control of the prison facility will find that interpersonal problems, conflicts, and grievances will escalate to the point that no system, no matter how infallible, will be successful. While accepting Wright's (2000) argument, it should also be noted that, new technologies have also proved helpful in making prisons safer, reducing costs and improving the effective management of facilities. Technologies like GIS and GPS can make prisons and jails safer for both corrections professionals and inmates (Hart, 2003). IT is progressively accepted as a valuable tool for correctional institutions around the world, especially in the United States, United Kingdom, and Australia. Rapid developments in computer technology, resulting in reduced costs of IT, have only increased the recent appeal of this technology to corrections. IT applications in the developed have taken their firm roots. Now, correctional institutions of less developed countries should take their strides in IT applications in corrections. To achieve this, nodal agencies to implement and manage IT in correctional institutions should be initiated in both the developed as well as developing nations.

References

BBC News. (2006). *Dutch open 'Big Brother' jail.* Retrieved on 15th August, 2010 from http://news.bbc.co.uk/2/hi/europe/4628186.stm

Bink.nu (2006). *Microsoft Gulf Inaugurates Training Centres in Dubai Correctional Facilities.* Retrieved on 15th August, 2010 from http://bink.nu/Article919.bink

Black, M., & Smith, R.G. (2003). Electronic Monitoring in the Criminal Justice System. *Trends and Issues in Crime and Criminal Justice series.* No. 254. Canberra, Australia. Australian Institute of Criminology.

Brennan, T.D., Wells, & Alexander, J. (2004). *Enhancing Prison Classification Systems: The Emerging Role of Management Information Systems.* July 2004 Northpointe Institute for Public Management, Inc. MI NIC Accession Number: 019687. U.S. Department of Justice and National Institute of Corrections.

Brown, M. (2000). Criminal Justice Discovers IT The Nature of Crime: Continuity and Change. *Criminal Justice 2000.* 1, 220-59.

Cadora, E.C., Swartz, & Stoe, D. (2000). *Corrections Mapping and Community Justice.* Abstract of the paper presented at the American Society of Criminology Conference, 14-18 November, 2000 at Los Angeles.

Crowe, A.H., L. Sydney, P., Bancroft, & Lawrence, B. (2002). *Offender Supervision with Electronic Technology: A User's Guide.* Kentucky: American Probation and Parole Association and National Institute of Justice.

Crown (2004a). *Over 50 prisons now using Video Link technology—08 Jul 05.* Retrieved on 15th August, 2010 from http://www.hmprisonservice.gov.uk/news/index.asp?id=3492,22,6,22,0,0

Crown (2004b). *Eye in the Sky to reduce re-offending - 02 Sep 04.* Retrieved on 15th August, 2010 from http://www.hmprisonservice.gov.uk/news/index.asp?id=1751,22,6,22,0,0

Fox, R.G. (1987). Dr Schwitzgebel's Machine Revisited: Electronic Monitoring of Offenders. *Australian and New Zealand Journal of Criminology, 20*(3), 131-47.

Harries, K. (1999). *Mapping Crime: Principle and Practice.* Washington, D.C.: National Institute of Justice.

Harris, R., C. Huenke., & O'Connell, J.P. (1998). Using mapping to increase released offenders' accesses to services. In N. La Vigne & J. Wartell (eds.), *Crime Mapping Case Studies: Successes in the Field* (pp. 61-66). Washington, D.C.: Police Executive Research Forum.

Hart, S. (2003). Making Prisons Safer through Technology. *Corrections Today*, 65(2) April 2003 issue.

IT Kerala (2006). *Akshaya to benefit inmates in prison.* IT Kerala Newsletter on IT in Kerala from the Kerala state IT mission. 49, May 2006. Retrieved on 15th August, 2010 from http://www.keralaitmission.org/web/main/default.asp?action=50&what=50&type=0

Jaishankar, K. (2005). Mapping and Corrections: Management of offenders with GIS. *Corrections Compendium,* 30(1), 7-9, 31 to 33, January/February, American Correctional Association.

Kichen, C., J. Murphy, & Levinson, R.B. (1993). *Correctional technology: A user's guide.* Washington, D.C.: U.S. Department of Justice, National Institute of Corrections.

Lawrence, S., & Travis, J. (2004). *The New Landscape of Imprisonment: Mapping America's Prison Expansion.* Research report. Washington, D.C.: Urban Institute, Justice Policy Center.

Liverani, M.R. (1998). Slow take-up for home detention: Magistrates cool, many lawyers unaware of the option. *Law Society Journal*, 42-48, February.

Mauritius Prisons Service (2006). *Computerization.* Retrieved on 15th August, 2010 from http://www.gov.mu/portal/site/prisons/menuitem.c9a355ecf9be5d2ff4a9e75b0bb521ca/

Maxfield, M.G., & Baumer, T.L. (1990). Home detention with electronic monitoring: Comparing pre-trial and post-conviction programs. *Crime and Delinquency*, 36(4), 521-36.

Miles, C.A., & Cohn, J.P. (2006). Tracking Prisoners in Jail with Biometrics: An Experiment in a Navy Brig. *NIJ Journal* No. 253. January 2006. Retrieved on 15th August, 2010 from http://www.ojp.usdoj.gov/nij/journals/253/index.html

New Zealand Department of Corrections. (2004). *IT Operational Strategy: Introduction.* Retrieved on 15th August, 2010 from http://www.corrections.govt.nz/public/news/strategic-documents/sbp/itstrat/

Niche (2006). *COMS: Corrections Offender Management System.* Retrieved on 15th August, 2010 from http://www.nicherms.com/coms_advantages.html

NIJ (National Institute of Justice) (2001). *A Resource Guide to Law Enforcement, Corrections, and Forensic Technologies.* Washington D.C.: Office of Justice Programs and Office of Community Oriented Policing Services, U.S. Department of Justice, Office of Justice Programs, National Institute of Justice.

O'Connell, M., & Fleury, J.K. (1999). *Mapping for Corrections*. Proceedings of the 19th Annual ESRI International User Conference in San Diego, California, held during July 26-30, 1999.

Olsen, J. (2003). Computerisation of legal institutions in Zambia: A comparative institutional analysis of administrative reform. A thesis submitted to the Institut for Statskundskab, Aarhus Universitet Specialevejleder: Mette Kjær 38.842 ordÅrskortnummer 990925.

Renzema, M. (1992). *The Electronic Monitoring Primer*. Mechanicsburg, PA: Tracking Systems Corporation.

Rich, T.F. (1995). *The Use of Computerized Mapping in Crime Control and Prevention Programs*. Research in Action Report: Washington, DC: U.S. Department of Justice, National Institute of Justice. Retrieved on 15th August, 2010 from www.ncjrs.org/txtfiles/riamap.txt

Richardson, R. (1999). Electronic tagging of offenders: Trials in England. *The Howard Journal*, 38(2), 158-72.

Rondinelli, V. (1997). Tracking humans: The electronic bracelet in a modern world. *Criminal Lawyers' Association Newsletter*, August. Retrieved on 15th August, 2010 from http://www.criminallawyers.ca/newslett/aug97/rondinelli.htm.

Rose, M.S. (1998). Mapping technology takes a bite out of crime. *Business Geographics*. Adams Business Media, June 1998. Retrieved on 15th August, 2010 from http://www.geoplace.com/bg/1998/0698/698maptc.asp

Rosica, J.L. (2000, May 8). New system will track criminals: CrimeTrax uses satellites to keep tabs on probationers and parolees. *Tallahassee Democrat* [Online]. Retrieved on 15th August, 2010 from http://www.tdo.com/news/local/0508.loc.crimetrax.htm.

Russo, J. (2001). Helping corrections inside and outside prison walls. *Corrections Today*, 63(7), 140-44.

Saylor, W.G. (1994). *The Design, Development, and Maintenance of Executive Information Systems for Corrections, Probation and Parole*. Paper presented in the Symposium on Criminal Justice Information Systems and Technology: Building the Infrastructure.

Schwitzgebel, R. (1968). Electronically monitored parole. *Prison Journal*, 48(2), 34-35.

Singapore Prison service (SPS) (2006). *Our Transformation*. Retrieved on 15th August, 2010 from http://www.prisons.gov.sg/our_transformation.html

Stark, J. (2003). Technology Tackles Troublemakers as the War on Crime Heats Up (Feb. 05, 2003) *Directions Magazine*. Retrieved on 15th August, 2010 from http://www.directionsmag.com/

Tamil Nadu Prison Policy Note (2005). *Home Department: Tamil Nadu Prison Department—Policy Note 2005-2006.* Demand No. 23, Retrieved on 15th August, 2010 from http://www.tn.gov.in/policynotes/pdf/home_prisons.pdf

Teale GIS solutions group. (1997). *State of California Prisons.* Retrieved on 15th August, 2010 from http://gis.ca.gov/catalog/docs/descriptions.html

TechBeat. (2002). *Cormap it.* National Law Enforcement and Corrections Technology Center, Summer 2002. A quarterly newsmagazine of the National Law Enforcement and Corrections Technology Center, a program of the National Institute of Justice, awarded by the U.S. Department of Justice, p. 5.

Thailand Department of Corrections (TDOC) (2004). *Video conference and online computer system.* Retrieved on 15th August, 2010 from http://www.correct.go.th/Innovation.htm

The Telegraph (February 8, 2006). *Prison data to go digital—Records, rosters in networked computers for instant access.*

Tihar Prisons. (2006). *Infrastructure: Computerization of Prisons.* Retrieved on 15th August, 2010 from http://tiharprisons.nic.in/html/infra.htm

Wright, K.N. (2000). The Evolution of Decision-making Among Prison Executives, 1975-2000. *Policies, Processes, and Decisions of the Criminal Justice System, Criminal Justice 2000, 3.*

15

Strategies for Revamping the Indian Prison System

Priti Bharadwaj

Introduction

India's prison system continues to be plagued by age-old myriad problems. The scenario has not changed until before independence. Overcrowded prisons, disproportionately high undertrial population, lack of sufficient resources, frustrated and overburdened prison staff, lack of escorts to produce prisoners in court, unnecessary detention of undertrials for undue period are among some of the major concerns weighing down the Indian prisons. Though the problems that plague the Indian prisons were highlighted in the previous chapters, I would highlight some of them specifically and provide some solutions to the problems and this chapter will serve as a conclusion to the book.

I. Lack of Political Will

Having curtailed their liberty, prisoners do not enjoy voting rights. Even though they can contest elections being in the prison, they cannot vote. This lack of power in deciding the next ruling party has made them forgotten souls behind bars. The 3,76,396[1] votes do not count and hence the politicians disregard spending any time or money to curb the challenges faced by both the prisoners and the prison administration. Even the society does not have a sympathetic attitude towards those imprisoned. A person in the prison, irrespective of the fact that s/he has not been proven guilty, is already considered a criminal in the eyes

---

1. National Crime Records Bureau (2007). *Prison Statistics India*, p. (i), Ministry of Home Affairs, Government of India.

of the community. Hence, reforming prisons has never been a priority on the agenda of a political party. In 1996, the National Human Rights Commission (NHRC) suggested a prison reform bill, which has been conveniently ignored by all the governments as prisons is not their priority.[2] The importance of political will in reforming prisons cannot be undermined. The United Nations report emphasizes "encouraging national ownership, generating political will, and civil society involvement in the prison system are complex and difficult processes, yet are key to success of programme support".[3]

II. Prison Overcrowding

"The occupancy rate of more than 100 per cent results in overcrowding in the jail."[4] One of the striking features of Indian prisons is the 141.4 per cent overcrowding across the 35 states and union territories. India was accommodating 3,76,396 prisoners in 2007 in its 1276 prisons having a capacity of 2,77,304 prisoners. 141.4 per cent is the overall average, with some states exceeding way beyond.[5] Uttar Pradesh reported the highest overcrowding of prisons (201.3%) followed by Chhattisgarh (193.3%) and Delhi (185.7%). Seventy-four per cent of the states struggle with overcrowded prisons. Only nine states and union territories[6] have their prison population within the prison capacity.

Overcrowded prisons is one of the root causes branching into several problems such as inadequate resources for every prisoner; increased burden on the limited prison staff; disgruntled and frustrated staff; lack of sufficient escort for the production of prisoners in court; delay in delivery of justice; deteriorating

2. Parwini Zora. (2005). *Fifty-four Years In Jail Without Trial: The Plight of Prison Inmates in India*, http://www.countercurrents.org/hr-zora260805.htm as on 20 August 2010.
3. United Nations. (2005). *Supporting National Prison Systems: Lessons Learned and Best Practices for Peacekeeping Operations*, p. 6.
4. As defined by National Crime Records Bureau. (2007). *Prison Statistics India*, Glossary, Ministry of Home Affairs, Government of India.
5. National Crime Records Bureau. (2007). *Prison Statistics India*, p. 15, Ministry of Home Affairs, Government of India.
6. Jammu & Kashmir, Manipur, Mizoram, Nagaland, Rajasthan, West Bengal, Chandigarh, Dadar & Nagar Haveli, and Daman & Diu.

hygiene and sanitation conditions; and inadequate health care facilities; etc. It also causes surveillance and security issues which ordinarily is one of the key concerns of prison officers. This has been identified by the Apex Court on several occasions including in *Ramamurthy* v. *State of Karnataka*[7], when a prisoner from Bangalore Central Jail complained about the general living conditions in a letter to the Chief Justice of India. The letter was treated as a writ petition and an inquiry was carried out by a District Judge who submitted a comprehensive report on the same. The Supreme Court observed the various problems that cropped as a result of the overcrowded prison.

III. Disproportionate Undertrial to Convict Ratio

Indian prisons have a strikingly high undertrial population. Undertrials are persons kept in prison (judicial custody) while the charges against them are being tried.[8] Undertrials are prisoners who are innocent in the eyes of the law. Yet, Indian prisons house prisoners of which 66.6 per cent are undertrials.[9] Only 31.9 per cent of Indian prison population are convicted. The highest number of undertrials at the end of 2007 were reported from Uttar Pradesh (53,992), followed by Bihar (33,316), Madhya Pradesh (16,537), and Madhya Pradesh (16,300).[10]

A lot of these prisoners continue to remain in prisons, despite being charged of bailable offences. In bailable offences, it is the right of the accused to be out on bail. However, since the bail system is biased and favours those that are economically well-off, it cannot be called impartial or fair. It is a challenge for the indigent to produce such huge monetary amounts for their release and so they continue to stay in prisons.

> Democracy's very life depends upon making the machinery of justice so effective that every citizen shall believe in and benefit by its impartiality and fairness.[11]

7. AIR 1997 SC 1739.
8. National Crime Records Bureau (2007). *Prison Statistics India*, Glossary, Ministry of Home Affairs, Government of India.
9. *Ibid.*, p. (i).
10. *Ibid.*, p. 29.
11. *MH Hoskot* v. *State of Maharashtra*, (1978) 3 SSC 544.

> With imprisonment, a radical transformation comes over a prisoner, which can be described as prisonisation. He loses his identity. He is known by a number. He loses personal possessions. He has no personal relationships. Psychological problems result from loss of freedom, status, possessions, dignity and autonomy of personal life.[12]

Just like Machang Lalung[13] and Syed Maqbool[14] Shah who had completely forgotten how life would be outside the four walls on their release after fifty-four and fourteen years respectively. While Machang, had he been convicted would have been given a maximum punishment of ten years imprisonment, was released after paying a token bond amount of one rupee. Syed was acquitted after serving fourteen years in prison. There are several Syed's and Machang's who continue to stay in prison without being given an opportunity to prove their innocence. The legislators identified this and in 2005 amended the Cr.P.C. to set a maximum period that an undertrial prisoner can be kept in prison. The 2005 amendment of the Cr.P.C. has brought some respite to a small section of undertrial prisoners. (See the section on *Release of Undertrial Prisoners*)

IV. Delay in Disposal of Cases for the Underprivileged

> Hundreds of them are dumb, simple persons, caught in the web of the law, unable to comprehend as to what has happened, what the charge against them is, or why they have been sent to jail. These are the people without a calendar or a clock, only a date in a court diary, extended from hearing to hearing.[15]

---

12. *A Convict Prisoner in the Central Prison* v. *State of Kerala*, 1993 Cri LJ 3242.
13. Parwini Zora (2005). *Fifty-four years in Jail without Trial: The Plight of Prison Inmates in India*. http://www.countercurrents.org/hr-zora260805.htm as on 25 August 2010.
14. Zahid Rafiq (2010). After 14 years, free 'strange' to acquitted man. http://www.indianexpress.com/news/after-14-years-freedom-strange-to-acquitted-man/610236/0 as on 19 August 2010.
15. K.F. Rustamji, Member of National Police Commission in 1978.

Most prisoners are poor and belong to the underprivileged sections of society. The state that deprives them of liberty is duty bound to provide them the basic necessities. The Supreme Court in *Hussainara Khatoon and Others (II)* v. *Home Secretary, State of Bihar* case found that "though speedy trial is not specifically enumerated as a fundamental right, it is implicit in the broad sweep and content of Article 21".[16] One of the critical problems plaguing Indian criminal justice system is the colossal delay in disposal of cases. This delay in disposal of cases may be attributed to three primary causes namely: large number of vacancies for the position of judicial officers; inability/failure of the police to complete investigation on a timely basis; and lack of police escort to produce the accused in court.[17]

All these challenges can be resolved, however due to a lack of political will and desire among the key players, nothing has been done to remedy the situation. Judges can be appointed, a dedicated branch of police can be appointed to look into investigations; and similarly with less overcrowded prisons, proper coordination between police and prisons, appropriate number of escorts can be managed. However, if there is no will among the police officers to complete investigation on a timely basis, and if there is no desire among the judicial officers to complete a case without prolonging it to more dates and letting the prisoners languish in prison, nothing can be done to better the situation.

Solutions to the Problems

1. Transition from State to Concurrent List

Prisons are a state subject. Each state has its own prison manual with detailed rules for the administration and management, regulating every aspect of prison life, both for prisoners as well as prison staff. Albeit these rules are framed following the framework established by the Prisons Act of 1894, there still exist discrepancies across states. Some state manuals

16. AIR 1979 SC 1369.
17. Bharadwaj, Priti. (2009). *Liberty at the Cost of Innocence—A Report on Jail Adalats in India,* p. 27. Commonwealth Human Rights Initiative, New Delhi.

have better provisions than others, which should be publicized and adopted by other states as well. This was the main reason why the Apex Court in 1997 issued directives on the framing of an All India Jail Manual.[18] For instance, the Maharashtra rules require every visitor to be provided with a copy of the rules at the time of their appointment.[19] It also has clear guidelines for the appointment of non-official visitors. The Mulla Committee recommended that "revision of jail manuals of states and union territories should be given top priority". Recommendations made by the committee and the Model Prison Manual may form the basis of such revision.[20] The All India Model Prison Manual Committee prepared a Model Prison Manual in 2003 to have one consistent set of rules for all prisons in the country, which was approved by the Central Government in 2004. Transferring prisons to the concurrent list will also make prison management more coherent across states.

2. Co-ordination among Criminal Justice Agencies

Prisons are not independent stand-alone systems. It is just one piece of the criminal justice fabric which needs to fit in perfectly with the other pieces, *viz.*, legislature, police, and the judiciary. While, the entry point for an offender into the criminal justice system is the police; the exit point is the prison, either after serving a sentence or as an undertrial being released after being vindicated. Few others are released without having to experience incarceration. While the legislature is bestowed with the role of lawmakers, the judiciary is given the multifarious task of being the human rights defenders, the monitors and the implementers. However, to ensure that every individual gets an equal opportunity to access justice, some other agencies come into play.

> It is high time that the public conscience is awakened and the government and the judiciary begin to realise that in the dark cells of our prisons there are a large number of men and women who are waiting patiently, impatiently

18. *Ramamurthy* v. *State of Karnataka*, AIR 1997 SC 1739.
19. Rule 9, Section I, Chapter XV, Maharashtra Prison Manual, 1979.
20. Rec 4.36.6, 1980-83, The Report of the All India Committee on Prison Reforms. Ministry of Home Affairs, Government of India.

perhaps, but in vain, for justice—a commodity which is tragically beyond their reach and grasp.[21]

Providing equal opportunity for justice for all is the fundamental duty of the state. Free legal aid is the fundamental right of a person accused of an offence and this right is implicit in the requirement of "reasonable, fair and just" procedure prescribed by Article 21 of the Constitution. It is the state's responsibility to ensure that every citizen irrespective of their economic background gets a fair opportunity to prove their innocence and contest their case. A significant proportion of those who enter the high gates of the prisons either as undertrials or as convicts are "people coming from poorer and underprivileged sections of the society with rural and agricultural background".[22] To ensure access to justice for all irrespective of their social or economic status, the *Legal Services Authority Act*, 1987 mandates every state government to constitute a body, i.e. the State Legal Services Authority (SLSA). The SLSA was mandated to provide free legal aid to all those who wanted with some criteria set in order to identify those that really needed it.

In addition, the National Human Rights Commission (NHRC) was established in 1993 as an independent statutory body, to periodically monitor and better protect rights of individuals. It was also responsible for monitoring prison conditions and issuing appropriate directions. Every state was required to constitute a State Human Rights Commission (SHRC) under the Protection of Human Rights Act, 1993. Nonetheless, in the past 17 years only 18 states[23] have formed a state human rights commission.[24]

---

21. *Hussainara Khatoon & Ors.* v. *Home Secretary*, Bihar, Patna. AIR 1979 SC 1360.
22. Letter from National Human Rights Commission, D.O. No. 11/1/99-PRP&P, dated 29 April 1999.
23. These states include Andhra Pradesh, Assam, Himachal Pradesh, Jammu & Kashmir, Kerala, Karnataka, Madhya Pradesh, Maharashtra, Manipur, Odisha, Punjab, Rajasthan, Tamil Nadu, Uttar Pradesh, West Bengal, Chhattisgarh, Gujarat and Bihar.
24. As reported by National Human Rights Commission website: http://nhrc.nic.in/ as on 2 September 2010.

3. Technology in Prisons

Presently, the involvement of technology in prisons is very limited. It is used in prison data management in very few states and recently has been used in facilitating video-conferencing between courts and prisons, without having to physically produce prisoners in front of the judge or magistrate. It is mostly being used to extend remand date of prisoners after every fifteen days. Proponents of video-conferencing argue that since the production of prisoners in court is often compromised due to inadequate escort provided by the police department, this is a good alternative.

However, this is just another patch-up remedy that our current justice system has installed which scapegoats the majority poor prisoner population. Undertrial prisoners were physically produced before the magistrate after every fifteen days, essentially to check if there were any signs of torture, and if they were being kept properly by the custodians. The Apex Court in *Ramamurthy* v. *State of Karnataka*[25] noted that the production of undertrial prisoners on remand dates is a statutory obligation. It gives an opportunity to the prisoner to bring to the notice of the court, of any ill-treatment or any other grievances that she/he might have regarding its custodians. This physical production also served various other purposes such as giving them an opportunity to see the outside world, to meet with their family members who would otherwise prefer not to come to prison because of the stigma attached to it, and thirdly and most importantly give them a chance to interact with their lawyers. Often the lawyers, both legal aid and private lawyers do not come to the prison to meet their clients. The courts are the only places where they talk to the prisoners. Having prisoners produced through video-conferencing also rips them off this one last opportunity to a legal representation which a fair trial guarantees.

However, technology can play a crucial role in simplifying and preventing duplication of a lot of the processes of prisons. If implemented to use the data management of prisons, it would ease the burden of the understaffed prisons. The prison staff is

25. AIR 1997 SC 1739.

overburdened and a lot of the reports are manually produced which takes them weeks to prepare. In some prisons there is a practice of shuffling the identity numbers of prisoners, at the end of the year. This when done manually takes them weeks at a time, however if done with the click of a mouse, can be done within minutes.

Technology, just like any other thing has its virtues and shortcomings. It is essential that the decision of implementing technology in prisons is a judicious one which does not compromise what fair trial guarantees and the rights of prisoners.

4. Release of Undertrial Prisoners

There have been some progressive amendments in the Cr.P.C. such as Sections 436 and 436A, which makes bail mandatory for those under bailable offences. It ensures that those who are unable to furnish bail amount within seven days, should be considered indigent, and be released on personal bond. It also prevents long periods of detention of undertrial prisoners, by setting a maximum detention period. Undertrials who have stayed for the maximum punishable sentence, had they been sentenced should be immediately released, and those who have completed half the period for offences other than those with a death penalty sentence, are eligible to be considered for bail. The overarching ideology of reform should be entrenched in the minds of the lawmakers, judicial officers and every such officer who works closely with the criminal justice system including police officers who are responsible for making indiscriminate arrests. Even though these amendments have been made, these have not yet trickled down to the roots, for the subordinate level prison officers to act upon.

5. The National Mission

The most recent prison reform initiative undertaken by the government as a part of the National Mission for Delivery of Justice and Legal Reform was launched on 26 January 2010. It envisioned 'timely delivery of justice to all' with a focused mission of strengthening the judiciary towards reducing pendency and delays. After recognizing the indiscriminate delays of cases of undertrials who continue to stay in prisons for long periods, it was proposed to operationalise a mission with the Chief Justices of the various High Courts. With an objective to reduce two-thirds of the undertrial population by 31 July 2010, the judiciary and the prison department have combined forces, appointed task forces, and released 85,782 undertrial prisoners by 26 May 2010.[26]

It has finally revived some hope among the citizens towards the justice system. However, it is imperative that the methods adopted be permanent and not temporary means of reducing undertrial population of prisons. Some of the methods adopted including identifying undertrial prisoners that fall under the ambit of the Sections 436 and 436A of the Cr.P.C.; those that are under petty offences; and those that have continued to stay in prison because of high bail amount. Such processes once started under this mission, should be made into an inherent continuous practice.

Conclusion

The Constitution of India guarantees certain fundamental rights to every individual, even those confined behind bars. However, the custodians forget that the offenders are sent to prison as punishment and not for punishment. How can a system be called restorative, if it still continues the practice of capital punishment, which imbibes and exudes a retributive philosophy? Capital punishment was conducted to deter people from committing such crimes.

> Any reform must be based on the idea that a prisoner is not punished but reformed and made into a good citizen. If this objective is once accepted; it would result in a complete overhauling of the prison system. At present few prison officials have even heard of such a notion.[27]

A drastic change in the ideology governing prisons is much needed. This entails sensitizing all those who are directly involved in the delivery of justice, including judges, lawyers, police officers, prison officers, correctional officers, social workers and civil society members. The change will not be imbibed unless these key players identify with the new ideology of correction and restoration.

---

26. See Press Information Bureau website, http://pib.nic.in/release/release.asp?relid=62125 as on 23 August 2010.
27. Jawaharlal Nehru. (1935). *India and the World*, p. 122.

Pandit Jawaharlal Nehru believed that

> ...the question of prison reform leads us inevitably to a reform of our criminal procedure, and even more so, a reform in the mentalities of our judges who still think in terms of hundred of years ago and are blissfully ignorant of modern ideas of punishment and reform. That of course leads, as everything else does, to a change of the whole system of government.[28]

It is about time, that the fundamentals of justice delivery, which the Constitution guarantees to every individual is resolved, and the focus is moved to the next step of restoration and reintegration of prisoners lives back in the society.

28. Jawaharlal Nehru documented in prison in 1935 which was also published in *India and the World*, p. 122.

Contributors

Amit Chaturvedi is presently a Doctoral Research Scholar in the University of Delhi, India. He has completed a Master's Degree in Criminology from the LNJN National Institute of Criminology and Forensic Science, Delhi, India. His research interests are communal violence, prison reforms and Indian Police Administration, and Victimology.

Arvind Verma is an Associate Professor at the Department of Criminal Justice, Indiana University, Bloomington, USA. Arvind Verma has worked in the Indian Police Service for several years. He has served as Superintendent of Police in the province of Bihar and occupied many senior administrative posts within the police organization. His doctoral work was concerned with the development of new tools of analyses using Fuzzy Logic, Topology and other "qualitative" mathematical techniques. He obtained his Ph.D. from Simon Fraser University, Canada. His research interests are policing, comparative criminal justice systems, policy issues, research methods, mathematical modeling, fuzzy logic and geographical information systems.

Debarati Halder is an advocate and legal scholar. She is the Managing Director of the Centre for Cyber Victim Counselling (CCVC) (www.cybervictims.org). She received her LLB from the University of Calcutta and Master's degree in International and Constitutional Law from the University of Madras and she recieved her PhD from the National Law School of India University (NLSIU), Bangalore, India. She has published many articles in peer reviewed journals and chapters in peer reviewed books. Her work has appeared in scholarly journals, including the *Journal of Law and Religion, Victims and Offenders, Murdoch University E-Journal of Law, ERCES online quarterly review, TMC Academic Journal (Singapore), Temida and Indian Journal of Criminology & Criminalistics* and edited volumes, *Crimes of the Internet, Trends and Issues of Victimology, Cyber Criminology,* etc. Debarati's research interests include Constitutional law, International Law, Victim Rights, Cyber Crimes and Laws. She has presented her research works in many international conferences including the Stockholm Criminology Symposium held during 11-13 June 2012.

Honey Aggarwal was a Master's student of Lok Nayak Jay Prakash Narayan National Institute of Criminology and Forensic Sciences (Ministry of Home Affairs, India). He is a Graduate in Social Work from Bheem Rao Ambedkar College, University of Delhi, New Delhi. He had been a Social Work Trainee at Akshay Pratisthan, Social Worker at Aradhaya and health social worker at Unique International Parivartan for a year. He was placed under block placement at Lok Nayak Jay Prakash Narayan Hospital as Medical Social Worker and in Prayas Observation Home as Counsellor. He has completed Mini Projects on Health Problems of Slum Dwellers and Socio-Economic Antecedent of Institutionalized Delinquent Children.

Jeevan Ballav Panda is an Advocate and is presently working as a Legal Associate at Khaitan & Co. Kolkata since May, 2008. He has recently completed his five years BA LLB (Hons.) from Hidayatullah National Law University, Raipur (Chhattisgarh) with an Honours degree in Intellectual Property Rights and Environmental Law. His areas of interest include—Litigation, ADR, IPR, Criminal Law and Environmental Law. He has gained some valuable work experiences and practical training through various internship programmes undertaken at trial court, appellate court, foreign law firm and law firms in India. He also has more than a dozen publications to his name in some of the reputed journals of the country and a few national as well as international journals. He has been associated as a Peer Reviewer for *International Journal of Criminal Justice Sciences*.

K. Jaishankar is a Senior Assistant Professor in the Department of Criminology and Criminal Justice, Manonmaniam Sundaranar University, Tirunelveli, Tamil Nadu, India. He is also a Member of Syndicate (Board of Management) of Manonmaniam Sundaranar University. He was awarded the National Academy of Sciences India (NASI)- SCOPUS Young Scientist Award, 2012—Social Sciences. He was a Commonwealth Fellow (2009-2010) at the Centre for Criminal Justice Studies, School of Law, University of Leeds, UK and has completed a research project on Victims of Cyber Crimes. He is the founding Editor-in-Chief of the International Journal of Cyber Criminology (www.cybercrimejournal.com) and Editor-in-Chief of International Journal of Criminal Justice Sciences (www.ijcjs.co.nr). He is the founder President of South Asian Society of Criminology and Victimology (SASCV) (www.sascv.org) and Executive Director of Centre for Cyber Victim Counselling (CCVC) (www.cybervictims.org). Jaishankar was a Discussant in the "Opening Discussion: Focusing on victims of crime—Comparing crime patterns and improving practice. Researchers' advice to policy" of the Stockholm Criminology Symposium held during June 11-13, 2012 at Stockholm, Sweden and responded to the questions of *Beatrice Ask, Swedish Minister for Justice*, and *Paula Teixeria da Cruz, the Portugese Minister for Justice*. Jaishankar was a *Keynote Speaker at the 14th World Society of Victimology Symposium* held during 20-24, May 2012, at The Hague, The Netherlands. Among the books he has written / (co) edited are: *Global Criminology: Crime and Victimization in a Globalized Era* (CRC Press, Taylor and Francis group, 2013), *Cyber Crime and the Victimization of Women: Laws, Rights and Regulations* (IGI Global, 2011), *Cyber Criminology: Exploring internet Crimes and Criminal Behavior* (CRC Press, Taylor and

Francis group, 2011), *International Perspectives on Crime and Justice* (Cambridge Scholars Publishing, UK, 2009), *Cyber Bullying: Profile and Policy Guidelines* (DOCCJ, Manonmaniam Sundaranar University, India, 2009), *Crime Victims and Justice: An Introduction to Restorative Principles* (Serial Publications: New Delhi, 2008) and *Trends and Issues of Victimology* (Cambridge Scholars Publishing, UK, 2008). His areas of Academic Competence are Victimology, Cyber Criminology, Crime mapping, GIS, Communal violence, Policing, and Crime prevention. URL: http://www.drjaishankar.co.nr

Manish Kumar is an MA in Sociology from Magadh University, Bodh Gaya, Bihar, India. He is also an MBA graduate from James Cook University, Australia. Manish Kumar has worked as a Senior Research Associate to Dr. Arvind Verma, Associate Professor, Department of Criminal Justice, Indiana University, USA for 8 and 1/2 years (July 1998 to January 2007). He has worked on various issues related to Criminology and Criminal Justice system in India funded by CPR and ICSSR. At present he is working as Deputy General Manager (marketing and branding) in an e-learning firm in Noida, India.

Megha Desai Asher holds an Under Graduate Degree in Criminology and Criminal Justice System and Post Graduate Degree in Journalism and Mass Communication from Griffith University, Australia. She is presently based in India as a freelance journalist contributing to *The Times of India*. She has also freelanced with India's leading women's magazine *Femina*. She is also an independent researcher, contributing articles to peer reviewed journals/books and presenting at international conferences. Her publications include a co-authored study on the Impact of media violence on Children, published in an Occasional series in Criminal Justice and International Studies, by RMIT press, Australia, co-authored study on the Victims of Sexual Harassment at Work Place: Prevalence, Characteristics and Response and also on Stalking Victims in India: A survey of college students, in the book *Trends and Issues in*

Victimology published by Cambridge Scholars Publishing, UK. She is also an editorial assistant of the *International Journal of Cyber Criminology* and the associate editor of the *International Journal of Criminal Justice Sciences.*

Megha Shree is a UGC Junior Research fellow and has completed her M.Phil, (Development Studies) at the Centre for Jawaharlal Nehru Studies, Jamia Millia Islamia, New Delhi, India and presently into PhD program. She has done Masters in Criminology from Lok Nayak Jayaprakash Narayan National Institute of Criminology and Forensic Science (Ministry of Home Affairs) and was awarded the Masters degree from Guru Gobind Indraprastha University. She has been an intern at reputed organizations, viz. National Institute of Social Defence (Ministry of Social Justice and Empowerment) and National Commission for Protection of Child Rights, Government of India. She has authored articles which are under publication on Criminology and Correctional Administration, Human Rights, Women, Migration and Domestic work, etc. She was an organizing coordinator for the First International Conference of South Asian Society of Criminology and Victimology held during 15-17 January 2011, Jaipur, India.

P. Madhava Soma Sundaram is Professor and Head of the Department of Criminology and Criminal Justice, Manonmaniam Sundaranar University, Tirunelveli, Tamil Nadu, India. He holds Masters and PhD degrees in Criminology from the University of Madras. Earlier he has worked for the Government of India to develop its policies on Juvenile Delinquency and substance abuse prevention by implementing its laws through National, Regional and State level consultations; working with National/state level NGOs by creating a network among themselves for urban crime prevention and designed, implemented and evaluated capacity building programs for Criminal Justice Professionals and civil society. Starting his career as a Lecturer in Criminology in 1992, he has authored many books, articles and monographs. In his long career in Criminology, he has picked up a few awards, like the ISC Prof. S.S. Srivastava Award for Excellence in Teaching and Research in Criminology (2009) and Fellow of the Indian Society of Criminology (FISC). His areas of academic proficiency are Juvenile Justice, Criminal Justice Studies, Victimology, and Crime Prevention.

P. Periakaruppan is the Professor and Head of the Department of Political Science, Madurai Kamaraj University, India and also the Coordinator of the School of Social Sciences.

Pradip Basu is currently Professor of Political Science, Presidency University, Kolkata. He was formerly an Associate Professor in the Department of Political Science, Scottish Church College (University of Calcutta), India. He is also Chief Editor, *Journal of Humanities and Social Sciences*, a refered International Journal published annually from the 180-year old Scottish Church College, West Bengal, India. He has authored numerous articles on Naxalism, Marxism and Postmodernism. His books include: *Towards Naxalbari (1953-1967): An Account of Inner-Party Ideological Struggle* (Kolkata: Progressive Publishers), 2000, *Postmodernism, Marxism, Postcolonialism*, (West Bengal: Avenel Publishers), 2010, and *Discourses on Naxalite Movement (1967-2009)*, (Kolkata: Setu Prakashani), 2010.

Priti Bharadwaj is an independent researcher specializing in prisoners' rights and prison reforms. She has an undergraduate degree with a double major in Criminology and Computing Science from Simon Fraser University, Canada. She worked as a Consultant for the Prison Reforms Programme in Commonwealth Human Rights Initiative (CHRI), an international nonprofit organization headquartered in New Delhi, India. During her tenure at CHRI, Priti analyzed government policies; advocated prisoners' rights; and organized awareness campaigns. She worked extensively for the release of pre-trial detainees (under-trials) unduly detained due to lack of legal representation, particularly in the eastern Indian state of Orissa. Her findings are reported in the publication—*Pre-trial Detention & Access to Justice in Orissa*. She has published six publications on various aspects of the Indian prison systems, including the only study in India critiquing the practice of Jail Adalats (prison courts)—*Liberty at the Cost of Innocence*. As a result of her interventions about the lack of basic amenities and inhuman conditions prevailing in the sub-jails of Maharashtra, the Bombay High Court ordered the Maharashtra Prison Department to take necessary actions and ensure the basic standards. To spread public awareness about the realities of the prison system, Priti conceptualized and developed India's first media campaign about the challenge of access to justice in the prison system. It was included as an insert in a Bollywood movie, and given the popularity and accessibility of cinemas across India. Currently, she is pursuing a Masters in Nonprofit Administration from the University of San Francisco.

S. Ramdoss is presently a Senior Assistant Professor at the Department of Criminology at the University of Madras, Chennai, India. Earlier he was a Lecturer in the Department of Criminology and Criminal Justice, Manonmaniam Sundaranar University, Tirunelveli (2003-05). Ramdoss's areas of special interest are: Victimology, Juvenile Justice, Crime Prevention, Human Rights and Correctional Administration. He holds Masters and PhD degrees in Criminology from the University of Madras. Ramdoss has contributed number of chapters in several national and international books besides publishing a number of articles in the various national level journals on the variety of issues pertaining to criminal justice science. Ramdoss has completed a number of research projects, *viz*., victim assistance program, and community crime prevention programs.

Sumit Mukherjee is a Professor of Political Science, University of Kalyani, West Bengal, India.

T. Lakshmi Narayana is a Research Scholar pursuing his doctoral research at the Centre for International Legal Studies, School of International Studies, Jawaharlal Nehru

University at New Delhi in India. Earlier as an advocate, he practiced in Criminal law before district courts for four years at Hyderabad, in Andhra Pradesh. He holds Bachelor's Degree in Law and Masters Degree in Public International Law from Osmania University, Hyderabad. He has also completed his Master of Philosophy in International Law on "Rights of Victims of Crime under International Law". His research interests are International Criminal Law and Victimology.

Tumpa Mukherjee is currently Assistant Professor in Sociology, Women's Christian College, Kolkata, India. She holds MA and PhD degrees in Sociology from University of Calcutta and Jadavpur University, Kolkata. She specializes in policing studies and has presented a paper at the 7th Annual Conference of Asian Association of Police Studies (AAPS) in Bangkok, Thailand, September 2006. She participated at the International Visitors Leadership Program on 'Human Rights Advocacy and Awareness' held at Washington D.C., Alabama, San Francisco, U.S.A. from 8th-19th March, 2010. The program was sponsored by the Department of State, U.S.A. She has been involved in teaching Sociology for more than a decade at undergraduate level in Scottish Church College, under University of Calcutta. She is a Visiting Fellow at Department of Law, under University of Calcutta. She is a Visiting Lecturer at the Central Detective Training School, Kolkata, under the Bureau of Police Research and Development, Ministry of Home Affairs, Government of India. She has been a Guest Faculty at the Swami Vivekananda State Police Academy under the Government of West Bengal. She has also been a Guest Faculty at the Regional Institute of Correctional Administration (RICA), Government of West Bengal, established to train correctional officers in West Bengal and North Eastern states of India. She was invited to deliver a lecture on 'Gender—the Concept, its Manifestations and Impact on Equality' to police officers of and above the rank of Superintendent of Police from the States and officers of equivalent rank from Central Armed

Forces at the Sardar Vallabhbhai Patel National Police Academy, Ministry of Home Affairs, Government of India, Hyderabad, in 2012. Her articles have been published in refereed journals, daily newspapers such as *The Telegraph* and *The Hindustan Times*. As a citizen journalist her articles have been published at merinews.com. Her book *Community Policing in India: A Sociological Perspective* has been published by Progressive Publisher in the year 2006.

Vijay Raghavan is the Chair Person and Associate Professor at the Centre for Criminology and Justice (CCJ), School of Social Work, Tata Institute of Social Sciences (TISS), Mumbai, India. Since 1990, he has been associated with Prayas, a field action project of the CCJ, TISS as its first social worker and currently, a faculty member. Through the work of this project, he has worked on or engaged with issues relating legal rights and rehabilitation of youth offenders, undertrial prisoners, women prisoners, commercially and sexually exploited women, children of prisoners and those vulnerable to criminalization or victimization, both at the field and policy level. He has been involved in highlighting the gaps in the implementation of correctional laws and policies towards prison reforms, legal aid, custodial conditions in women's institutions and rehabilitation of vulnerable groups in criminal justice.